MEMORY AND TRADITION IN THE BOOK OF NUMBERS

In *Memory and Tradition in the Book of Numbers*, Adriane Leveen offers an imaginative rereading of the fourth book of Moses. Leveen examines how the editors of Numbers crafted a narrative of the forty-year journey through the wilderness in order to shape Israelite understanding of the past and influence the world-view of future generations. Leveen's book explores religious politics, the complexities of collective memory, and the literary strategies used by the editors of Numbers to convince the children of Israel to accept priestly rule. Leveen considers how this process took place in the face of the horrifying memory at the heart of the Book of Numbers: the death of an entire generation of Israelites in the wilderness, struck down before their children's eyes by divine decree.

Adriane Leveen joined the faculty of Hebrew Union College in 2007 after three years as a senior lecturer in Hebrew Bible in the Department of Religious Studies at Stanford University. She has published in the *Journal for the Study of the Old Testament* and *Prooftexts*, and she is a contributor to the forthcoming volumes: *Women Remaking American Judaism* (2007), *Healing in the Jewish Imagination* (2007), and *The Torah: A Women's Commentary* (2007).

∾ *Memory and Tradition in the Book of Numbers*

Adriane Leveen

CAMBRIDGE
UNIVERSITY PRESS

CAMBRIDGE UNIVERSITY PRESS
Cambridge, New York, Melbourne, Madrid, Cape Town,
Singapore, São Paulo, Delhi, Mexico City

Cambridge University Press
The Edinburgh Building, Cambridge CB2 8RU, UK

Published in the United States of America by Cambridge University Press, New York

www.cambridge.org
Information on this title: www.cambridge.org/9781107407831

First published 2008
First paperback edition 2012

A catalogue record for this publication is available from the British Library

Library of Congress Cataloguing in Publication Data

Leveen, Adriane (Adriane B.)
Memory and tradition in the book of Numbers / Adriane Leveen.
    p.   cm.
Includes bibliographical references and index.
ISBN 978-0-521-87869-2 (hardback)
1. Bible. O.T. Numbers – Criticism, Redaction.   2. Memory – Biblical teaching.
3. Tradition (Judaism).   I. Title.
BS1265.2.L48   2008
222′.14066 – dc22   2007006726

ISBN 978-0-521-87869-2 Hardback
ISBN 978-1-107-40783-1 Paperback

To Three Generations:

Pauline and Seymour Leveen

Arnold Eisen, Shulamit and Nathaniel Eisen

We have found a way to transcend the limitations of our individual minds and brief life spans through our scribbles and inscriptions, our runes and hieroglyphs, our palimpsests, holographs, and multiple printings, our *furor scribendi.*

Tony Eprile, *The Persistence of Memory* (2004)

Contents

Contents

Acknowledgments

I would like to thank Robert Alter, who has consistently encouraged my teaching and scholarship from my days as a graduate student. More than anyone else, Uri has taught me how to closely read and elucidate the text. Through his teaching, writing, and commentaries he has memorably brought the biblical text alive in its richness and nuance to a growing audience. Israel Knohl taught me how to hear the "Divine Symphony" that is Torah, allowing me to appreciate the text in its multivocality. My first professor of Bible, Edward Greenstein, taught me how to value my own insights into the text and encouraged me to pursue the study of bible as a vocation. Benjamin Sommer encouraged my work in the wilderness and along the way offered useful advice and insight. His own work remains a model. Steve Weizman carefully read and critiqued the entire manuscript. His comments were invaluable. At a crucial moment in the process Steve was extraordinarily generous with his time. I hope to repay his kindness by following his example with others.

Three texts guided my reading of Numbers. Hayyim Nahman Bialik's search for the buried generation resulted in *The Dead of the Desert* and my entry into the wilderness. Stephen Owen's reflections on the cultural persistence of memory in *Remembrances* informed almost every aspect of my own analysis of memory. I thank Lee Yearley for sending Owen my way. Finally, the recently published *Dominion of the Dead* by Robert Pogue Harrison allowed me to complete my own work, knowing that my instinct to reflect on the meaning of the deaths of an entire generation would eventually lead me out of the wilderness.

I would like to thank the following people who over the years read some version of the text or listened patiently to my ideas: Isa Aron, Daniel Boyarin,

Bill Cutter, Tamara Eskenazi, Charlotte Fonrobert, Sharon Gillerman, David Kaufman, Robert Kawashima, Chana Kronfeld, Sarah Luria, Ilana Pardes, Barbara Pitkin, Amy Sapowith, George Savran, Bill Schniedewind, Tom Schwarz, Vered Shemtov, and David Stewart. I would also like to thank my students whose reactions to the biblical text offer their own satisfactions.

I would like to thank the Memorial Foundation for Jewish Culture for a fellowship to complete the early stages of the present work as a dissertation in 2000. A version of chapter 4 was published as "Variations on a Theme: Differing Conceptions of Memory in the Book of Numbers," *Journal for the Study of the Old Testament* 27, no. 2 (2002): 201–221, and is reprinted by permission of Sage Publications. A version of chapter 6 was published as "Falling in the Wilderness: Death Reports in the Book of Numbers," *Prooftexts* 22, no. 3 (2002): 245–272, and is reprinted by permission of Indiana University Press.

I dedicate this work to three generations. I am grateful not only for my parents' continued faith in me but for my mother's passion for ideas and my father's creative joy. My husband Arnie Eisen has always loved Torah. His seeking after its wisdom has buoyed my own pursuit. I thank him for his love, unceasing support, and, especially, his exuberant partnership in parenting and in everything else. My children Shulie and Nathaniel carry me forward into the future with a purpose and hope without which I would never have completed this book.

ONE

Desert Bound

> For league upon league no voice, no syllable breaks the stillness; oblivion has swallowed forever the victories of a bold generation. Whirlwinds have razed the footprints of the terrible warriors of the wasteland, sand has piled up around them, rocks thrust out through the dunes; the desert holds its breath for the brave sunk in endless sleep.[1]

> [H]e must unpack the concentrated focus of memory: he must "write" it as narration, description, reflective interpretation.[2]

Shortly after God denies him entry to the promised land, a fate Moses shares with an entire biblical generation, the prophet nonetheless proceeds to set a course there on behalf of the generation to follow. That course would take the people Israel across the territory of Edom. In seeking the permission of the king of Edom to cross his land, Moses can think of no better opening to his request than a brief recital of Israel's past:

> Thus says your brother Israel, you know all the hardship that has found us; our ancestors went down to Egypt and we dwelt in Egypt many days and Egypt caused us and our ancestors harm; And we cried out to YHWH and He heard our voice and sent a messenger and took us out from Egypt and behold we are in Kadesh, a town at the edge of your border. Please let us cross through your land. (Num. 20:14b–17a, translation mine unless otherwise noted)

Moses' recourse to prior events as a prologue to present exigencies is a fine example of the persistent turn to the past in biblical narrative. What happens there, or, more precisely, what one remembers to have happened there, repeatedly impacts the present. Current actions and requests can be understood, so our example argues, only in a context provided by the past.

Moses' attempt to persuade the king of Edom rests on that assumption. As will become clear, Moses hopes to persuade not only a foreign king of the worthiness of the journey and its destination, but even more so, his own people. His attempt reflects in microcosm what the editors of the fourth book of Moses – Numbers – attempt in broader, more ambitious fashion.[3] Numbers presents its audience, the people Israel, a narrative of past events in order to explain present circumstances, opportunities, and dangers. It also attempts, just as crucially, to chart a course for the future. In the process, the editors of Numbers construct a unique and troubling version of the events of the wilderness journey that contributes to the stock of biblical traditions of that early period in Israel's history.[4]

Among the events to be remembered, Numbers singles out, and makes central to its account, the failure of the entire wilderness generation, so recently liberated from Egypt, to enter the land promised them by God. Every freed Israelite, so carefully "counted" at the beginning of Numbers, is held accountable for the people's later failure of will, sentenced to die in the wilderness, abandoned without trace. Why include this dismal punishment in a book meant to inspire later generations of Israelites on their many journeys to faith and covenant? I shall argue that its editors recognized in the tales of the wilderness rebellion and the fate suffered by an entire generation a most dramatic and highly useful deterrent. By the end of Numbers the children of that generation must come to realize that they cannot survive for long in a wilderness dominated by appetites, a wilderness in which law and God can be so disastrously defied. Indeed, they are last glimpsed readying themselves to enter the land under God's commandments and priestly leadership, obliged and guided by their tradition to build a certain type of nation. The editors insist that each subsequent generation, especially their own, make that same choice. The present work analyzes the sophisticated, and at times coercive, ways in which the editors of Numbers attempt to persuade the people of their particular vision. Such an analysis highlights the often neglected, but crucial, role of Numbers within the larger biblical corpus in forging the people Israel into a unified whole.

For the sake of convenience, I sometimes refer to this later editorial hand in the singular, but as I argue in a later chapter, the editing of Numbers should be considered a group, rather than an individual, project. Most likely originating in a priestly school, such a project took place in stages over a period of many decades sometime between the seventh and the fifth century B.C.E. The priestly editors organized the various stories of the wilderness period, some of which dated from much earlier times, into a coherent whole while creatively editing or adding other materials to the mix, including their own comments, in order to ensure the success of their endeavor.[5] A variety of agendas powered this project. Explain the past. Shape collective memory. Ensure the means of transmission. Prevent recurrence of disaster.

And secure the proper leadership. As they shaped earlier priestly and non-priestly materials alike into a carefully redacted priestly account, the editors placed the priestly leadership exclusively in the hands of the sons of Aaron. In so doing, they supplied the priestly hierarchy of their time with an origin in the wilderness period, thus creating a powerful legitimization for that hierarchy. Only the sons of Aaron could ensure the proper functioning of the wilderness camp with its tabernacle, and, by extension, only the sons of Aaron could ensure the proper functioning of the nation and its Temple.

Thus Numbers provides a particularly rich example of how a select group asserts its version of tradition, using narrative to impose its will on a particular audience by controlling the process of retelling the past: "it is the recognized ability to expound the true memory of the group that constitutes the core of religious power."[6] I provide evidence of this priestly assertion of control by elucidating an editorial process that shapes various materials of varying dates into an overarching narrative of the journey, subtly does away with other sources of authority that compete with their own, goes on to examine the uses and abuses of collective memory during that long journey on behalf of a later time, preserves a record of the political battles in the wilderness camp and their resolution (again with an eye to a later time), reports on the death of a generation, and in concluding, secures a more promising future for the next generation. The culmination of these editorial strategies makes a highly specific construction of tradition compelling, authoritative, and, finally, binding on a later audience.

That vision is best conveyed via the dramatic narratives of the wilderness journey. The editors have other types of material at hand, including two censuses, ancient poetry, diverse laws, an inventory of tribal gifts, and a priestly calendar. They strategically place those materials within the larger work. But their creativity and persuasion appear most evident in their use of the tales of rebellion. Beginning with the moment of rupture that occurs in chapter 11 as the people first begin to complain, the editors highlight the repercussions of glorifying the Egyptian past. A single memory of Egyptian delicacies spreads throughout the camp like wildfire, triggering the downward cycle of the generation. Before the fire is extinguished – three chapters later – God condemns an entire generation to death. A generation temporarily bound for the desert on the way to the promised land ends its life bound by the desert. It is this image of the generation bound by the desert that the editors brilliantly exploit. The generation's fate pervades – even haunts – the rest of the book.

It also haunts readers of a later time. The modern Hebrew poet Hayyim Nahman Bialik beautifully captures that sense of hauntedness in his epic 1902 poem, "Metei Midbar," or "The Dead of the Desert." His poem first taught me to pay attention to the repercussions of such wholesale devastation and to reflect on its meaning in the biblical narrative. Bialik's resurrection of the ancient tale, itself an act of memory, provides a testament to the power of the biblical text and its tenacious hold on later readers. The poem especially invites contemplation of the desert as the setting for the unfolding tragedy. "Whirlwinds have razed the footprints of the terrible warriors of the wasteland, sand has piled up around them."[7] The poet imagines the burial grounds of the entire biblical generation as nearly unrecoverable, abandoned to a wilderness waste shrouded in the distant reaches of time. The eternal rhythms of nature, the movement of open, barren desert, the recurring silence serve notice in Bialik's view that those buried long ago will not easily be found again.

In a more recent work that also takes memory and death as its themes, *The Dominion of the Dead*, Robert Pogue Harrison evokes the power of the sea and in so doing unwittingly captures the terrible dilemma produced by the wilderness setting as it is expressed both in Bialik's poem and in the biblical text. Harrison's passage is worth quoting at length:

> It is its [the sea's] passion for erasure that makes it inhuman. Erasure does not mean disappearance only; it means that the site of the disappearance remains unmarkable. There are no gravestones on the sea. History and memory ground themselves on inscription, *but this element is uninscribable.* It closes over rather than keeps the place of its dead, while its unbounded grave remains humanly unmarked.[8] (emphasis added)

The same could be said of the desert setting of Numbers. It is conceivable that such a threat of erasure motivated Bialik. For he refused to leave the dead of the desert alone. The poet was compelled to disturb their obscure burial ground, to wake the dead by writing about them, inscribing them in his poem, fixing them in collective memory. Perhaps he was reacting to the sheer terror of the biblical text. For Numbers does nothing less than turn Harrison's image of an unbounded grave into the wilderness in its entirety. It is a site of disappearance. And it is unmarked.

But what triggers such a fate? According to Numbers, in spite of being witness to the greatest feats their God had performed on their behalf – liberation from slavery, a miraculous crossing of the Reed Sea, and, in a thunderous moment of divine revelation, the granting of a covenant – the people Israel failed nonetheless to grasp hold of the radical promise of nationhood in their own land. No doubt Bialik would be interested in such a failure considering the climate of Jewish nationalist stirrings in which he lived and wrote. Bialik's poem exemplifies how tradition may be used to ask questions about one's own time, a topic of great interest to the present work. At the same time, his poem and Harrison's meditations exemplify the way in which certain texts or images from the past unsettle us enough to compel a sustained reflection on the past.

And in fact the intense desire to understand what lay behind the failure of the generation liberated from Egypt fuels not only the interest of later readers such as Bialik but the earliest readers – the editors of Numbers themselves. How to account for the generation's frightened and feeble response to God's grand plans for them? Seemingly, the editors hoped that in understanding that tale, they could prevent a recurrence of failure in their own time and place. But how? In other words, how should the wilderness generation be remembered and to what end exactly? What meanings should be derived from its fate? How best determine and fix those meanings? What form should the generation's story finally take?[9]

In answering those questions, the priestly editors of Numbers rely on a primary function of narrative, its ability to make sense of breakdown and disorder. "In search of meaning, [a narrator may] narrate the unexpected or disturbing, creating a sense of order – a sense that things make sense after all – through the imposed order of narrative."[10] In fact, Numbers' editors succeed in moving from the total breakdown of God's plan for one generation and the haunted arena in which they die to restored order and purpose in the next. They dare to narrate a path out of that unmarked wilderness into the promised land for all time.

Yet the editors of Numbers face a daunting, even formidable, task. Engaged in a crucial struggle for the content and shape of Israel's identity as a certain type of nation guided by a certain type of priest, the editors simultaneously leave behind evidence of the difficulties and dynamics of that struggle. In consequence, the final form of Numbers comprises a set of reflections on the uses of the past *and* the limits of such use. The book vividly illustrates the results of imposing an authoritative, priestly version of tradition, intended to be binding, on a people who repeatedly threaten, much like the generation we first encounter in the shifting sands and unmarked territory of wilderness, to come undone. Along the way, it also illustrates the extent to which prior textual materials may have claims that the editors cannot ignore. Compelled to include in their final version older fragments of known texts or poetry associated with the journey in the wilderness, the editors preserve complaints and memories that become, perhaps inadvertently, a de facto resistance to the priestly attempt.[11] That resistance is not as easily overcome as Moses – or the editors – could have wished. Halbwach contends that religious memory is "highly conflictual ... combining, as it always does, a plurality of collective memories in a state of tension one with another."[12] As we shall see, in the end the editors' manipulation of the competing memories of that time does succeed, creating an unflinchingly critical tale of the wilderness generation. Yet that very criticism provides the means through which the priestly editors ultimately hope to redeem the people Israel.

In sum, the present work offers a rereading of Numbers that highlights the role of the editors in shaping a view of the wilderness period as a time not only of disaster but of renewed determination. That priestly determination shapes a vision for the future that is paradoxically placed in the distant past. Yet it is their contemporaries whom the priests most hope to sway through their editing of the tale. As the editors devise the means to transmit and impose their narrated version of the wilderness period, they leave behind a richly layered record of the process as well as a set of remarkable reflections on the uses of the past.

Before proceeding to a description of such editorial strategies and the results in subsequent chapters, let me first address a number of introductory matters. These include the placement of Numbers in the context of the rest of the Five Books of Moses, known as the Torah, and a consideration of the two terms, memory and tradition, that are key to the priestly uses of the past. Both contemporary and biblical conceptions of tradition and memory will aid such an analysis.

◁ In the wilderness

After beginning with the story of the world's creation, Genesis narrates the tale of the founding family of Israel, headed by Abraham. The remainder of Genesis is concerned with this particular family and the often contentious relationships that exist among husbands and wives, parents and their children, and brothers and sisters. Genesis is equally concerned with the relationships of the members of Abraham's family to God. Exodus takes this interest further, moving from the story of a family to that of an entire people. Born into slavery in Egypt but liberated from the oppression and enslavement of the Pharoah by God, the people Israel are headed back to the land God promised to Abraham and to a better future.

The primary interest of the book of Exodus is the relationship of the people with Moses and, above all, with God as they begin their journey to the promised land. What the people Israel witness at Mt. Sinai – God's presence, the granting of laws and the establishment of a covenant – is meant to cement their commitment to God. Subsequent chapters of Exodus and all of Leviticus focus on the details of that commitment – the rules of sacrifice and the priestly supervision of the people Israel, centered on the tabernacle. Thus the design and building of the tabernacle and the regulations involving the priests, the delimitation of their authority and the development of their expertise, dominate the rest of Exodus and Leviticus. These two books provide a blueprint of the tabernacle and a description of the cult under priestly authority meant to be precisely duplicated in the land of Israel.

Following what can best be described as a momentum toward promise and fulfillment, the events in Numbers force the people to halt in their tracks and nearly abandon their plans. But it is not immediately clear that such a crisis will occur. The first section of Numbers (described in more detail in subsequent chapters), continues to focus on the tabernacle and the various responsibilities that the priests, and a newly established subordinate class, the Levites, have for its functioning. We also observe the counting and placement of the entire people within the wilderness camp as they ready themselves to conquer the land. Suddenly, even abruptly, reality intrudes. Nothing prepares the reader for what happens next: an outpouring of Israelite complaints that disrupt the carefully orchestrated and ordered narrative until that point. Turning their thoughts back to Egypt, the people Israel allow memories of its delicacies to overcome them, weakening their resolve to follow God's lead and overwhelming them with doubt that they have the strength or ability to conquer the promised land. Furthermore, nothing prepares us for God's angry and lethal condemnation of the people. After all, they had complained about food earlier in their journey, way back in Exodus shortly after leaving Egypt. What stands between that moment and the present crisis of Numbers is Sinai, with the people's promise of fidelity to God. After Sinai everything is different. Deeply disappointed, certainly enraged, in Numbers God vows to destroy an entire population, including the children. Only Moses' skillful intercession and the actions of the high priest Aaron stand between the people and utter destruction. Moved by Moses' words, God relents and allows the members of the new generation to continue toward the promised land, but only after the deaths of their parents in the wilderness.

Numbers thus creates an atmosphere of crisis and near catastrophe in the wilderness camp that is distinct from what came before. Its emphasis on crisis sets up, in the starkest of terms, a choice that Israel must make between the order and control of priestly rule, abundantly represented at the beginning of Numbers, and the chaos and disaster that follows. It is the children of those killed off in the wilderness who must make that choice and, in so doing, leave their parents behind. It must be noted that the final chapters of Numbers conclude on a more hopeful note than we would have supposed in the midst of such devastation and destruction. That hopeful note is restored by an unlikely source, the non-Israelite prophet Balaam, who sees in the Israel encamped in the valley below a flourishing people – recipients of God's blessing – simply too vast to count. The optimism of Balaam's vision of Israel is justified in what follows in the concluding chapters of Numbers. Moses and the people become engaged in matters such as inheritance and a calendar of annual holidays that can only be implemented once Israel is settled in the land.

In some ways, Deuteronomy, the final book of the five, functions as a review of the books that precede it, recounting the events of the Exodus and the forty years of wandering that are narrated as an eyewitness account in Exodus-Numbers. Moses is the dominant figure of Deuteronomy, while the priests who play such significant roles in Exodus-Numbers retreat decidedly into the background.[13] Among other things, Deuteronomy could be considered an inner biblical interpretation and elaboration of the laws given to the people in Exodus 21–23. Deuteronomy ends with the death of Moses. Thus concludes the Five Books.

We are now in a position to observe the larger trajectory in which Numbers takes its place. Each book interacts with the next as the action unfolds over hundreds of years but also retains its own discrete content and structure. Genesis focuses on the founding family and the descent into Egypt, Exodus on liberation from Egypt and the construction of the Tabernacle, Leviticus on the priests and their cult, and Numbers on the journey and its obstacles on the way to fulfillment. Because Deuteronomy functions more as a review of the wilderness journey as the people camp on the other side of the Jordan, just prior to crossing over, action largely ceases at the end of Numbers. The present work treats Numbers as a book that is an integral part of the larger Torah, referring to, and even at times replicating, earlier scenes or episodes and anticipating later ones, such as the death of Moses at the end of Deuteronomy. But I also treat Numbers as a work with its own internal structure and content that sets it apart from the other four works. Principally, Numbers must deal with the near extinction of a project that God first set before Abraham and then Moses. That project, whose success is presumed by Exodus and Leviticus, entails the successful settlement of Israel in the promised land. No other book of Torah has to grapple with the consequences of that divine threat of extinction so urgently and so immediately as Numbers.[14]

At the conclusion of Numbers the children of Israel have survived, encamped at the very edge of the promised land. It should be no surprise that issues of transmission and inheritance take on a poignant urgency at journey's end. The children of Israel, literally bereft of their parents, have little left but their traditions and memories as they prepare to enter the promised land.

∼ Tradition and memory

As Harrison reminds us, the living are linked to the dead "in the modes of memory, genealogy, tradition, and history."[15] In a later chapter I briefly refer to the role of genealogy in categorizing the Israelites as families, clans, and tribes over several generations in the two censuses of Numbers. The actual historicity of the wilderness journey lies beyond the scope of this study, though I should mention in passing two important, recent archeological finds that are of direct relevance to Numbers. These discoveries date from a period much later than the alleged journey through the wilderness. They are most likely to be contemporaneous with some of the written materials of Numbers, though earlier than its final editing. This external archeological evidence has confirmed the accuracy of two of the texts or characters of Numbers – the priestly blessing found in Numbers 6 and the figure of Balaam in Numbers 22–24. I refer to texts found at Deir 'Alla in the Jordan Valley from around the middle of the eighth century B.C.E. that describe the activities of Balaam the prophet and to silver amulets discovered at a site known as Ketef Hinnom, just outside Jerusalem that date approximately to the sixth century B.C.E. One of the silver amulets contains the priestly blessing recorded in Numbers 6. These examples suggest the extent to which the editors of Numbers may have had in their possession, and artfully drawn on, an array of preexisting materials that they could use to develop, and lend an air of verisimilitude to, their account of the wilderness period.[16]

Again, modes of genealogy, history, memory, and tradition link the living to the dead. The other two terms on Harrison's list – memory and tradition – are indeed indispensable, as I have suggested above, in linking the living to the dead in Numbers. Therefore, they are indispensable to the present study. In consequence, I devote the rest of this introduction to a discussion of these terms as they are used both within contemporary theoretical literature and within biblical texts.

Let me begin with tradition and its discussion by Edward Shils. He offers the reader a simple and straightforward definition: "in its barest, most elementary sense, it means simply a traditum; it is anything which is transmitted or handed down from the past to the present."[17] But then Shils immediately challenges such a broad definition of tradition. So does the book of Numbers. "Anything" suggests an endless inventory of elements. But in Numbers, tradition quickly becomes specific laws, rituals, hierarchical arrangements, and stories. I am interested in how Numbers goes about determining its particular list – which customs, laws, and stories should be transmitted and why. Furthermore, in claiming that particular laws, customs, and stories originate during the wilderness journey, the editors defy a definition of tradition as an impersonal transference of past experience to the present independent of human agency or intervention. What becomes "tradition" is consciously chosen over time (though of course not entirely). As they impose their particular version of tradition on a contemporary audience, the priestly editors do indeed use the weight of the past to legitimate their choices. Yet in so doing they do not allow the past to limit or constrain their appropriation of it.

Eric Hobsbawm identifies several motives for the borrowing of the past's authority on behalf of present interests. Such motives include the legitimization of current institutions, hierarchies, and status relationships.[18] By means of illustration, a particular group of priests, those who identify themselves with the line of Aaron, edit the book of Numbers to impose and strengthen their current authority through the shaping of tradition. Thus the exploitation of tradition is entangled with politics and is in itself a highly political act. To a large extent, the present work is in sympathy with this notion of tradition as an intentionally selective construction and representation of past events that are appropriated for present purposes rather than a set of givens. Other aspects of the past are in fact forgotten or ignored.

But not entirely; it is not as simple as suggested thus far. For instance, in spite of the priestly attempt to select only certain aspects of tradition, the editors do not have complete freedom over the process. Other traditions, even if ignored, cannot be discarded. They also have claims on the community and will impose themselves on the final form of the work. In consequence, when tracing traditions in biblical materials, one needs to formulate a series of questions, including how do traditions originate, by whom are they sustained and transmitted, and how do different and often competing traditions interact with each other?[19] This last query is of particular interest to the present work. At times, as we will see, it is complementarity that drives the editing of multiple traditions rather than conflict and supremacy. The layers of tradition are respectfully preserved. This has been noted by Marc Brettler. "Probably the earlier documents had a certain prestige and authority . . . the redaction of the Torah from a variety of sources most likely represents an attempt to enfranchise those groups who held those particular sources as authoritative."[20] I take up the editorial use of different traditions in chapter 4.

Thus the process of shaping tradition is more complex and convoluted than Hobsbawm's thesis would allow. Nonetheless, in the end certain traditions do become dominant if they succeed in acquiring the status of "taken for granted" in the present. Shils emphasizes this point, arguing that literary

works "often contain normative intentions ... they praise one set of arrangements and beliefs and attempt to show the wrongness of another."[21] One
can assume then that the transmission of set arrangements and beliefs in
a literary work such as Numbers involves not only a great deal of persuasion but powerful polemic. If that polemic is successful, certain traditions
succeed in becoming dominant and normative.

Yet what makes Numbers an interesting study in the shaping of tradition has to do with its simultaneous evidence for the assertion of authority
and for its opposite – a lack of consensus or widespread acceptance of too
recent a past expected to compel the people's adherence. Even in its final
form, the text almost longingly envisions a future time when the rites and
symbols it commands will be widely practiced, familiar parts of daily life.
The repeated insistence that those laws are binding on Israel for all time
reflects an assessment that acceptance of those laws as a given has yet to be
accomplished.

To bolster that acceptance, the editors of Numbers rely not only on the
sanctity of the past but even more so on the authority of divine injunction.
"Therefore you shall be reminded to do all My Commandments and be holy
to your God ... I, YHWH Your God" (Num. 15:40a, 41b). The notion that
God's law is meant to be an ongoing, binding force, beginning in the past of
the wilderness but continuing forward in time, is captured in God's use of the
phrase והיו לכם לחקת עולם לדרתיכם, meaning "an eternal law throughout your
generations." In a study of this phrase Israel Knohl argues that its repetition
in Numbers, always spoken by God, aims to ensure that a particular law
not only be considered binding on the generation that receives it but will
become an unquestioned given over time.[22] Note just how far we are from the
straightforward acceptance of "tradition" simply because it is handed down
from one generation to the next. The priestly attempt is not automatically
guaranteed success but demands specific sources of legitimization (the past,
divine injunction) and, as we shall see, both highly developed narrative
strategies and the command of memory. Thus tradition can be understood as
an interaction between "what was" and present need, a need that emphasizes
certain objects or texts from the past over others in order to forge ahead into
an envisioned future.

If they can control memory, the priestly editors might just succeed in
transmitting one tradition over any other. As put by Margalit: "Tradition is
one form of shared memory, one in which the line transmitting a version

from the past is sanctified, authorized, or even canonized in such a way that it is immune to challenges based on alternative historical lines."[23] Margalit's notion of immunity captures what I consider to be the goal of the editors of Numbers. They envision a flourishing people securely in their own land under the guidance of priestly traditions and arrangements – but only if they succeed in discounting, or dismissing other alternatives, other memories, of the past.

Thus memory is integral to a discussion of tradition. In its barest sense, tradition can be considered a collection of laws, customs, and stories that are transmitted and received in a later time. Memory is the means by which some of those traditions are retained and accepted, while others are minimized or rejected. Yet just as we saw with the term "tradition," remembering is far more complex than such a terse and straightforward description would suggest.[24] The control of memory requires specific legitimatizing strategies, much like tradition. In fact, memory and tradition correspond in the fluid ways in which their contents may be manipulated on behalf of present exigencies. At the same time both processes resist easy appropriation.

The editors of Numbers appear to have identified that resistance. Positive memories of Egypt have so many destructive repercussions among the people Israel that the only way to curtail the damage is to destroy those who hold them. In consequence, Numbers treats memory as a terribly potent force and makes its reliability and limits a recurring focus of concern. To elaborate on a possible understanding of memory within Numbers, I offer a brief synthesis of the contemporary theoretical literature. This is followed by an equally brief detour into Exodus and Deuteronomy in order to highlight the distinctive emphasis on memory's destructive power found in Numbers. I conclude with a reference to a previous scholarly consensus on biblical memory that the present rereading of Numbers will challenge.

Theoretical literature on collective memory rather than that of the individual is far more germane to the present study. Numbers simply does not describe the memories of individuals. Nor does it evince any interest in individual acts of remembering. Instead, Numbers focuses on the people Israel who remember Egypt in a collective voice.[25] But the idea of collective memory poses a problem for certain theorists of memory who go so far as to reject it as a legitimate subject of scrutiny. For instance, Gedi and Elam argue that memory can be analyzed and made sense of only as an individual process: "All collective terms are problematic – because they are conceived of as having capacities that are in fact actualized only on an individual level, that is, they can only be performed by individuals."[26] They dismiss the usefulness of the term, insisting that

> the only legitimate use of the term "collective memory" is, as was claimed before, a metaphorical one, namely as some property attached to some generalized entity such as 'society.' It has the advantage of being a vivid and illustrative description, but as an explanatory tool it is useless and even misleading.[27]

Individuals certainly have unique experiences that they remember. However, such memories are often inaccessible if unexpressed and are therefore not a readily available topic of study. But more than scholarly pragmatism is at work. A community will often publicly commemorate events experienced on a collective scale. Therefore, the forms taken by commemoration *are* available to an observer. Within the United States in the last fifty years we may include in the collective memory such public events as the Vietnam and Iraq wars, the assassination of a president, a candidate, and a civil rights leader, as well as a terrorist attack against the World Trade Center. In response we observe anniversaries and birthdays, commemorate events, and establish monuments. No doubt individuals remember those shared events differently and through the lens of their own experiences, but they are in turn exposed to a public rendering of events that then corrupt and transform their individual recollections. Numbers is fascinated by, and depicts, that collective expression and corruption of memory.

In describing the shift between individual and collective memory as a topic of study, Jonker writes: "The isolated 'user' who calls up ready-made memories is replaced by the social interaction of a society within which memories are 'produced.'"[28] Margalit makes a similar point in his study of collective memory. He identifies the "agents and agencies entrusted with preserving and diffusing it."[29] In other words, when memory is invoked in the biblical narrative, we should consider as a working principle questions quite similar to those asked above about tradition: "by whom, where, in which context, against what?"[30]

I assume with Pierre Nora that collective memory "takes root in the concrete, in spaces, gestures, images and objects."[31] Therefore, in subsequent chapters of this study I analyze the symbols, practices, and names of places in which collective memory takes root.[32] The present study especially includes the textual landscape of Numbers in such a catalog. Its words and verses provide an accessible arena, one that embodies collective memory of a wilderness journey thousands of years ago as well as the appropriation of memory by its editors. Stephen Owen elegantly proposes how such a recourse to the text in fact bridges and resolves the tension between individual and collective memory. The transformation of memory through writing "aspires to carry memory outside the self."[33]

By now we recognize that collective memory, like tradition, is a contested process. In Numbers that contestation is represented in a final portrait of the wilderness past that emerges out of competing versions of the period. The dominant narrative emphasizes the wilderness as a period of liberation and covenant. Yet a "counternarrative," complaint and longings for Egypt, also exists in Numbers. To complicate matters further, the priestly editors chose to preserve and transmit *both* narratives. Narrative and counternarrative illustrate the point that more than one past may be retrieved and remembered. Are the people to be considered a holy army or a motley group of complainers? Depending on the interest of the rememberer and on what aspects of tradition are to be emphasized, first one, then the other image may be heightened. *In the end both are used.* Thus in this view, memory, just as tradition, is understood as a highly constructed and edited process.

At the same time, memory, even more so than tradition, resists easy manipulation and, in fact, undermines any attempt to rely on it completely. For instance, Numbers illustrates the extent to which a single memory of Egyptian delicacies, uttered aloud, impinges on the present in disturbing and unpredictable ways, nearly unraveling the future of an entire people. Richard Terdiman notes this "involuntary" aspect of memory, writing:

> I think involuntary memory ... represents, with an extraordinary but displaced intensity, the pervasive and continuing perception at the heart of the memory crisis: that rather than being subject to our recapture, the past in fact malignantly captures us.[34]

Involuntary memory is often triggered by something in the present, for instance, a physical smell or sensation, such as hunger or thirst. Involuntary memories are also fragmentary.[35] Such memories are heightened to the exclusion of more precise or accurate ones. The notion that the past may in fact exert its control over us in unexpected or even distorted ways is certainly a commonplace after Freud. Yet it is fascinating that the story in Numbers highlights precisely the physical elements of involuntary memory and does so on a collective level. The people, sick of their bland desert diet, suddenly remember the delicacies left behind in Egypt that exert more and more control over their behavior, "malignantly" capturing them.

The collective nature of the complaint narrated in Numbers confirms another aspect of memory remarked on in contemporary theory: the repercussions of the public expression and dissemination of memory. The collective often embellishes what is remembered. Because the complaints are altered in collective revision, one can no longer distinguish between the actual and the invented. For instance, as they cry out for Egyptian delicacies, the people seem to forget altogether the hardship of their lives as slaves in Egypt. As David Lowenthal has observed: "Contrary to the stereotype of the remembered past as immutably fixed, recollections are malleable and flexible; what seems to have happened undergoes continual change."[36]

In sum, contemporary theory sheds light on different and even contradictory aspects of biblical expressions of collective memory found in Numbers. Different types of memory – constructed and involuntary – are depicted. The process of retrieval may be highly controlled or sudden and erratic. The collective traditions to be remembered are often shaped by those with vested interests. Nonetheless, by its very nature, memory may elude such control. Memory may often be unpredictable, selective and disturbing. In surprising ways, Numbers has anticipated many of these conclusions. However, this work argues that the priestly editors have no choice but to manipulate memory cautiously on behalf of a future community imagined securely in its own land. They do so out of necessity.

That the editors appear conscious of the deleterious effects of memory, even citing it as a cause of Israel's rejection of God's plans, while at the same time relying on it, marks Numbers as an intriguing and complex study of memory. Such complexity warrants a sustained analysis, especially since Numbers has been largely overlooked in recent discussions of biblical memory. Memory poses an extraordinary problem for the book. In contrast, other biblical works tend to have more confidence in the efficacy of memory, therefore paying less attention to its more troubling dimensions. To get at that contrast, a brief perusal of the term (in the verbal imperative "remember" and the noun form "remembrance") outside Numbers is warranted even if a detailed study of memory outside Numbers lies beyond the scope and interest of this book. Such a comparative study, even if brief, will heighten what can be considered distinct to Numbers. I briefly examine the two books of Torah in addition to Numbers that extensively rely on memory on behalf of nation building: Exodus and, in particular, Deuteronomy.

∼ Ritual and rhetoric: memory in Exodus and Deuteronomy

Exodus repeatedly concretizes memory in ritual and symbol, using the noun form "remembrance" (זכרון) to suggest the importance of a material or concrete signifier as an aid to memory.[37] Let us briefly look at Exodus 12–13, a premier illustration of this practice.[38] The topic of these chapters is the Passover observance. They literally overflow with ritual instructions and behavior. God begins by marking the month in the yearly calendar in which Israel should observe the day. God then describes the details of slaughtering the paschal lamb, marking the doorposts with the blood of the sacrifice to ward off the Destroyer, and eating of the sacrifice with the matzah and bitter herbs. While Israel does these things, the Destroyer will simultaneously destroy the first born of Egypt. Suddenly, God interrupts instructions given in a present moment to command future actions. That day shall be a זכרון, a day of remembrance and celebration *throughout the generations* (Exod. 12:14). But how is the day to be commemorated? God commands a concrete action coupled with a warning. Israel reenacts the last night in Egypt by eating the unleavened bread in the future. Every generation will eat matzah in order to commemorate the very first time. Those who do not will be "cut off from Israel" (Exod. 12:15). In a second and purposeful temporal shift, ritual instruction for the future is suddenly replaced by a reversion to the present moment in Egypt. In 12:21 Moses summons the elders and then, more terribly, in 12:29 God inflicts the tenth plague. The narrator moves back and forth from present to future, intermingling present dread and haste with an anticipation of calm future celebration. The temporal integration between present and future brilliantly makes the point that the taste of matzah throughout the generations will return the people Israel, so to speak, to that long night of waiting in Egypt conjured up through the details of Exodus 12.

Chapters 12 and 13 assume that concrete ritual behavior and objects are the best means for securing such a highly specific memory. For instance, in chapter 13 Moses again exhorts Israel to remember that day in which

God took them out of Egypt by avoiding leavened bread (13:3), actualizing memory through action, albeit this time through inaction. The injunction against eating leavened bread is repeated and culminates in 13:9 with another material reminder, or זכרון, that Israelites are to place between their eyes (13:9). Just as matzah functions as a mnemonic device, so too the sign between their eyes reminds the people that God took them out of Egypt with a mighty hand. Memory of God's action in Egypt on behalf of Israel justifies ongoing obligation to God. Hence it is absolutely necessary to the building of the nation.[39] Strikingly, throughout the two chapters God's ability to command memory, and control its content and expression, is a given.

In the rest of Exodus, the noun "remembrance," זכרון, continues to dominate, suggesting that a reliance on concrete objects is the chief strategy deployed by Exodus to control memory. In addition to examples from Exodus 12–13 cited above, other concrete triggers include writing on a scroll (to destroy Amalek in 17:14), stones on the shoulder pieces of the ephod (28:12 and 39:7), the names of the children of Israel on Aaron's breast piece of decision (28:29), and the money of atonement (30:16). The repeated reliance on these objects implies belief in their efficacy.

In contrast, the term זכרון doesn't appear in Deuteronomy at all! While there are plenty of ritual instructions and objects in the work, including the written text itself (see Deut. 31:26), memory is not summoned with the aid of a concrete object.[40] This distinction between Exodus and Deuteronomy is quite interesting. In fact, Deuteronomy replaces the confident strategy of Exodus with a certain amount of anxiety that Israel might in fact forget the events of the Exodus, Sinai, and the wilderness journey. Perhaps that anxiety is due to the lack of concrete memorials in Deuteronomy. In this regard, Deuteronomy's anxiety echoes the caution and wariness toward memory found in Numbers. But Deuteronomy resorts to two strategies of its own to combat such anxiety that are almost entirely missing from Numbers. It replaces the cacophony of voices found in Numbers (God, the people, Moses and Aaron, and the rebels) with that of a single speaker, Moses. And it revels in the power of writing, a technology barely mentioned in Numbers, to preserve those words, laws, events, and teachings that Moses most wants the people to remember. In Deuteronomy it is Moses who controls the retelling of the wilderness journey just completed, and it is Moses who writes down a record of that journey for future generations. Rabinowitz reminds us of the importance of a written text on behalf of memory: "writing fixes, preserves, renders permanent what otherwise might be changeable, evanescent, impermanent."[41]

As an example of Moses' use of rhetoric to shape the collective memory, consider Deuteronomy 4:9. Moses raises the possibility that the people might forget, but only after he commands the people to "take utmost care and watch yourselves scrupulously lest you forget the things that you saw with your own eyes." Moses seems to assume that it takes but a conscious act of vigilance to overcome forgetfulness and keep memory focused. In another example, Moses rhetorically turns to the past for justification as he announces to the people:

> You have but to inquire of former days that were before you, ever since God created a human on earth, from one end of the heavens to the other: has there ever been such a grand thing, or has its like been heard? Has a people ever heard the voice of a god speaking out of a fire, as you have, and lived? (Deut. 4:32–33)

Moses makes a lofty appeal to the past his chief rhetorical device. It is in the nature of rhetoric to go unanswered. His is an unquestioned declaration that the past exists as a trustworthy witness and allows for no alternative view. In fact, the people offer no objection but remain silent. The text projects an assumption of agreement. They will remember what Moses, in passionate speech, tells them to remember. The past as Moses retells it becomes the premise of present action as well as a guarantor of future events.

Moses spells out precisely what Israel is to remember in historical and abstract terms. For instance, Israel is to remember God's saving acts and interventions. The list of course includes the fact of their slavery (15:15, 24:18, 22), what God did to Pharoah (7:18), the hardship of the wilderness (8:2), and their own provocations (9:7). They are also to remember that God steadfastly remains the source of their power (8:18). They are exhorted to remember the afflictions of Miriam, the behavior of Amalek and especially the days of old. God in turn is exhorted by Moses to remember the patriarchs in Deuteronomy 9:27 (in a repetition of Exod. 32:13).

In sum, in his rhetoric Moses highlights key events of the recent past and ignores others, acting all the while as if the past he recounts is already a well-established and shared entity. In fact, Moses acts with a certain amount of urgency. The future Moses envisions for the people Israel depends on their acceptance of his particular version of the past and the lessons thereof.

In spite of that urgency, Deuteronomy does not resort to the drastic actions or consequences portrayed in Numbers. Rather, Deuteronomy ensures the memory of Moses' words even after he is gone by relying on, and celebrating, writing. Moses writes an extensive version of his teachings, calling it *torah* in Deuteronomy 31:9, 11, 12, and 24. In fact, it is in the book of Deuteronomy that the term *torah* is expanded from specific instruction for a particular addressee, usually a priest, to a written text that becomes central to Israel's life as a community, containing as it does God's rules for all of Israel. The people are to hear the written words of the Torah read aloud at a public gathering every seven years (Deut. 31:10–13). The centrality of writing in Deuteronomy, and its usefulness in shaping and preserving collective memory long into an anticipated future, is noticeably absent in the book of Numbers.[42]

This brief digression identifies the material objects of Exodus and the lofty rhetoric and written Torah of Moses in Deuteronomy as strategies deployed by the writers of the two books to control what it is that Israel shall remember from its past. Because memory is crucial to the agenda of each book, it is given significant attention but in a fairly straightforward and uncomplicated way. Above all, both books emphasize God's saving acts as the core memory that Israel must transmit from generation to generation.

✑ *Different conceptions of biblical memory*

This assumption that memory can be commanded, and that it can be used on behalf of the covenant between God and Israel, confirms classic definitions of biblical memory by Childs and Schottroff. Both argue that the bible uses זכר in its different forms for largely theological purposes. H. Eising interprets Schottroff's view of memory as expressing "a continuous adherence to a historical tradition."[43] God's saving acts form the greatest portion of that tradition. The cult then functions to remind later generations of those acts on their behalf. Childs echoes this view as he defines Israel's attempts to reinterpret the significance of its tradition in theological terms: "Israel testified to the continuing nature of her redemptive history by [interpreting] the events of the past in the light of her ongoing experience with the covenant God."[44] God's redemption of the people becomes the recurring content of collective memory throughout the generations. This holds true for Exodus and Deuteronomy but, as we shall see, is greatly modified in Numbers.

In his treatment of biblical memory Yosef Hayim Yerushalmi begins by acknowledging that memory is "always problematic, usually deceptive, sometimes treacherous."[45] Yet in discussing the Bible's conception of memory Yerushalmi assumes that memory can in fact be manipulated successfully. He notes that "the Hebrew Bible seems to have no hesitations in commanding memory."[46] Indeed, the bible assumes an uncomplicated conception of memory as static, universal, and indispensable. Memory does nothing less than form the basis of Israel's faith and its very existence. Sinai anchors that faith: "What took place at Sinai must be borne along the conduits of memory to those who were not there that day."[47] The biblical appeal to remember has little to do with curiosity about other events of the past. The principle behind the bible's selection of collective memories is apparent and clear: "God's acts of intervention in history and man's responses to them, be they positive or negative ... must be recalled."[48] Thus, though Yerushalmi notes a "desperate pathos about the biblical concern with memory, and a shrewd wisdom that knows how short and fickle human memory can be," his emphasis remains, just as that of Schottroff and Childs, on the widespread use of memory in the bible for theological purposes and its ready appropriation in doing so.[49]

All three critics develop their notions of biblical memory in readings of Deuteronomy, of the history of ancient Israel thought to emerge from the Deuteronomic school, and of the major prophetic works.[50] What happens when we turn to Numbers? We can certainly identify several examples of the use of memory that are at one with the assumptions made by Exodus and in Deuteronomy, especially in Numbers 10, 15 and 31, chapters in which God commands the creation of particular objects or acts of commemoration.

Yet as the rest of the present study will argue, at least one other tradition within Numbers vehemently and persuasively challenges such a fixed, static view of biblical memory. Beginning in chapter 11:5 memory introduces havoc into the camp and becomes an extraordinary problem for Moses. The opening verses of the chapter describe a collective, public remembering of Egyptian delicacies that trigger a series of disastrous events that end up challenging the wisdom of relying on memory at all. Hesitations concerning its malleability are fully justified in light of what follows – the death of an entire generation in the wilderness. Thus a discontinuity with what preceded Numbers 11 and with what will follow in Deuteronomy has occurred. The presence and juxtaposition of this strikingly different notion of memory with the far more common biblical understanding of memory demands an explanation that this work intends to provide.

Thus in subsequent chapters I focus primarily on Numbers. There is a distinct advantage to such a singular focus on Numbers. It allows me to highlight Numbers' unique contribution to the story of the beginnings of the people Israel, redressing the neglect of Numbers' role in prior studies. The priestly vision and concomitant assertion of power in Numbers (and not only in Leviticus) should be considered alongside other attempts to shape the Israelite community, namely, that of the Deuteronomists and the Prophets. In addition, the editors of Numbers not only have created a usable past on behalf of a later community but have left behind sustained reflections on such an attempt. Yet the resulting examination of the problematic dimension of memory as well as its potential has been consistently overlooked in other studies of the role of memory in shaping the people Israel into a unified whole.[51] Turning memory itself into an object of scrutiny as Numbers does can be quite fascinating and absorbing: "narration, description, reflective interpretation. And strange forces are at work in this process of unpacking memory, forces that we, in our turn, may want to unpack."[52]

∼ Re-reading Numbers

As a result of the skillful activity of its editors, Numbers offers the reader a rich and complex portrait of the events of Israel's long and difficult journey through the wilderness while simultaneously using that portrait to promote a priestly vision for Israel. That vision emerges out of an arrangement of multiple texts, derived from a collection of sources, at the disposal of the editors. As they communicate their vision of Israel to the reader, the editors do not conceal their editorial interventions. They are quite transparent. For instance, one can readily observe that different texts have been juxtaposed to one another or placed in an order that is not patently logical. I intend to illustrate that as they put these texts together, the editors of Numbers left the seams exposed in order to create the maximum amount of flexibility in shaping a final narrative of that time. By preserving opposing views on any given topic, such an editing project explicitly creates possibilities for inner biblical dialogue. Such a dialogue is a necessary prerequisite for any serious reflection on matters as weighty as establishing a collective narrative of origins, one that hopes to deter future mistakes and offer a commanding platform for the proper behavior of Israel in its relationship to God. Such dialogue ultimately becomes part of the skillful rhetorical persuasion of Numbers' priestly editors.[53]

Perhaps this type of editing can be understood by analogy to the careful observation of an intricately designed quilt. One detects the individual panels out of which a quilt may be sewn, yet also observes it as a whole, a perspective that creates the dominant impression. If Numbers is viewed in that fashion, in detail and as a whole, it becomes a series of separate episodes in the wilderness and, at the same time, a broad, searing meditation on the establishment of tradition and the use of memory and power to achieve it. Power – its pursuit and the ravages left in its wake, especially on the character of Israel – becomes a major subtext of the work. In the next two chapters I identify how the editors were able to transform an earlier, rather unruly, collection of texts into a complex but coherent narrative of the wilderness journey. I begin in chapter 2 by identifying evidence of the priestly editorial presence in Numbers and will continue in chapter 3 by examining the possible interests of those editors, especially vis-à-vis other figures of authority (such as the prophet). The evidence for particular priestly interests will also lead to a tentative proposal for the historical context of the editing of Numbers.

In its final form Numbers does not shirk from illustrating the many difficulties inherent in the attempt to constitute the people Israel out of a narrative of its past. Yet Numbers concludes on a positive note as the new generation prepares itself to enter the promised land rather than remain in the chaos of wilderness. They will do so under priestly control as proposed by God and Moses. According to its editors, each generation must make that same choice. And to make the proper choice, Israel must come to remember the wilderness journey in a highly specific way. A description of the struggle to understand and exploit collective memory to achieve such a goal provides the content of chapter 4.

Chapters 5 and 6 illustrate the strategies employed by the priestly editors to appropriate memory in a way that continues to strengthen, rather than subvert, their purposes. Those strategies are political in nature. In fact, politics pervades the portrait of the wilderness camp. Chapter 5 examines the tense struggles over the proper leadership, priestly or nonpriestly, and over the proper leaders – Moses, his siblings, or, albeit briefly, his cousin Korah. Questions over access to the holy sites, even access to God, trigger dangerous, at times lethal, confrontations. In chapters 15–17 of Numbers ritual objects – tassels on one's garment, plating on the altar, and a flowering rod – come to be associated with the resolution of those struggles. Each is meant to influence the way in which future generations will come to remember Israel's past in the wilderness. Each reinforces the priestly authority. Chapter 6 identifies and investigates the most powerful means used by the editors of Numbers to convince their audience to submit to that authority – death itself. The generation's grim abandonment in the wilderness colors the reports of its fate, reports that illustrate the political (and heartbreaking) nature of death and burial.

Finally, in a brief conclusion to the present study, I consider the pragmatic and anti-climactic way in which Numbers ends. As the new generation is about to inhabit the land, a law regulating female inheritance is revisited and revised. How can such an ending possibly be considered a fitting conclusion to the long and often tragic journey through the wilderness? As we shall see, by focusing on future inheritance once in the land Numbers assumes not only that there is a way out of the morass of wilderness but that the people Israel are, at long last, about to arrive in the promised land.

TWO

Weaving by Design

The complex reflections on tradition and memory embedded in the narrative of Numbers are made possible by the book's long and interesting compositional history. Numbers comprises a collection of materials dating from fairly early in Israel's history to post-exilic times and includes a noteworthy variety of genres: ancient poetry, narratives of complaint and rebellion, a legendary tale involving a talking ass, law and ritual, two censuses, a travelogue, and an archival list. These different materials, by their careful placement within the larger narrative, create an inner-biblical dialogue that allows different aspects of tradition and memory to be illustrated, considered, rejected, and/or promoted. Those differences are precisely the point, for the final version of Numbers is forged out of a chorus of different voices in interaction, advancing an argument that manages nonetheless to unify the book through a vision of the wilderness period in its entirety. My rereading of Numbers traces competing versions of what took place in the wilderness after the people Israel left Egypt and the uneasy fusion of those discrete materials into a final form.

Several methodological assumptions shape this way of reading. I assume that only some of the multiple traditions found in Numbers neatly fall into sources as identified by the documentary hypothesis, namely, priestly versus nonpriestly sources. Others clearly lie outside the scholarly categories generated by that hypothesis.[1] For instance, Numbers 21 refers to an obscure work, the book of the Wars of YHWH, and two archaic poems, one about a well, the other an ode to the ancient city of Heshbon. None of these texts readily fits the description of those proposed in the documentary hypothesis. In fact, Numbers contains the most diverse and far-ranging collection of materials within the Five Books of Moses. A number of those texts fall outside the hypothesized sources. In the present work, I am not interested in, and do not take up, the precise dating of those obscure independent traditions nor am I interested in microscopically identifying segments of narrative verse by verse so as to claim that they belong to one source or another. Others have done that type of detailed analysis.[2] But neither do I intend to ignore or minimize the variety of texts and traditions in Numbers. The multiple sources of Numbers are significant precisely because of their richness and diversity. I am simply interested in more broadly identifying and analyzing them as they are preserved *both in their separateness and in their interactions* within the final form.

I believe there are advantages to this approach. Reading the text as composed of multiple traditions allows one, as Ernest Nicholson has put it, to hear "the testimony of many voices at different stages in the history of Israel."[3] Just such a purposeful preservation of discrete texts allows the text's final form to become a record of the past. As put by Tigay: "By not imposing unity and consistency on the sources, the compiler preserved the variety and richness of ancient Israelite belief, tradition, law and literature."[4] In what follows I am interested in how the variety of biblical materials that comprise Numbers function as independent units. In consequence, I briefly elaborate on the contours of such materials in this chapter.

Yet these different stories and texts *are* undeniably linked together in a larger whole. Only by observing that larger whole can I detect how the *placement* of discrete materials functions. In other words, why weave the cloth in one particular way and no other? The final product, whether in the hands of a single or multiple editors, does produce a design that is different from its parts. Therefore in this chapter and throughout the present work I am equally interested in the weaver or editor of the whole. Richard Elliot Friedman succinctly captures the weight of an editor's influence on his given materials: "The combinatory design which this redactor conceived did more than house the received texts. It gave birth to new narrative syntheses . . . the Priestly tradents's contribution [is] . . . no less significant and no less creative than that of the authors who, knowing or not, bequeathed their work into his care."[5] Note Friedman's identification of the tradent as priestly, an identification I suggested in chapter 1 for the editors of Numbers due to their striking preoccupation with priestly concerns and with a change in the priestly hierarchy. For these reasons and others that I enumerate in the course of my argument, I have concluded that the editorial presence I seek to highlight is a priestly one.

Thus, throughout this work I attempt to strike a balanced reading that takes into account both the final form of Numbers with its priestly editors and the earlier materials that they edited. I assume throughout that the editors skillfully and purposefully used the earlier materials to great effect. At certain points the editors were compelled to go out of their way to preserve traditions in their separateness, even in their contradictoriness, within a narrative synthesis. Yet they also edited those traditions into a coherent whole. In so doing they functioned not as mere compilers or anthologists but as highly creative writers who affected the material they had at hand by adding to it, however sparingly at times. The editors had a clear design in mind, one that fulfilled a highly ideological agenda identifiable from the results of the editorial placement of, and additions to, prior materials. They envisioned and argued for a life under specifically priestly control yet reached that conclusion, and hoped to convince others, by navigating a journey through earlier textual traditions that they used to the fullest.

Before proceeding I want to again raise the issue of treating Numbers largely on its own rather than as part of the Torah as a whole. I do so in light of the present chapter's interest in the editors of Numbers. Those editors probably combined Numbers with the other four books of the Torah. In addition, Numbers contains sources (i.e., "J" and "P") that begin in Genesis and run through Exodus and Leviticus. And in its present placement, Numbers certainly functions to continue an ongoing narrative that began with God's promises to Abraham, promises that encountered enormous obstacles in Numbers that were met and overcome by journey's end under the leadership of Moses. Thus Numbers and its editorial project are part of an even larger whole. Yet each of the Five Books is often fruitfully considered on its own terms as well. Each book depicts and responds to a particular moment in that ongoing narrative or to a particular undertaking (such as the construction of the tabernacle) before the people Israel settle the land. Within each work, certain themes, even those we encountered in prior works, are taken up and explored anew. This is true even when stories seem to repeat themselves, such as the episodes of complaint found in Exodus and in Numbers. Within each book they lead to different consequences – reproach and accommodation in Exodus versus outright condemnation in Numbers. Furthermore, each book may introduce new material that legitimates an examination of that particular work in detail. For instance, Numbers introduces and makes much of a priestly hierarchy consisting of sons of Aaron over against other Levites and makes much of the ramifications of such an innovation. Baruch Levine highlights this distinctive aspect of Numbers when he observes that Numbers 8 confirms "the position of the Levites as an order subordinate to the Aaronide priesthood.... In this respect the book of Numbers parts company with Deuteronomy, and in its emphasis is distinctive even within priestly literature itself."[6] Thus, without losing sight, when relevant, of Numbers vis-à-vis the other books of the Torah, especially the other priestly materials and parallel episodes in those books, the present work treats Numbers and its editors largely on their own terms.

In the rest of this chapter I briefly describe the separate materials that comprise Numbers and then propose how we can discern the editors at work as they combine and add to the texts they received. I conclude with a brief evaluation of at least some of the results.[7] To obtain those results, the editors deployed a rhetoric whose power lay in "an articulating and structuring of words intended to constitute or prefigure actualities of the 'real world.'"[8] In its final form Numbers was meant to do nothing less than shape the community of readers and listeners into a united audience with a common purpose – the building of a life for the people Israel in the promised land. It did so in part by relying on narrative, revealing "its function in creating a people in politics and history."[9]

⬦ The sources

In recent years the status of the documentary hypothesis as an adequate explanation for the composition of the Five Books of Moses has been subjected to intense criticism. There are many dissenters in the scholarly literature concerning not only the number, identification, and breakdown of sources, but in thinking of the Five Books as composed in this fashion. In consequence, other models have been proposed, such as that of Rolf Rendtorff. He suggests that the Torah developed out of a series of compositional accretions, or "a number of 'larger units,' each of which has its own respective profile and history and which were brought together at a later stage."[10] In the same essay he asserts that the assumptions of the documentary hypothesis are in such serious doubt that "the main pillars of that theory are no longer taken as valid."[11] Yet in 2003 Richard Elliot Friedman published *The Bible with Sources Revealed*, in which he not only provides a thorough and highly accessible justification and explanation of the documentary hypothesis but highlights those sources throughout the Five Books of Moses in shades of green and blue. This is not the place to account for those disagreements. I have described them elsewhere, as have others.[12] For now, I simply want to acknowledge that as a result of my encounters with the diverse texts of Numbers my approach falls somewhere in the middle of the continuum of rejection and acceptance. In other words, I do not wholly subscribe to the neat categories of the documentary hypothesis but neither do I reject at least some of its proposals.

Let me begin by briefly reminding the reader of the proposed sources of the documentary hypothesis. Two sources are labeled in reference to alternative names for God – J for Jahweh (YHWH) and E for Elohim (and now RJE, referring to an edited J and E source) – while two others are labeled for the figures involved in preserving a particular source – P for priests and D for those who contributed to the content and editing of Deuteronomy.[13] Over time the P source came to be understood as containing both early and late materials, designated as P and H (whether H predates or follows P is still debated). H is engaged with issues of holiness. Finally, R refers to the redactors. Note that these letters do not necessarily refer to an individual but rather to a group of writers and editors over time.

With this basic hypothetical description of sources in mind, what can be discovered when one turns to the actual biblical book of Numbers? The first impression is one of stylistic order, and a reliance on formulas and genealogical lists, established hallmarks of the P source. The second impression is that priestly concerns do indeed dominate as I shall describe in much greater detail in chapter 4. For now, let us note some of those priestly concerns: transporting the tabernacle, the role of the Levites vis-à-vis the sons of Aaron, and several communal and personal issues that require priestly supervision. There is little controversy or disagreement that a significant amount of textual material in Numbers shows evidence of a priestly provenance, even if the dating of that material is contested (a debate I describe in the next chapter). For instance, in his commentary on Numbers Baruch Levine cites the preponderance of priestly materials, including documents that he classes as administrative. These include census records and a list of donations to the tabernacle as well as the description of priestly rituals, and an abundance of priestly language.[14] In an even more recent work (2005), Knierim and Coats identify the emphasis on Aaron and his sons as the primary evidence that the editors of Numbers represent priestly interests. They characterize all of Numbers 1–10 as a priestly program for the future of the people Israel.[15] In my own survey of Numbers, I have observed that in a book of thirty-six chapters the priests play an important supervisory role, develop priestly legislation, perform a ritual act, or provide a calendar of sacrificial offerings in at least twenty-four of those chapters.[16] Thus I accept P as the likely source for many of the materials in Numbers.

But what of H, an additional priestly source, and its relationship to P? Here I rely on the argument of Israel Knohl, who defines H as a priestly source that follows P. According to Knohl, H added new priestly materials to an earlier priestly corpus while also editing nonpriestly materials into a final form. Therefore H could be R as well! In other words, this later priestly source could at some point be responsible not only for adding more material to the work but in editing and completing Numbers. Knohl's proposals strike me as sensible on historical grounds. It is plausible to suggest that a group as influential as the priests, whose roles only grew in importance from late First Temple times into the period of the Second Temple, would have recorded and provided a great deal of textual material such as ritual and legal instructions that make up the Torah. To survive over such a long period of time, such a group would inevitably adapt to changing circumstances. According to Knohl, such a changing circumstance might include the rise of a prophet, such as Isaiah, who attacked the priests with pointed criticisms for what he considered their intolerable priestly insularity. This tension between priest and prophet can also be identified within Numbers itself as I shall discuss in chapter 3. Knohl's identification of the later editorial layers of Numbers as priestly is considered uncontroversial.[17] For instance, Baruch Levine emphasizes that the restructuring of earlier material in the book of Numbers is done by priestly writers. Knierim and Coats emphasize that later priestly layers within Numbers are expansions of earlier priestly materials.[18]

So far I have accepted that P and H/R originate in a priestly class over a long period of time and are crucial sources for many of the early and later materials and the later editors of Numbers. Numbers contains few materials that originate with the D source, writers of Deuteronomy. That leaves only the sources labeled J and E. The materials in Numbers that do not originate in the priestly class simply do not fit two such discrete and self-contained sources. Materials outside the purported sources include early poetry in Numbers 21, the many citations of battles, the travelogue of Numbers 33, and the legend of the talking ass, thought to originate in Trans-Jordanian materials. I consider the cited texts to be independent traditions (perhaps originally oral) that came into the hands of the later editors of Numbers. On the other hand, the content of some of the texts in the middle chapters of Numbers does seem to fit the concerns of the sources described in scholarly literature as J and E. These chapters, particularly Numbers 11–12, dramatically raise and resolve prophetic concerns and rivalries concerning the figure of Moses.[19] I am willing to concede these obvious nonpriestly chapters might match descriptions of J or of E, especially because they also portray the people Israel, Moses, and his siblings in a critical and complex light. Such psychologically astute portraits of biblical characters can be found in the portraits of the patriarchs in Genesis that are considered J or E, even though those attributions have also been subjected to criticism. Hopefully, the reader can begin to appreciate the amount of detail open to dispute and controversy in the proposals of the documentary hypothesis. That complexity has repeatedly led even the supporters of the hypothesis to disagree over its particulars.

For present purposes, I assume that a significant amount of Numbers originates in priestly circles, and that at least some of the nonpriestly material might fit J, E, or RJE, while other material does not. No matter the origins of those texts, later priestly figures put the earlier materials together over a period of time. To a large degree my proposal for the compositional history of Numbers agrees with a broader consensus for the composition of the first three books that precede Numbers. Each book contains its own balance of early and late materials, while it is assumed that some priestly figure put these works and Numbers together with the fifth book of Moses, Deuteronomy, probably during the early years of the Second Temple period. The priestly editors appear more obviously active in Numbers than in the other books, perhaps because the traditions of the wilderness period that they received were a fragmentary or particularly diverse collection in greater need of their active interventions. The editors of Numbers certainly made their presence felt in their introduction of a priestly hierarchy that is considered a relatively late innovation within the Five Books, largely absent from Exodus or Leviticus. The subordination of Levite to Cohen might have even originated during the final stages of the redaction of Numbers.[20]

I refer to Numbers 11 and 12, and portions of 13, 14, and 16 – all distinct from priestly materials in language, content, tone, and style – simply as nonpriestly texts. The other texts I cited above, such as the records of battles and early poems, will also fall into the category of "nonpriestly." The later priestly editors use these nonpriestly materials to dramatic and rich effect as they juxtapose them with earlier priestly texts about the wilderness period, sometimes even within the same chapter. It is in the use made of these materials that the skills of the priestly editors are most apparent. Let us now turn more specifically to the evidence for that later editorial presence.

∼ Editorial interventions

Several types of editorial interventions can be discerned in Numbers. Cumulatively, the evidence confirms a "mediating intelligence."[21] Interventions include the structural framework for Numbers, especially the placement of the two censuses that anchor the book. Minor interventions weave together or connect the separate materials or narrative episodes within that frame through the use of formulaic phrasing, repetition, and the deployment of key words over a section of material rather than in a single passage. The results produced are discernible in both minute and broad fashion. I elucidate some of those results on a micro-level, examining chapters 32–34, and on the macro-level, briefly stepping back to perceive the design of the whole. Through careful and quite precise placement, chapters 32–34 provide a discrete example of the more general editorial interventions throughout the book. The three distinct events narrated in those particular chapters work together like a puzzle when placed in chronological succession. The broader mediating presence of the editors can be determined by looking at two crucial topics that weave Numbers into a coherent whole: Israel's relationship to Egypt and the configuration of time in the wilderness. Returning for a moment to the metaphor of the weaver, in the rest of this chapter I examine the framing of separate biblical materials, the weaving together of the pieces, and the effect thus produced when taken as a whole.[22]

∿ *Framing the wilderness journey*

The opening and concluding chapters of Numbers provide a frame in which the rest of the book is placed. One can detect that frame by noting two concrete topics that are initially elaborated on and then returned to at the end of the book. These are the naming of the tribes and the singling out of the Levites. The placement of the censuses that name the tribes in chapters 1 and 26 anchor the materials and are then followed in each instance with an explicit reference to the Levites. That symmetry suggests an editorial hand.

I begin with a brief description of the opening chapters in order to highlight the return to that content in the concluding chapters of Numbers. Chapter 1:1 concretizes the situation of the Israelites in a detailed and, at the same time, remarkably concise report. The reader learns the location and setting of the story, the wilderness at Sinai. A site within the wilderness is singled out as the setting for God's commandment to Moses. Their conversation occurs not just on any day or year, but on a specific day in a specific year, anchored of course in a momentous past event:

> And YHWH spoke to Moses in the wilderness of Sinai in the tent of Meeting on the first day of the second month in the second year after their leaving the land of Egypt. (Num. 1:1)

This careful rendering of the scene purposefully roots the opening chapters, using the Exodus as starting point. The first census follows.

The census categorizes the group by tribes, listing the descendants of Jacob's twelve sons as head of each division.[23] A single formula is repeated twelve times. Verses 26–27 of chapter 1 are typical: "Of the children of Judah, their generations, after their families, by their ancestral house, as listed by name, aged twenty years and over, all who were able to go forth to war – those enrolled from the tribe of Judah: 74,600." The entries are largely identical. Only the names and numbers vary. Reuben, Simeon, Gad, Judah, down to the descendants of Naphtali, thousands are recorded by their tribal names and numbered. The listing of the descendants of the twelve sons of Jacob, each in turn, provides a coherent structure for this opening census.

By structuring the census around the twelve sons of Jacob, Numbers is linked to Jacob's dying testament to his sons at the end of Genesis.[24] The list in Numbers reiterates one of the functions of genealogies in Genesis. Every list of descendants fulfills God's promise of the blessing of vast numbers of offspring throughout the generations. The current census refers to those promises made in the past but kept in the present, fulfilled in the image of thousands camped in the wilderness.

However, in contrast to Jacob's genealogy, the tribe of Levi is singled out in Numbers 1:47–53 for greater attention. The Levites hold a special responsibility for the transportation and guarding of the wilderness tabernacle (at times referred to as the Tent of Meeting), a role that did not yet exist at the time of Jacob's death. The brief but noticeable singling out of the Levites in Numbers 1 is very suggestive, anticipating in microcosm the later and innovative elaboration of the relationship of the tribe of Levi to the rest of the children of Israel, including the sons of Aaron, that is a hallmark of Numbers.

The description of these tribal arrangements is interrupted by a notice in chapter 2 that locates the Tent of Meeting in the very center of the camp: "And so moved the Tent of Meeting, of the camp of the Levites, in the midst of the camps. As they camped so did they move, each in position, by their standards" (Num. 2:17). The tribal arrangements, the exact physical locations, and the Tent's placement provide the reader with a striking blueprint of the camp, making an actual model of the wilderness camp a fairly easy undertaking.[25] It is meant to be duplicated – again and again – vividly fixing it for all time, if only in the reader's imagination.

Chapters 3 and 4 focus on the Levites. They are placed at dead center of the assembled group, a center containing the Tent of Meeting, which they surround. The detailed discussion of the Levites, their special responsibilities for the Tent of Meeting (guarding its implements, setting it up and taking it down, carrying the tent on the journey through the wilderness) and their relationship to Aaron, high priest, is, as I have noted, a particularly important topic. It is also unique to Numbers. The Levites join Aaron and his sons in forming a priestly hierarchy in which the Levites are subordinate, creating further order within the Israelite organization as well as considerable tension and even violence within in the priestly group. For now, the naming, numbering, and placing of the Levites in the camp replicates in miniature the larger census and mapping of the Israelites contained in Numbers 1 and 2, suggesting that the Levitical group is fitted into the larger scheme of the opening census.

Finally, one other piece of evidence signals the editorial presence. The concluding verse in each of the first four chapters, identical in at least one phrase, firmly shapes the four chapters into an integrated unit. Each of these verses contains the following phrase: אשר צוה יהוה את משה, "as YHWH commanded Moses." In addition, the concluding verses of chapters 1 and 2 subtly move the narrative forward. The first two concluding verses are as follows:

> And the children of Israel did all *as YHWH commanded Moses*, so they did. (Num. 1:54)

> And the children of Israel did all *as YHWH commanded Moses*, so they camped according to their banners and so they traveled, each according to his clan by his father's house. (Num. 2:34, emphasis added)

Note that both verses contain the identical phrase. However, 2:34 moves beyond "so they did" to the far more specific "camped" and "traveled," conveying the impression of movement and emphasizing that Israel is indeed on a journey. The concluding verses of chapters 3 and 4 emphasize their unity with the above two verses through the repeated use of the same phrase, placed now as the conclusion of each verse.

> And Moses gave the redemption money to Aaron and his sons according to the bidding of YHWH *as YHWH commanded Moses.* (Num. 3:51)

> At the bidding of YHWH they were accounted by the hand of Moses, each individual to his service and his porterage and his record *as YHWH commanded Moses.* (Num. 4:49)

Thus chapters 1–4 reveal a pattern that in its repetition appears purposeful rather than random. Such repetition demarcates and sets apart the initial chapters from what follows.

The striking duplication of the content of chapters 1–4 in the closing chapters of Numbers reinforces the impression of a purposeful frame. Naming and numbering the Israelites and Levites recur, beginning with another census in chapter 26, this time taken by Moses and Eleazar, son and successor to Aaron. The two censuses anchor the book's structure while also highlighting the fate of the wilderness generation. Before I examine the census of chapter 26 in more detail, let me first elucidate the ways in which the activities of the opening chapters are duplicated, though admittedly more broadly, in the closing chapters of Numbers that follow the second census.

At the end of chapter 34:16–29, the reader hears a familiar echo of the earlier naming of the twelve tribes as they are about to be positioned in the wilderness camp. But this time the naming of the tribes pronouncedly shifts the reader's attention to the future life lived in the land. Moses is once again instructed by God:

> And you shall also take a chieftain from each tribe *to divide the land for possession*. These are the names of the men: from the tribe of Judah: Caleb son of Jephunneh. From the tribe of the children of Simeon: Samuel son of Ammihud. (Num. 34:18–20, emphasis added)

Those now explicitly mentioned inherit territory in the land, rather than reside in the wilderness. They will finally achieve the goal their parents were denied. In fact, a form of inheritance, נחלה, surfaces in these latter chapters in numerous examples: Numbers 26:53–56, 27:7–11, and in the chapter just quoted, 34:2, 5, 13, 14, 15, 17, 18, 29 (not an exhaustive list). The repetition of נחלה in the narrative of the second generation typifies the biblical use of a leading word, reinforcing the shift in focus from wilderness to the impending entry into the Land. Such a use should not be considered coincidental but rather the means of thematically unifying the various chapters that form Numbers' conclusion. Finally, the Levites as a separate entity are reintroduced in chapter 35 much as they were introduced as a separate entity in the opening chapters of Numbers. Chapter 35 discusses the inheritance of the Levites, because they too are about to enter the land with the rest of Israel.

Chapters 26, 34, and 35 provide a clear parallel in miniature to the book's opening chronology as it lists the descendants of Jacob's sons and then lists the Levites. This is hardly coincidental. Yet in spite of this type of evidence, many commentators argue that the wide array of materials constituting Numbers results in an unruly, chaotic book, preventing a coherent structure from emerging in its final form.[26] I would disagree. By paying attention to framing devices, the two censuses and the deployment of a leading word over several chapters, the current argument suggests that the design of the book has an unmistakably purposeful order. Much like book ends, these devices support the story. At its core, the wilderness journey depicts the many difficulties that threaten the successful completion of the journey – murmurings, disorder, rebellion – all kept at bay and ultimately overcome with enormous difficulty, at least in the new generation. The repetition of names and numbers of Israelites in the second generation confirms that success while reminding the reader how it all began forty years earlier.

∿ Counting the children of Israel a second time

The extent to which the second census found in chapter 26 adds to the purposeful design of the materials becomes clear on closer scrutiny. All those so carefully numbered in the opening census are condemned by God to die in the wilderness. The second census in chapter 26 explicitly confirms the implementation of those deaths:

> These are the persons enrolled by Moses and Eleazar the priest who enrolled the Children of Israel on the steppes of Moab, at the Jordan near Jericho. Among these there was not one of those enrolled by Moses and Aaron the priest when they enrolled the Israelites in the Wilderness of Sinai. For YHWH had said to them, "They shall die in the wilderness." Not one of them remained, except Caleb son of Jephunneh and Joshua son of Nun. (Num. 26:63–65)

Almost nonchalantly the verses confirm the astounding result of God's punishment – not a soul remains of all those thousands recorded in the opening census except for the leaders – Moses, Eleazar, Caleb, and Joshua.

Dennis Olson builds an entire thematic and structural interpretation of Numbers out of the two census lists. His work's title, *The Death of the Old and the Birth of the New*, introduces the argument. He sees "the two census lists of the twelve tribes of Israel in Numbers 1 and 26 [as providing] the major structural edifice of which the organization of the book as a whole stands."[27] Identical language links the two lists, as God commands Moses:

> *Take a census of all the congregation of the people of Israel* by families, by fathers' houses, according to the number of names, every male, head by head, from twenty years old and upward, all in Israel who are able to go forth to war. (Num. 1:2–3, Olson trans., emphasis added)

> *Take a census of all the congregation of the people of Israel,* from twenty years old and upward, by their fathers' houses, all in Israel who are able to go forth to war. (Num. 26:2, Olson trans., emphasis added)

Olson's emphasis on the structure provided by the census lists provides a counterweight to the majority of modern commentators on Numbers, who fail in his view to propose a "coherent, convincing and meaningful structure for the book."[28] His analysis of Numbers provides the starting point from which the current argument is developed.

Olson shows that the census of chapter 26 confirms the survival of the Israelites in spite of the condemnation of the wilderness generation. To make that point, the names of the various sons or clans of each tribe are extended one more generation than those mentioned in the earlier list found in chapter 1 of Numbers.[29] Such an extension of generations seems quite pointed. The fortunes of the second generation and their children, as recorded in the latter half of Numbers, will be radically different from those of the first generation. Indeed, future life in the land will replace the pervasiveness of death in the wilderness. The placement of the second census immediately after the deaths of the wilderness generation, but immediately prior to the shift in emphasis to the future, allows the census to serve as the bridge between narrative sections. Its placement argues for an editorial intervention.

In one rather intriguing respect, the second census differs from the first. Chapter 26 contains a fascinating series of asides that are missing from the earlier census. Those asides selectively shape the past by alluding to and ordering the narrative materials that precede chapter 26. The allusions even extend back to Genesis and include Exodus and Leviticus as well as Numbers. Those asides give the entire narrative a sense of coherence both internal to the book of Numbers and as a bridge to material found in the first three books of Moses. In addition to the conventional list of names, the topics found in chapter 26 include, in the order of their mention (which is not chronologically accurate): the departure from Egypt; the deaths of Korah and the rebels; the deaths of Judah's two oldest sons (which predate the descent of Jacob and his sons into Egypt); the names of the daughters of Zelophehad, anticipating their narrative appearance in the following chapter; an obscure but intriguing reference to Serah, daughter of Asher; the births of Moses, Aaron, and Miriam in Egypt; the deaths of Aaron's two oldest sons; the first census; and, finally, God's condemnation of the entire wilderness generation.[30] Some of these asides can be accounted for by the typical interest in births and deaths expected in a census. Other asides highlight key points in the narrative, such as the births of Israel's leaders, the departure from Egypt, and the crisis created by Korah's rebellion. But a few notations in chapter 26 cannot be explained so readily. They suggest an underlying agenda. For instance, the mention of the deaths of Judah's sons reminds us that nonetheless the rest of that important tribe will survive. Or alternatively, perhaps mention of Judah's loss of his two sons is meant to parallel the loss of Aaron's two sons in Leviticus 10 in some type of balance between families or political alliances, between secular and priestly rule. However intriguing the details in the second census, these speculations lie beyond the present argument.

For now, it is the evidence of a reciprocal relationship with the prior material, a relationship that works in both directions, that is most pertinent. Chapter 26 could represent an older kernel out of which the prior narratives are elaborated. Or, without contradicting that conjecture, one could also argue that chapter 26 functions as a summary of those same events. Even if the census itself is an independent document, written long before the editors used it (a highly probable conjecture), its *placement* in chapter 26 of the narrative creates possibilities not necessarily present if read only in isolation.[31] In its current placement, the second census not only functions retrospectively to remind us of past events, but also looks forward, setting the stage for the anticipation of the impending future in the land found in the remainder of the wilderness narrative in Numbers. This weaving of the past into a bleak present while awaiting a better future is a striking dimension of Numbers and among the best evidence for a mediating editorial intelligence.

～ *Present, past, future: Numbers 32–34*

Medieval commentators of the Bible, such as Rashi, assumed that seemingly distinct biblical events found in a narrative sequence were linked by purposeful association. The commentators strove to supply the meaning of such linkages as part of their commentaries.[32] I too ascribe importance to the interconnections between distinct materials. In addition, I want to argue that the editorial placement of independent, distinct materials that leads to such connections is intended to invite not just medieval commentators but all subsequent readers to consider the sequencing of chapters, their interactions, and their meaning. Chapters 32–34 of Numbers provide an extended example of such editorial activity. Each chapter is distinct from one another in content, tone, and provenance, yet when read together, the three chapters convey one of the core, and increasingly urgent, messages of Numbers: the necessity of reading the lessons of the past correctly (as defined by the book's editors) in order to reach the promised land.

As chapter 32 opens the Gadites and Reubenites request permission to remain outside the land, on the other side of the Jordan. Moses interprets their request as a serious threat to the whole enterprise, immediately reminded of the older generation's refusal to cross over the Jordan. He angrily retorts: "And now you, a brood of sinful men, have risen up in place of your fathers, to add still further to the wrath of YHWH against Israel" (Num. 32:14). Moses' anger at the tribes must surely be exacerbated by the fact of his own impending death, as he identifies their request to remain on the other side of the Jordan as a rejection of his life's work – the safe and successful arrival of the new generation in the promised land. He can think of no better response to the two tribes than by using past events to threaten them as he accuses them of repeating the mistakes of their fathers.

Immediately after this confrontation, Moses again turns to the past in chapter 33, but this time, *to record it formally* in a self-contained document, the itinerary of the wilderness wandering. The context of the itinerary's placement suggests that Moses understands that his time to persuade the people is fast slipping away. All he will be able to leave behind to guide the present generation is a record of the prior generation's punishing journey as they wandered through the desert for forty long years. Moses recalls each physical site along the way with remarkable precision.

Subsequently, chapter 34 records the exact boundaries of the land, providing both destination and reward for the new generation after the exhausting travels listed in such detail by Moses. The choice between the geography of wilderness and that of the homeland is made marvelously tangible to the children of Israel and all future readers through the linked descriptions of physical place. Thus disparate pieces of narrative – chapters 32–34 – fit together like a puzzle. The threat to the entire enterprise leads to a formal recording of wilderness space traversed over forty years only to be followed by imagining the intended space of promised land. By observing the skillful weaving together of chapters 32–34, a discernible design emerges that at the same time testifies to the editorial presence.

Nowhere is this presence more evident than in the placement of the itinerary in chapter 33 with its record of the past squarely positioned between the present crisis of chapter 32 and the future hope of chapter 34. The editors of Numbers repeatedly argue that only the correct reading of the past can lead to the desired future. Most likely an independent document of 49 verses, the itinerary, placed very near the end of the entire narrative (in chapter 33 of 36 chapters), not only functions as a bridge between chapters 32 and 34, but does nothing less than recapitulate the entire journey in the wilderness until that point.[33] We have seen the shrewd placement and use made of an independent document before in the placement of the second census found in Numbers 26 that summarizes what preceded it and anticipates what will follow. Chapter 33 functions precisely in this manner. But unlike the census, which refers to characters and events as long ago as Genesis, thus hundreds of years earlier, the itinerary begins with the very day of the Exodus from Egypt. It then focuses almost exclusively on the journey through the wilderness, a mere forty years. In so doing it provides a fine example of the editors' overarching attempt to shape the wide-ranging collection of materials that describe the wilderness period into a coherent whole. In fact, the itinerary provides a paramount example of biblical material preserved and exploited in the service of building a collective memory of the wilderness. Yet its use in the preservation and shaping of the just completed past – in fact, its turning that past into an object of scrutiny – has been largely ignored. Thus it warrants further analysis as an extended example of the results when the editors skillfully place independent materials where they will do the most good in reinforcing larger editorial goals.

⤳ Travels in the wilderness

Chapter 33 begins by stating:

> These are the marches of the children of Israel who left the land of Egypt, according to their armies, in the charge of Moses and Aaron. And Moses wrote their goings out according to their journeys by the order of YHWH; and these are their journeys according to their goings out. (Num. 33:1–2)

The reference to writing is quite unusual in Numbers. Here Moses writes the record of the journey as demanded by none other than God. The chapter recapitulates the exact stops along the way in the wilderness, providing an itinerary of the trip not yet completed. It is a rare record of travels within the biblical corpus. The vast wilderness spaces crossed by the Israelites are labeled in minute detail, turning anonymous desert into a memorable series of stops along the way.[34] The geographer Yi-Fu Tuan describes the effects of naming place: "If we think of space as that which allows movement, then place is a pause; each pause in movement makes it possible for location to be transformed into place."[35]

In addition to the detailed listing of the stations along the way, Moses highlights several events that occurred on the journey. If the itinerary actually predates other materials found in Numbers, then these asides could theoretically form the kernel of the prior narrative. Yet, much as we saw with the placement of the second census in chapter 26, regardless of its original function or dating, it is the *final placement* of the itinerary with its asides located almost at the conclusion of Numbers, certainly at the end of the journey, that most captures our attention. The itinerary functions to organize the prior narrative into a coherent whole yet does so not only by summarizing the events of the wilderness journey but by signaling which of those events should stand out for special notice. It is not sufficient to recall the past. The past must be recalled in specific and polemically useful ways. The asides found in chapter 33 include four key topics: the moment Israel left Egypt, the naming of sites either lacking in water or overflowing, the announcement of Aaron's death, and the first battle against a Canaanite king.

To begin, verses 3–4 depict the moment of leaving Egypt the morning after the Passover. The Egyptians are busy burying their dead:

> They set out from Rameses in the first month, on the fifteenth day of the first month. It was on the morrow of the Passover offering that the children of Israel started out defiantly, in plain view of all the Egyptians. And the Egyptians were burying those among them whom YHWH had struck down, every first-born, and upon their gods YHWH executed judgment. (Num. 33: 3–4)

Mention of the first Passover reinforces the connection of the present moment not only to the flight from Egypt described in Exodus but to additional references to those events in Numbers (i.e., God's reference to the slaying of the first-born Egyptians in Num. 3:13 and to laws of Passover observance in Num. 9:1–14). The Egyptian burial of their dead refers to the tenth plague, the slaying of the Egyptian first-born, the climax of God's plan to liberate the Israelites. The narrator of Numbers 33 could have mentioned all of the plagues as an entity, the "signs and wonders" frequently mentioned elsewhere in the Torah. Yet the particular act of burial is selected, even though, or perhaps because, it is omitted in the earlier story in the book of

Exodus. Thus Numbers 33:4 returns to the terrible events that occurred at the moment of departure forty years earlier but adds further information, as if only now completing the tale. Certainly, the singling out of the tenth plague here reinforces its importance to the story of the Exodus. But perhaps the emphasis on burial has a further meaning within Numbers. In chapter 6 of the present work I take up the lack of *Israelite* burial in the wilderness as a significant fact in need of interpretation. Perhaps the reference in Numbers 33 to the Egyptian care of their dead is meant to contrast with the treatment of the Israelite dead left largely abandoned in the anonymity of wilderness. Such a contrast heightens the severity of the punishment of the entire Israelite generation liberated from Egypt only to die in the wilderness.

The lack or provision of water during the wilderness journey provides the second topic of concern. Verse 9 states: "And they traveled from Mara and came to Elim and in Elim were twelve fountains of water and 70 palm trees and they camped there." But verse 14 states: "And they traveled from Alush and camped at Refidim but there was no water there for the people to drink." Concerns for water surface repeatedly throughout Numbers, often causing the people to complain and ultimately triggering the punishment of Moses and Aaron. God condemns both men to die in the wilderness, outside the promised land.

As if aware of that connection, the next aside in the itinerary informs us of the age of Aaron at his death as well as the site of that death:

> Aaron the priest ascended Mount Hor at the command of YHWH and died there, in the fortieth year after the Israelites had left the land of Egypt, on the first day of the fifth month. And Aaron was a hundred and twenty-three years old when he died on Mount Hor. (Num. 33:38–39)

Interestingly enough, as in verse 4, this aside also offers additional information – details of Aaron's age and the precise day of his death – missing from the report of Aaron's death in chapter 20.

Finally, verse 40 informs the reader that the Canaanite king of Arad has learned of the impending arrival of the Israelites. The battle against this king, described in detail in chapter 21, just after the death of Aaron (thus precisely duplicating its order in the itinerary), marks a turning point in the fate of the Israelites. After this battle, they will be victorious in all subsequent battles as they head toward the promised land.[36]

In sum, within its self-contained structure, the itinerary reveals which topics are essential to highlight along the journey through the wilderness for the sake of collective memory, at least to its compiler. These asides also remind the reader of two overwhelmingly important figures in the narrative of the wilderness journey: God and Aaron the high priest. God's importance is underscored by the reminder of God's actions on the people's behalf in the Exodus, in God's supplying basic needs such as water, and of God's granting victory in battle. The brief mention of the lack of water reminds the reader of the darker, more ominous side of God's relationship to the people who repeatedly complain due to the lack of water. Their complaints lead to catastrophe for an entire generation, including Aaron the high priest. He of course is denied entry to the land due to an incident involving water. The repetition of Aaron's death notice signals that connection as well as his importance as the first high priest – the source for much of the priestly politics that motivate the book of Numbers. Taken together, these asides remind the people Israel of their continuing obligations both to God and to their priestly leaders. Taken together, the events of the journey and the retelling of them almost at journey's end give form and unity to the entire wilderness journey being pieced together by the priestly editors while fixing its contents for the collective remembering of that time. We are to remember, almost at the very same moment, the liberation and the complaints that are meant to serve as a deterrence. Above all we are to remember the hopeful ending of that extraordinary and painful forty-year journey through the wilderness.

❧ Egypt and the pull of the past

If we were to step back from the micro-level to discern the design of the whole of Numbers, we might observe that design emerging through two rather broad but significant topics that overlap: the attractions and repulsions of Egypt for the people and their leaders and the way in which Egypt functions as a sieve through which narrative time is organized. Each is best observed through the detailed rereading of Numbers to follow in subsequent chapters. For now, let me briefly sketch the contours of that design and how Egypt and time marvelously intersect in Numbers' final form.

The exodus from Egypt is mentioned in the very first verse of Numbers 1, signaling its importance to the subsequent narrative. It functions as a temporal marker, measuring the various communications from God to Moses and the people as well as the events of the wilderness journey through distance in space and in time from that crucial event. God refers to the exodus at least two times in the early chapters, reminding Israel both of God's virtues in liberating the people from oppression and of their subsequent obligations to God. In Numbers 3:13 and again in 8:17 God reminds Moses that God both destroyed the first-born Egyptians and consecrated the first-born Israelites. In Numbers 9, an extensive discussion of the first observance of the Passover since Israel left Egypt ensues, including detailed discussion of who should observe the Passover and when, exceptions to that observance, and accommodation of late observance. The repeated reference to Egypt as well as detailed rules of commemoration of the Passover suggests its importance as testimony to God's great care of the people Israel. The exodus becomes the chief motive for their subsequent relationship to God, strengthening and making such a relationship permanent.

And yet, rather unpredictably if one relies only on the matter-of-fact tone of the use made of Egypt in the first ten chapters, in Numbers 11 Egypt comes to represent the opposite. Memories of Egypt can and will undo that seemingly permanent relationship between God and those liberated from Egypt. Egypt triggers a dramatic breach by becoming the site of Israel's desires, a place of security and comfort instead of a nightmare that Israel gladly escapes. Such a paradox becomes only more pronounced in the events that follow the first outpouring of desires for Egyptian delicacies in Numbers 11. By Numbers 14 those events end in catastrophe for an entire generation. The opportunity created by the abrupt juxtaposition of different views of Egypt is brilliantly exploited by the editors. I will return to, and elaborate on, this editorial exploitation of Egypt in Numbers.

As we have already seen in Numbers 1:1 Egypt becomes an anchor that organizes narrative time. But it also functions as more than mere anchor and starting point of the journey. It represents the past. The different views of the life lived in Egypt by the people Israel and the repercussions of those views on the fate of the wilderness generation are organized along a broad temporal continuum (duplicated in miniature in the present/past/future orientation of chapters 32–34). Chapters 1–10 take place in a *present* moment in the Sinai wilderness under God's watch. We observe Moses and the people preoccupied with organizing the camp in preparation for conquest, happy to leave the oppressions and slavery of Egypt behind them. But chapters 11–25 completely overturn the goals of the present through pervasive longings for the Egyptian *past*. That past becomes an obstacle to a successful future. Only after the death of those seduced by the Egyptian past can the next generation proceed to fulfill a *future* in the promised land, as suggested in chapters 26–36. Such a strong choreography of the flow of time in the wilderness comes about through the careful placement of materials in a narrative that situates events in a present moment, suddenly shifts to eruptions of memories of Egypt, and ends by imagining the future life in Israel.[37] Only a highly creative redaction of the materials could produce such a haunting mosaic of Israel's wilderness wanderings over forty years. I return to this point in chapter 4.

Numbers presents a paramount example within the bible of weaving by design. We have observed the framing of separate biblical materials, the weaving together of the pieces, and the effect thus produced when taken as a whole. I have identified the possible range and identity of separate texts and materials, and have described the framework in which to place that array of materials in the opening and closing chapters of Numbers. We have seen the "pieces" woven together through the use of brief formulaic insertions, the accumulating effect of a key word, and the strategic placement of independent documents, such as the second census and the itinerary. Finally, by stepping back from the micro-level to the macro, we have observed the effect of the whole in the brilliant use of Egypt and its intersections with the flow of time.

We should now be in a better position to understand Friedman's concept of a "combinatory design" that emerges out of the careful placement of materials. The interventions cited above do in the end create such a grand design. Subsequent chapters of the present work explicitly focus on that design, seeing in its contours the persistent and careful shaping of the wilderness traditions on behalf of a priestly agenda. But before analyzing that agenda and the strategies used to achieve it, I first turn in the next chapter to the question of the possible identity and historical context of the editors of Numbers.

THREE

Priestly Purposes

From time to time in the Torah, God will appear to an individual and strike up a conversation. Sometimes God makes a demand that includes ritual or legal instruction. At other times God takes the opportunity to communicate divine intentions or feelings. In Numbers, God conveys a special attachment to, and appreciation of, both the prophet Moses and the priest Phinehas, grandson of Aaron. In the first instance, after witnessing Miriam and Aaron challenge the sole authority of Moses as prophet in the camp, God rises to Moses' defense, severely rebuking the two of them and punishing Miriam.[1] God angrily (and poetically) informs them: "When a prophet of YHWH arises among you, in a vision to him I make Myself known, in a dream I speak with him. Not so with My servant Moses. Throughout My house he is trusted" (Num. 12:6–7).[2]

In the second episode, it is the turn of the priest Phinehas, grandson of Aaron, to rise to God's defense. Phinehas slays two idolaters within the camp. While such an act might jar the sensibility of a modern reader, God rewards Phinehas, graciously announcing: "behold I give him my covenant of friendship. And it shall be for him and his seed after him a covenant of priesthood for all time" (Num. 25:12–13a).

Thus both prophet and priest are singled out for God's special attention. Both episodes are located in the middle of the book of Numbers in the midst of a widespread crisis in the wilderness camp. The first instance examines the extent to which prophetic status and authority could be shared. It also highlights God's concern with preserving the honor of Moses and their singular relationship. In the second instance, God grants extraordinary legitimacy to the descendants of Aaron via Phinehas as the first family of the priestly community.

The tales of Moses and of Phinehas illustrate the extent to which the *type* of leadership – as well as its privileges and legitimacy – attracts the attention of the writers and later editors of Numbers. In this chapter, I briefly take up the political maneuverings of the priest and the prophet as found within particular traditions (i.e., Num. 12 or 25) and as those traditions are edited together in the final form of Numbers. I examine how the editors manage to preserve the enormous prestige of the prophet Moses while nonetheless making sure that the predominant rule of the community is a priestly one. The ultimate curtailment of the prophet Moses in Numbers provides one of the most interesting and persuasive pieces of evidence for a priestly editor.[3] But as we will see, the politics *within* the priestly class are just as interesting, providing not only further evidence for the priestly editing of Numbers, but also suggestive information for locating that literary activity historically.

Let us briefly return to our two examples. Each story suggests that the authority of the main leaders in Numbers – the prophet and the priest – is not an established given. Each figure requires nothing less than divine intervention of a rather dramatic kind. God shores up and protects Moses' power against usurpers, including the high priest Aaron, but then goes on to ensure the legitimacy of the descendant of Aaron, Phinehas the priest, over any other. Considered together, the two episodes suggest that prophet and priest exist in an interesting tension with one another – at times vying for God's singular favor, while at other times joining together to repel significant challenges to their shared authority. Consider our first episode. The prophet is pitted against the high priest and his sister. Read on its own, Numbers 12 seems a clear affirmation of prophetic power at the expense of priestly. The high priest cannot save his sister but is reduced to pleading with Moses to intervene with God on her behalf. Yet the second episode mitigates the first. The grandson of that very Aaron is singled out in Numbers 25 for an eternal covenant of friendship with God, thereby providing priest as well as prophet with divine endorsement.

As we will observe, the editors of Numbers go out of their way to resolve the tensions between priest and prophet. If one understands the extent to which the depiction of the wilderness camp is meant to be a model for the future community in the promised land, then the overwhelming attention paid to communal arrangements, and especially to the leaders of that community, makes sense. In its final form Numbers repeatedly raises the issue of legitimate power and its transfer from generation to generation.

Who makes legal decisions for the community? How is a new ruler chosen? Should there be a balance between prophetic and priestly interests? Of course a society imagined and described *biblically* will be one in which religious and cultic life will dominate. What is the proper worship of God and who will ensure it? Whose vision of that life is fortified and communicated? Finally, who gets the last word on these matters? The weight of the evidence suggests that in the end the authority that preserves and edits the tale in Numbers is a priestly one intent on legitimating priestly rule even at the expense of Moses.

To understand both the dynamic of prophet and priest and how it is resolved in the course of Numbers, let us begin by looking more broadly at the role of the prophet and of the priest and then focus on how the prophetic power is curtailed. I conclude this chapter by briefly leaving the biblical text behind to examine the possible historical context in which that curtailment is accomplished and the priestly editing achieved.

～ *The prophet Moses*

The figure of Moses looms over the Torah attributed to him, including the book of Numbers. Moses appears in almost every chapter, receiving God's instructions, transmitting those instructions, and supervising the camp. Many of these activities would not be considered "prophetic," if one defines that term largely as the act of intercession between God and the people. In Numbers Moses functions in many capacities. Principally, he is the highest political authority in the camp.[4] In the first ten chapters alone, he is chief administrator, keeping lists of the tribes, organizing the transport of the Tabernacle, and giving new instructions to the people concerning such matters as adultery, the Passover sacrifice, and the blowing of trumpets. However, it is quite striking that most of those instructions require a priest rather than Moses to implement them. In fact, in the first ten chapters Moses is intimately involved in creating a priestly hierarchy that consists of the sons of Aaron and the Levites but that excludes Moses. In creating that hierarchy Moses advances the tribe of Levi to serve Aaron. Thus we could describe Moses as in charge of the camp. At the same time, he is busily advancing the priestly structure of rule.

On the other hand, Moses does serve as an intercessory. As an intercessory, a biblical prophet serves as God's prosecuting attorney while also defending the people. Ultimately, if successful, the prophet gains God's agreement to relinquish or modify the divine punishment. Thus intercession and reconciliation are key goals of the prophet.[5] And in Numbers, as we shall see, Moses does serve in this role on occasion and on occasion gets God to relent. Ultimately, of course, God is beyond even the persuasion of Moses and condemns an entire generation to death in the wilderness.

Numbers 11–14 are the primary chapters in which the prophetic, rather than administrative, role of Moses is emphasized. Suddenly, even abruptly, in Numbers 11 the more prophetic side *and* the more distinctly human side of Moses appear. In this chapter Moses prays for the people after a furious God aims a devastating and destructive fire at the outskirts of the camp. In good prophetic fashion, Moses gets God to rescind the fire. Yet, in a sign of how unusual this chapter is, things do not return to normal. Instead, more complaints follow. Moses even joins the complainers! He wishes to "beg off" the job of guiding and protecting the people Israel. He even expresses the wish that the prophetic spirit be spread widely among the camp. While his more human side is part of what makes him a psychologically appealing character, at this particular juncture it does not necessarily make him a great prophet. Because he thinks of his own predicament and of his own weariness, he fails to obtain further protection for the children of Israel. Numerous Israelites go on to die as a result of God's continuing anger.

The placement of Numbers 12 after 11 could be understood in part as a response to such a recognizably human Moses. As we have seen, God vigorously defends a largely silent Moses, restoring his singular role as trusted adviser to God. Moses does briefly intercede on Miriam's behalf after Aaron urges him to do so. Thus his superiority to the priest is also reinforced. Both moves strengthen Moses' stature as prophet.

Moses' greatest hour as intercessor is still before him in Numbers 14. But at this juncture in his career he is only partially successful. Moses attempts to convince God to rescind a blanket condemnation of the entire people by addressing God's reputation among the Egyptians and reminding God of Divine forbearance and forgiveness. He fails to obtain a reprieve for the generation who left Egypt. They will perish in the wilderness. But he succeeds in saving the next generation, who will be allowed to settle the promised land. Thus Numbers 14 leaves no doubt that Moses' role as prophet remains crucial for the people Israel. He does nothing less than secure their future.

Almost as if that reminder of Moses' prophetic accomplishment is sufficient to secure his unquestioned authority, these episodes are followed in Numbers 16–17 by a rebellion that Moses decisively puts down on behalf of Aaron. He publicly defends Aaron, grandly legitimating his role as high priest. After that public defense Moses returns to his role as political leader, among other things worrying about who will succeed him, supervising the succession of Aaron's son as the new high priest, and allotting portions in the land. These actions signal that Moses not only is occupied, as many of the other biblical prophets, in a present community, but also is occupied in planning, as concretely as possible, for the future of the community he has led for so long.

There is one simple way to observe the prevalence of the prophet in the book of Numbers. The formula "and God spoke to Moses" occurs forty-two times; clearly, the chain of authority is God to Moses to the people. But if one observes what follows that formula, it often involves the priest, who must implement God's instruction.[6] Thus let us turn to the other chief figure of authority to be found in Numbers: the priest.

∼ *Priestly purposes*

Who are the priests? The broadest possible definition would emphasize their role in expunging sin and winning absolution for the people Israel through the sacrificial system. In other words, they assure "divine favor for Israel by means of sacrifice."[7] The many rules of sacrifice and the types of offenses and bodily processes that require sacrificial offerings form the content of Leviticus. In Numbers, in light of the emphasis on the journey through the wilderness, we learn much more about the priestly duties concerning the transportation of the tabernacle. We learn that the priests are in charge of erecting the tabernacle, dismantling it, paying special attention to its sacred vessels, and, of course, implementing a plan of transport (at the order of Moses as signaled by God). While it is stationary, they are also in charge of guarding the tabernacle and taking care of its lamps, shrine, and altar. It is the central site within the camp for the activities of the cult.

The priests are also in charge of the sacred vessels and the trumpets to be used in battle. For example, Phinehas, son of Eleazar serves "as a priest to the army, with the sacred vessels and the trumpets for sounding the blasts in his hand" (Num. 31:6). There are several biblical examples of the connection between the military and cult within ancient Israel, suggesting an understanding of the tabernacle and its vessels as representing and ensuring God's presence with Israel on the battlefield.[8] In addition to their responsibilities for the tabernacle, the priests implement many of the ritual and legal instructions God gives to Moses and supervise a variety of personal issues, such as the handling of a corpse. They accompany Moses in officiating at judicial matters (Num. 15:33), and most memorably, they formally bless the people (Num. 6:22–27).

Yet if we look more closely at the examples just cited we see that in Numbers there is a distinct division of labor within the priestly class. Those activities that require supervision of the people, officiating at sacrifices, involvement in communal matters, and the priestly blessing are specifically fulfilled either by a generic priest, labeled in Hebrew "Cohen" (and *not* Levite), or, more often, by a priest specifically affiliated with Aaron.[9] The more manual tasks connected to the tabernacle are assigned to the Levites who are supervised by Aaron and his sons. Three subgroups of Levites are named: Gershonites, Kohatites, and Merarites. They are counted and assigned different functions in dismantling and carrying the tabernacle. The Gershonites are in charge of hangings, the Merarites the planks, bars, post, and sockets. The Kohatites are assigned the most important task: to carry the sacred vessels from the inner part of the tabernacle. However, as I examine in detail in chapter 5, the Kohatites are immediately made subordinate to the sons of Aaron. Only the sons of Aaron may handle the sacred vessels. Only after they are completely covered may the Kohatites even enter the tabernacle to carry the vessels on the journey.

Within just a few verses, the distinct split between Levite and Aaron and his sons, hinted at in the division of labor, is made explicit. We learn that the Levites are to attend to Aaron (Num. 3:6), while at the same time Aaron and his sons must protect their priestly prerogatives and responsibilities (Num. 3:10). I would suggest that the Levites are now defined by their service to a higher order of priest, Aaron and his sons. A distinction has been made and a hierarchy established. As bluntly put by Levine, in Numbers the Levites are not "officiants or celebrants, but … servitors."[10]

This arrangement leads to a great deal of tension within the priestly class. Thus not only do we have the politics of priest and prophet in the book of Numbers, but of Cohen and Levite. As we will see, the division created between Cohen and Levite probably reflects particular historical developments within the priestly class that in turn allow us to hazard a historical period for the editing and final form of Numbers. But before turning to such evidence, now that we have a sense of the priestly activities and interests in Numbers, let us examine the ways in which those interests might be further strengthened by diminishing the stature of the prophet. Such a curtailment of the prophet sets the stage for the dominance of priestly rule and a priestly vision for the people Israel.

∾ *"Because you did not trust me enough": Numbers 20:12*

Moses is the dominant figure of the Five Books attributed to him. Nonetheless, while his is a looming presence, a given within the camp, he is gently overshadowed in Numbers by the force of a priestly vision in which the people settle in the land guided by priestly arrangements, such as the priestly calendar, and by priestly leaders. This is accomplished in several ways, some of which we have already observed. We have seen Moses' reliance on the priests to implement much of God's plan for Israel in Numbers 5–6. We have also seen the human side of a battered, frustrated, and weary Moses as portrayed in Numbers 11. In addition to these examples, Moses' stature comes under the harshest of attacks from the most surprising source of all – God. I refer to the incident in which Moses strikes the rock rather than ordering it to produce its water. As a result God denies Moses (and his brother Aaron, who is somehow implicated in the act) entry to the promised land: "Because you did not believe in Me to sanctify Me in the sight of the children of Israel, therefore you shall not bring this assembly into the land that I have given them" (Num. 20:12). Many possible interpretations, most unsatisfactory, have been offered to explain this incident and God's motives. For present purposes, suffice to say that the incident provides a dramatic opportunity to lessen the prestige of Moses. And even though it also diminishes the prestige of Aaron at the same time, the end result opens the way for a shift in the balance of authority between leaders in the next generation.

This becomes obvious in the arrangements made for Moses' successor. At that moment the balance ever so subtly shifts to the priest. When the time comes for Moses to appoint a successor, God singles out Joshua and announces:

> And give him some of your authority in order that all the community of Israel may listen. And he should stand before Eleazar the Priest who shall seek the decision of the Urim on his behalf before YHWH. (Num. 27:20–21)

God is quite explicit that Moses is to give Joshua only *some* of his authority. After all, there is no one like Moses. Then, Joshua must stand before the priest on whom he is publicly dependent to inform him of God's intent via the Urim, a device used in an oracle. Thus Joshua's direct access to God is limited. Note that the prestige of Moses not only survives intact but is strengthened in contrast to that of Joshua, who has only "some" of Moses' authority and, unlike Moses, must rely on the priest. But as this episode also affirms, in the larger scheme of things within Numbers it is the priest, not the prophet or his successor, who becomes ever more crucial to the future rule of the community.

I would like to propose one other way in which the prophetic authority of Moses is curtailed in Numbers. I refer to the prominent role of the non-Israelite seer Balaam, whose poetry could be considered a subtle rebuke of Moses' angry (and tired) words aimed at the children of Israel.[11] In the discussion that follows, I emphasize the extraordinary nature of Balaam's vision of Israel, rather than the way in which Balaam's authority is itself curtailed through the story of his talking ass, who sees much more than Balaam himself. If we put aside that satirical tale, the remainder represents a rather positive view of the non-Israelite visionary.

To begin, it hardly seems a coincidence that the events of Balaam's entanglements with Israel occur soon after the announcement of Moses' death outside the land due to his digression from God's precise instruction in Numbers 20. Perhaps we are meant to consider such a contrast every time we hear Balaam repeatedly announce: "I could not of my own accord do anything good or bad contrary to the command of YHWH" (Num. 24:13).

In fact, the contrast in imagery and language to be found more broadly in the juxtaposed chapters create a comparison that is unfavorable to Moses. Called on to curse Israel by Balak, enemy king of Moab, Balaam can do nothing but shower blessings on Israel. In so doing, he envisions the glory of Israel encamped below him in a fashion that seems wholly lost to the people themselves, and even to Moses, in the midst of one of the darkest moments of their journey through the wilderness. Listen to Balaam:

How fair are your tents, O Jacob
Your dwellings, O Israel!
Like palm-groves stretched out,
Like gardens beside a river
Like aloes planted by YHWH. (Num. 24:5–6a)

In other words, Israel is flourishing and fragrant, fertile and abundant. Yet juxtapose that image of the fair tents of Israel with another image of those tents – this one up close. In the midst of yet another crisis in the camp Moses observes the people weeping, "each person at the entrance of his tent" (Num. 11:10). Moses then rightly rails against the rebellious Dathan and Abiram, ordering the people to move away from "the tents of these wicked men" (Num. 16:26). Or consider the words of Moses in chapter 20 just moments before Balaam's praise of Israel. Moses cries out: "Listen you rebels." In contrast, Balaam continues to develop his optimistic vision, prophesying a future in which the people Israel successfully destroy their enemies and are triumphant. The exuberance of the non-Israelite Balaam versus the anger and weariness of Moses is striking. Balaam's profoundly positive vision of Israel and its future is so necessary at that juncture in the narrative because of its utter absence in the camp of Israel and in Moses' view of his people.

It is fairly well established that the tale of Balaam and his poetic blessings is an independent literary tradition placed in the book of Numbers.[12] Again and again in Numbers we can observe independent materials that are purposefully used within the broader narrative. Whoever chose to place Balaam's effusive words in Numbers 22–24 so soon after Moses' cries in Numbers 20 allows Balaam's very presence and activity on behalf of Israel to impact critically the reader's assessment of Moses, even if only during Balaam's oratory. The editorial intervention that allows Balaam's presence to throw a shadow over that of Moses should be considered in light of the other interventions we discussed earlier – the censuses, chapters 32–34, and the itinerary. The placement of Balaam's tale reflects the same type of editorial method – an imaginative and effective juxtaposition and interaction with surrounding texts to make a larger point. Could it be coincidence that before Balaam's blessings, Moses is rebuked by

God and after Balaam, God publicly endorses none other than the priest Phinehas?

Moses remains the great figure of the period in the wilderness. Yet at least in Numbers his presence is balanced to a certain degree by that of the priest. After God singles out Phinehas, the remainder of Numbers is taken up with the structures and rules of life in the land, much of which falls under priestly supervision, providing further evidence of the priestly imprint on Numbers. Let us now turn to the editors who left such a design behind.

∾ *The editors of Numbers*

I begin with a disclaimer. I do not know the specific identities of the editors of Numbers or the precise dating of their activities. But that lack of certainty does not prevent me from identifying the editorial goals and vision found in Numbers. As we have begun to observe, some sense of the possible interests of the editors, particularly in a work as political as Numbers, is accessible. So are hints of the audience those editors sought to sway with their strategies of deterrence and of promise. Whose interests are being served, what are those interests, and to what end?

Numbers offers a highly specific setting with which to begin reconstructing a plausible answer to those questions. The people Israel are camped in a wilderness space *outside the land*, planning to conquer it, but not yet successful. Second, as we have seen, the Levites are clearly subordinate to Aaron. Such a priestly hierarchy is largely absent from the other four books of Moses. Both the setting and the priestly innovation provide suggestive data for the editing of Numbers.

A wilderness setting could suggest a period in which the people Israel again found themselves residing outside the land, namely, during the Babylonian exile that began in 586 B.C.E. The detailed vision of a renewed life in the promised land found at the end of Numbers would provide hope for an audience in the Babylonian wilderness, an audience perhaps tempted by the desires of exile much as Israel lusted after the delicacies of an earlier exile in Egypt. Mary Douglas succinctly draws the same parallel: "Egypt, where the people of Israel endured their first bondage, would be matched by Babylon, where they endured the second."[13]

The priestly innovation found in Numbers, as well as the dominance of priestly material, provide a different and more concrete type of data. That Numbers is peopled by priestly figures is beyond dispute. By my count, in at least twenty-four of the thirty-six chapters in Numbers, Aaron, his successor Eleazar, or his grandson Phinehas appear as major actors. Those numbers suggest that many of the narrative materials originated in a priestly group connected to the line of Aaron or, at the very least, quite sympathetic to priestly concerns.

To better observe the rather unique emphasis on Aaron's line at the expense of the Levites in Numbers, consider the description of the priests in Deuteronomy. The reference is usually to "the priests, the Levites," as one indistinguishable unit (i.e., Deut. 17:9, 18, and 18:1), or simply to "the Levites." While the tribe of Levi is singled out, no mention is made of a distinct class of priest, the sons of Aaron, except for one reference to Eleazar taking over after the death of his father (Deut. 10:6). Rather, Deuteronomy emphasizes that the entire tribe of Levi is to serve God, in contrast to Numbers where they are to serve Aaron and his sons. Not only that, but the entire tribe is to bless the people in God's name, not just Aaron and his sons: "At that time YHWH separated out the tribe of Levi to carry the ark of the covenant of YHWH, to stand before YHWH to serve him and to bless in his name until this day" (Deut. 10:8). The Levites have significant responsibilities in Deuteronomy. They consider difficult matters and controversies. They utter the warning curses against the people if they break the covenant near the end of Deuteronomy. Finally, they are in charge of the written Torah of Moses and shall teach its judgments (33:10). Yet curiously, on first crossing over the Jordan, it is the *people*, not the Levites, who are commanded to offer sacrifices.

The evidence from Deuteronomy leads to two observations. First, the priests are an important part of the community in Deuteronomy but are not primarily in charge of ruling it. They remain largely in the background. Rule after rule is spelled out without reference to the priests as those who might implement such rules. Second, and more significant for the present argument, there is simply no hierarchy between Levites and sons of Aaron, and no distinction made between the Levities as a class of servitors and the sons of Aaron as the head of the cult.

In comparison, in Numbers the priests are in charge of a great deal of communal life, while the Levites are their seconds. Numbers seems to go out of its way to subject the Levites to Aaron.[14] As summarized by Baruch Levine:

> The priestly texts of Numbers constitute . . . a major departure within Torah literature, even within priestly literature itself. We are presented with a class of cultic servitors known as Levites who are genealogically related to the Aaronide priests, yet subservient to them and differentiated in terms of their functions.[15]

As narrated in Numbers, the attempt to subject the Levites to the authority of Aaron results in a hotly contested hierarchy between the sons of Aaron and the Levites. In the end, the sons of Aaron decisively gain the upper hand. Therefore we should be considering a historical context in which the priestly hierarchy might be in some disarray and in need of reorganization. Furthermore, the text itself points to a period in which the claims of a group closely aligned with the figure of Aaron might need to be legitimated by recourse to arrangements anchored in Israel's distant wilderness past.

At least two historical periods within Israelite history necessitated priestly reorganization. The period following the fall of the North in 722 B.C.E. led to a flood of refugees, including Northern levitical priests, into a Jerusalem governed by Hezekiah.[16] Alternatively, the potential or actual return of the priestly class to the newly rebuilt Second Temple also triggered priestly adjustments and literary activity. I will briefly describe each period and its priestly realignments. Before doing so, let me be quite explicit about the priestly material found in Numbers. There is abundant priestly material that originated during the First Temple even if the priestly editors we seek emerged during the restoration of Yehud in the Persian period. We need to distinguish that material's presence from a possible later use of it. Of course the editors intended the work to be timeless, pertinent in any historical exigency or setting.

There are three scholars whose work I would like to briefly mention in reconstructing a possible setting for heightened priestly activity, if not a final redaction of Numbers, in light of priestly turmoil during the First Temple period. These three are Jacob Milgrom, Israel Knohl, and William Schniedewind. In his magisterial commentary on Numbers, Milgrom argues for the antiquity of much of the priestly material in Numbers. To name just a few of his examples, Milgrom cites and dates as ancient the following: Israel's square-shaped camp in the wilderness; the division of the tabernacle's custody between priests and Levites, a tradition found in the Hittite cult; and the similarity between the description of the menorah in the tabernacle and lamp stands found in the late Bronze Age.[17] Milgrom also argues that a priestly hierarchy would have ample time to emerge during the period of the First Temple and inevitably would emerge. In particular, Milgrom elaborates an argument first proposed by S. E. Loewenstamm that the literary rendering of the rebellion of Korah, a Levite, against Aaron found in Numbers 16 does not fit the reality of a Second Temple priestly organization. By that point the conflict had been decisively settled, because Korahites in the Second Temple held roles with a lower status, as singers and doorkeepers. Therefore, only in the First Temple period could a literary depiction of the Korahites in rebellion against other priests make any kind of sense.[18]

Israel Knohl makes the case, as referred to earlier, that the editors most likely emerged from a group composed of Jerusalem priests whom he considers the Holiness School (HS). This group responds to the influx of new priests from the north as well as challenges leveled against the Temple and cult by the prophet Isaiah. (Could the tensions between prophet and priest in Numbers reflect a priestly response to the criticisms of Isaiah?) Hence Knohl identifies the crucial period as that in which Isaiah was thought to prophesy – the reigns of Ahaz and Hezekiah, sometime from the eighth century B.C.E. Knohl argues the following:

> Would the Jerusalem priests allow the Levite families of Judah and Israel to participate in the Temple cult, thus giving up their exclusive rights as priests of the king's Temple of Jerusalem? ... HS sought to resolve this question by distinguishing between the Aaronide priests – that is, the ancient families of the Jerusalem priesthood – who retained the exclusive privilege of serving in the inner areas of the Temple, and the other Levite families, who are assigned the guardianship of the sacred enclosure and other service tasks.[19]

Knohl offers extensive detail for the particular interests and editorial interventions of the priests connected to the Holiness School. Those editorial interventions encompass not only earlier priestly materials but more popular, nonpriestly materials. As a result HS turns its attention to both priestly and popular experience. Knohl describes the project in the following terms:

> The revolutionary project of HS was guided by its vision – to create a broad, all-inclusive framework of faith and cult, in which the mutlifarious values

of the religious experience would be combined; it would express both the reflections of the priests serving in the Sanctuary and the innermost needs of the people in the fields.[20]

Thus the vision of HS translates into an editing project that preserves side by side and merges together not only the different interests of the priests and the people but the different vocabulary and styles found in the priestly and epic sources, *precisely the kind of composition we find in the final form of Numbers.* This description is very persuasive, as it so well fits the evidence of Numbers. It should be noted that Knohl leaves open the possibility that such editorial work could, and most likely, did continue into the period of exile and perhaps the early period of return. Thus he does not place the *final* editing of Numbers in the period of Hezekiah but rather places the *beginning* of such editorial engagement with earlier priestly texts.

William Schneidewind argues that the period of Hezekiah's rule was crucial for the writing of the Torah in consequence of the fall of the Northern Kingdom. Due to social and economic factors, including the growth of Jerusalem as the administrative center of Judah, Jerusalem became a site of great literary activity as well as increasing literacy. Schneidewind extends the likely writing of sections of the biblical corpus from the time of Hezekiah to that of Josiah.[21] He notes that the collapse of the north and the reforms of Hezekiah gave the priestly aristocracy in Jerusalem an advantage over their rural counterparts, fleeing from the north to the safety of a still independent Jerusalem. A hierarchy consisting of Jerusalem priests as more prominent than those from the rest of the country would be a likely outcome of these rapid changes. Later, under Josiah that advantage remains, as is clear from a reading of the relevant passage in II Kings 23:8. The priests from outside Jerusalem are distinct from those in Jerusalem and even subjected to condemnation.

However, Schneidewind, like Knohl, also concludes that the Second Temple period provides the more likely context for the rise of the priestly class as the *editors* of the Five Books of Moses.[22] Based on these arguments it seems reasonable to identify the First Temple period as the provenance of many of the materials found in Numbers, possibly including those narratives that describe the tensions between Levites and Aaron and his sons. But it is likely that the book's final editing took place during the early Second

Temple Period. If so, that would also explain Numbers' setting outside the land.

Baruch Levine and Joseph Blenkinsopp explicitly place the editing of Numbers in the period at the end of the exile or in a Yehud under Persian authority. Like Milgrom, Baruch Levine identifies the rebellion of Korah in Numbers 16 as providing important data for a possible reconstruction of the setting for the editing of Numbers, though with conclusions very different from those drawn by Milgrom. Levine begins by noting that the priestly writers delegitimized the Kohatites (the clan of Korah), and thereby established Aaron's clan as the legitimate priests. Precisely because the subjection of Levites to the sons of Aaron was an innovation, it would have been imperative to legitimate that arrangement by describing its inception during the wilderness period. Levine succinctly sums up the innovation:

> The book of Numbers, as restructured by the priestly writers, focuses our attention on the cultic and religious policies of the priestly school in ancient Israel. In its historiography, P establishes the sole legitimacy of the Aaronide priesthood within the tribe of Levi and legislates the functions of the Levites as a separate corps of temple servitors relegated to non sacral functions.[23]

Levine observes that the subordinate position of the Levites in Numbers strikingly parallels the description of their status in Ezekiel 44:9–14. He writes: "the consecrated priests and subordinate unconsecrated Levites can be traced to a policy *first advocated* in Ezekiel 44:9–14."[24] If so, then the hierarchical arrangement found in Numbers originated either in the time of Ezekiel and the exile or in the early postexilic period. Levine prefers an early postexilic provenance, because renewed priestly creativity during the late sixth century B.C.E. would make sense. "The newly constituted Jewish community, in Jerusalem and Judea with its restored temple, was preoccupied with the reordering of religious life under new conditions of collective existence."[25] Note how Milgrom and Levine can draw opposite conclusions from the same data. For Milgrom the fact that the Levites are subordinate to Aaron suggests a parallel to the Hittite model and thus an early date. For Levine the same data suggests a parallel to Ezekiel 44:9–16, hence at the very least exilic, though more likely during the early years of the restoration.

Levine of course argues that Numbers is late due not only to the evidence of Ezekiel 44 but for a variety of reasons, including the use of particular terms found in late biblical Hebrew under the influence of the Aramaic obtained in Exile.[26] Thus Levine ascertains that Numbers is late due to the textual institutionalization of the Levities as distinct and the linguistic evidence. However, couldn't Numbers contain a priestly arrangement originating during the First Temple period that is developed by Ezekiel for his own purposes? At the same time, couldn't Numbers contain loan words from the Aramaic of exile and yet be editorially completed only in the early Second Temple period? Perhaps the textual description of the Levites as subordinate in Numbers originated in the time of Hezekiah-Josiah, reflecting their edicts and the reorganization of the First Temple, but was preserved and used by later editors for their own purposes. This in fact is a conclusion arrived at by Levine for the priestly materials of Leviticus: "priestly law and literature took form over a protracted period of time.... it would be inaccurate to assign all of their contents to a single period of ancient history. This approach helps to explain the presence of some relatively early material in Leviticus while at the same time allowing for the inclusion of exilic and postexilic creativity."[27] Such a conclusion could hold for Numbers as well.

It is indisputable that the priests become increasingly powerful in the period of Persian rule partially as a result of the Persian preference for priesthoods and temple communities.[28] Based on the Persian context, Blenkinsopp identifies the early period of the second commonwealth, either shortly before or shortly after the rebuilding of the Jerusalem temple, as crucial for the consolidation of priestly power.[29] The key issue facing the priests in the first century of Persian rule would involve control over the operations of the temple. Whoever obtained such control would enjoy "not only spiritual hegemony but a large measure of political and economic power as well."[30] As a result of political machinations, those connected with the figure of Aaron came to dominate other priests, particularly the Levites. At that point "the Aaronite claim, successfully pressed, to exclusive title to the priestly office displaced the traditional generic designation Levite so that it acquired the more restrictive connotation of minor clergy."[31] Numbers certainly provides an etiology for such a change in its depiction of the relegated status of the Levites. Blenkinsopp dates any literary description of the conflict between sons of Aaron and Levites decisively to the return from Babylon. He writes:

> In the account of the wanderings, the intent is to create a paradigm or model of the ideal polity for Israel, as viewed from within the conceptual world of

the Aaronite priesthood ... the actual political and social reality of which the paradigm was meant to apply was *the new commonwealth in the process of formation during the first century of Persian rule.* (emphasis added)[32]

In sum, both the period of Hezekiah with the influx of priests from the north and the rebuilding of the Second Temple with the reinstitution and realignment of a priestly leadership suggest plausible contexts for priestly tensions. It is tempting to assume that both periods provide the basis for the priestly politics in the text. The historical period of redactional activity could have begun during the time of Hezekiah and continue into the restoration, spanning roughly two to three hundred years. My earlier claim should now make sense. I use "editor" as a term of convenience, but the actual editing of Numbers might very well represent several generations of editorial interventions but by a group closely aligned with, and attuned to, internal priestly interests concerning the line of Aaron. The editors of Numbers held fast to a vision of a community in the ancient land promised Israel by God, perhaps beginning in the reforms of Hezekiah but newly imagined several hundred years later in a reconstituted Yehud under Persian rule. The targeted audience would be repeatedly encouraged to choose the life offered to them in that land according to the plan set forth by the priests – none other than those descended from the sons of Aaron.

By way of conclusion, let me cite Mary Douglas:

> There is a general scholarly consensus that the book of Numbers received its final form during the exile in Babylon and shortly after the return. It is also well understood that the materials from which it was compiled are very ancient, some coming from oral traditions, some written, some laws, some stories. ... the book has been carefully constructed ... the many repetitions and jumps of context are not accidental.[33]

In sum, I propose that the editing of Numbers in its final form originated in a priestly class intent on legitimizing a particular priestly group's move to take power. This could have occurred over several hundred years, but the end point of that final form, so "carefully constructed," very likely came about during the Exile or during the early years of the Second Temple period. And yet the end result – the book of Numbers – offers us such a rich portrait of the journey through the wilderness because the ancient materials out of which the priestly editors shaped its final form do not disappear. They hold their distinctness either in spite of or, I think more likely, because of their skillful placement and editing. Of course the final editors could not entirely control the process. The variations in language, the presence of contradictory versions of the wilderness journey, each with a separate claim, the very elusiveness of memory and the complexity of shaping tradition all collude to preserve a far more complicated and compelling story of the wilderness period than any single agenda could produce. It is to that story that we are now in a position to turn.

FOUR

Variations on a Theme: Shaping Memory in the Wilderness

Again and again memory keeps its attention riveted on the present, even on present and future conduct.[1]

Nearly at journey's end two of the tribes of Israel – the Reubenites and Gadites – suddenly approach Moses without warning to demand land on the other side of the Jordan. No vignette in the Book of Numbers better conveys the pronounced importance of memory to its continuing concerns than in the curious negotiations conducted by the two tribes with an increasingly furious Moses. One can imagine that Moses would find this new crisis to be a particularly cruel one, as it occurs so near to the borders of the promised land and so close to his own death. Undaunted, the Reubenites and Gadites approach Moses, Eleazar the priest, and the chieftains of the community to request the lands of Jazer and Gilead, excellent lands for cattle. "Ataroth, Dibon, Jazer, Nimrah, Heshbon, Elealeh, Sebam, Nebo and Beon – the land that YHWH has conquered for the community of Israel is cattle country and your servants have cattle" (Num. 32:3). Each and every foreign place uttered in this speech must surely gall and provoke Moses. Each is located on the wrong side of the Jordan, outside the boundaries of the land to which the Israelites are headed. In fact, the Reubenites unwittingly emphasize the point when they beseech Moses: "Do not move us across the Jordan" (Num. 32:5). Furthermore, earlier in the journey through the wilderness this very tribe played a particularly ignominious role in a disastrous revolt against Moses' leadership, a revolt led by none other than the Reubenites Dathan and Abiram along with Moses' cousin, Korah the Levite.[2] Not surprisingly, Moses perceives this new request as a renewed challenge from the same quarter.

Their request provokes a blistering torrent of reproach from Moses, as if to deaden the sounds of foreign sites under the counterweight of his rage. Significantly, Moses couches his rage in a calculated use of the past, perhaps relying on the fact that in "dangerous times [memory] . . . opens a possibility for overcoming a dire crisis."[3]

> Are your brothers to go to war and you stay here? And why will you turn the hearts of the children of Israel from crossing to the Land that YHWH has given them? *That is what your fathers did* when I sent them from Kadesh Barnea to see the land. . . . And YHWH was incensed at Israel and he made them wander in the wilderness for forty years, until the end of the whole generation that did evil in the eyes of YHWH. And now you have risen up in place of your fathers, a brood of sinful men, to add still further to the wrath of YHWH against Israel. If you turn away from Him and he abandons them once more in the wilderness, you will bring ruin upon all this people.[4] (Num. 32:6–8, 13–15, emphasis added)

In just a few verses this brief interaction encapsulates the equivocal dimensions of memory found in the book of Numbers while also illustrating memory's persistence as a vexing concern throughout the wilderness narrative.

In his doubt that the Reubenites and Gadites can remember even their own parents' fate and draw the proper lessons, Moses expresses his hard-won understanding of memory's problematic, unreliable nature. It may show itself as an obstacle to his ultimate aim – that the entire new generation make it across the Jordan together. Yet in spite of his skepticism toward memory's usefulness, Moses has no choice but to resort to specific memories of the wilderness generation's demise when facing this new threat from its children. Thus we see Moses lacing his rhetoric with pointed references to past events that culminate in his dramatic warning of repeated disaster. In their subsequent responses, the Reubenites and Gadites confirm Moses' efficacious use of memory as a means of ending the crisis. They reassure Moses of their intention to avoid their fathers' mistakes. In fact, they will serve as the vanguard of the conquering forces. In the end, this episode clearly endorses memory's usefulness in accomplishing Moses' aims.

In this chapter I examine the textual background to Moses' skepticism toward memory even while he simultaneously relies on it to influence the behavior of the new generation. As we will see, due to a series of encounters with the people, experience has taught Moses, and communicates to the reader, a complex understanding of memory. In fact Numbers makes memory, its reliability and limits, a recurring and pressing focus of concern. In particular, Numbers 10 and 11 highlight the issue through a juxtaposition of two competing, even contradictory notions of memory. Each is embedded and developed in a narrative trajectory – chapters 1–10 versus 11–25. Each is taken up in turn.

As I describe in more detail momentarily, chapters 1–10 understand memory as a stabilizing force, used to forge Israel's identity as a collective with a shared past dominated by God's saving acts. Such memories oblige the people to serve God and Moses and submit to priestly regulation, successfully preventing dissent and ensuring harmony in the camp. The focused intensity of the attempt to build a community under priestly leadership is captured in the very noticeable use of the term פקד, translated as "to count or keep track of," especially in the opening chapters. By the end of chapter 10 the priestly use of memory has become a successful means of social control.[5]

Beginning in chapter 11, subsequent events subject this rather authoritarian and over-confident use of memory to a blistering critique. The priestly narratives are exposed as thoroughly naïve, failing as they do to acknowledge memory's extraordinary elusiveness. In place of God's saving acts, desire for the Egyptian past dominates popular collective memory. These chapters grimly narrate the disastrous consequences. Memory subverts Moses' project of unification and control, undermining his authority and even threatening the very continuation of the people Israel. Indeed, by the end of chapter 25 all those liberated from Egypt and so carefully "counted" at the beginning of Numbers are killed off and abandoned without trace in the bleak wilderness landscape.

Such a careful and skillful juxtaposition of the different views of memory in chapters 10 and 11, as well as the exploration of the consequences in the larger narratives in which they are embedded, provides yet another example of the editorial method we have already observed in Numbers.[6] The juxtaposition of diverse materials produces an "echo chamber . . . [a] mix of actual events and different memories of them that informs the Bible's representation of the past."[7] In Numbers an "echo chamber" is created when the priestly editors encounter both earlier priestly memories of the events at Mt. Sinai and an account of the people's shocking and misplaced memories of Egypt. By combining these materials, the editors preserve and represent the past in its complexity. This weaving together of Numbers 10 and 11 provides a paramount example of the interaction among an editor, the older texts he has at hand, and his audience. This has been described as "a repeated process of older traditions being retold in a new context and in a new form with the resulting composition on the one hand faithful to the spirit of the old traditions and their intent, and on the other creatively revised to teach the people and help guide their future destiny."[8] Of course the possibility remains that the process is more haphazard: "The modified biblical narrative often left vestiges of older versions of the past, issuing in a text with a dialectic between the master narrative and other earlier, or even contemporary conflicting versions. Israel's representation of its past in the Bible also incorporates competition and compromise over the meaning of that past."[9] I suggest that both descriptions of the process – an intentional editorial retelling of the past and/or the inadvertent result of preserving contradictory textual traditions – are at play in the final form of Numbers.

Either way, as it now stands, the final form of Numbers has turned the nature of memory itself into an issue and an urgent topic of exploration. Woven together, these different accounts of past events illustrate the ways in which memory is conveyed, sustained, and/or subverted.[10] Such an examination of memory has immediate implications for the success of the priestly project to fashion the narrative of the wilderness journey for the audience of their time. In fact, the priestly editors succeed in offering the reader a richly layered past while capturing the vivacity of a tradition that finds itself capable of repeated adaptation, dialogue, and self-critique. The biblical writers and their later editors are even able "to write back through the past . . . to enable moving through present loss . . . toward the future."[11] Of course, as we shall have opportunity to observe, that vision of the future rests on an uneasy accommodation of memory as both necessary and relentlessly problematic.

∼ Textual analysis of differing views of memory

On their return from viewing the promised land for the first time, the scouts inform the people that, just as they had been told, the land indeed "flows with milk and honey" (Num. 13:27). The scouts then list the many difficulties, which they consider insurmountable, to their successful conquest of that land. Caleb attempts to silence them while motivating the people to proceed. He can think of no better argument than the desirability of the land promised them by God, echoing the scouts' description of the land offered moments before. It is "a land that flows with milk and honey" (Num. 14:8). Unmoved, the generation refuses to march forward, bringing upon itself a series of disastrous punishments that culminate, perhaps at one of the lowest points of the narrative, in the defiant cries of Dathan and Abiram. These two dare to describe Egypt in terms reserved exclusively for the promised land: "Is it not enough that you brought us from a land flowing with milk and honey to have us die in the Wilderness"? (Num. 16:13). Their appropriation of those words of praise signals the extent of the crisis facing Moses, especially because they are in fact only a magnified echo of the people's desire to return to Egypt. The misremembering of Egypt – in startling contradistinction to their actual experience there, and in blatant opposition to the views of Moses and God – forms the core of the people's memory. These popular utterances are especially shocking because of their striking contrast to the depicted state of the people, and of memory, just prior to this rebellion. Therefore, to make sense of the dramatic crisis in the camp, one must first begin with the content of chapters 1–10 that sets up this study in contrast.

The first ten chapters of Numbers contain a variety of materials dated to different periods of time. Nonetheless, they share a priestly provenance that can be ascertained by paying close attention to the content, language, and structure of these chapters. I examine each in turn. Together they coalesce into a distinct editorial unit that is internally coherent. By the end of chapter 10, the reader will observe a smoothly functioning wilderness camp inhabited by a unified and compliant people on their way to the promised land. A precise numbering and placement of the twelve tribes in the camp, with the tabernacle in its midst, provides a blueprint for order and a clearly structured hierarchy. The priests are in firm control.

As we have already had occasion to note, concerns relevant to the priestly class are paramount throughout the first ten chapters of Numbers. Priestly topics include the initiation of the Levitical class in subordinate roles to the sons of Aaron, thus establishing a clear priestly hierarchy; instructions to the Levites for transporting the tent of meeting; cultic matters requiring priestly expertise and intervention, such as corpse contamination, various impurities, and the ritual of jealousy; the outpouring of gifts at a celebration marking the consecration of the tabernacle; and the priestly blessing of

Aaron.[12] As depicted in these chapters, life in the wilderness unfolds "in an orderly manner according to a pre-established plan."[13]

The appropriation of the past and the shaping of collective memory reinforces priestly control of the social order. In chapters 1–10 the past justifies ongoing obligations to God (Num. 3). Memory is used as a tool of instruction, warning, and ritual control (Num. 5). An act of memory, the establishment of an archive, commemorates the celebration of the tabernacle's completion (Num. 7). Finally, being remembered by God over time and commemorating that remembrance creates an ideal means through which events in the wilderness will be linked to the future and to the strengthening of priestly authority in the promised land (Num. 10). An understanding of memory as amenable to exploitation is implied in each of these examples of its use. In fact, memory provides the chief motivation for the current arrangements of the people, especially their willing submission to the priestly authority of Aaron and his sons as established and legitimated in the wilderness.

∼ Being held to account

Thus the opening chapters of Numbers illustrate an attempt to control the social body through the careful use of memory. The pervasive attempt at social control is best captured by the term פקד, "to keep track of." פקד is unmistakably prevalent in Numbers. One only has to search a concordance for the deployment of the term within the five books of Moses to confirm that the word predominates in Numbers over the other four books.[14] Just in qal, the root appears six times in Genesis, sixteen times in Exodus, once in Leviticus, and twice in Deuteronomy. In contrast, in Numbers פקד appears about ninety-three times, especially in its opening chapters. In chapters 1–4 of Numbers the term is simply used above all others. Such dense repetition requires an explanation.

To begin, what does the term mean and how is it connected to remembering? In the other four books of Moses, פקד refers to God's remembering a promise made either to an individual or to the people. For instance, in Genesis 21 God remembers Sara as he had promised, opening her womb so she could conceive: "And YHWH took account פקד of Sara as he had said and YHWH did to Sara as he had spoken" (Gen. 21:1). In another example, as Joseph is about to die in Genesis 50:24–25, he declares to his brothers that God will remember them and take them out of Egypt:

> And Joseph said to his brothers "I am dying and God will surely take account פָּקֹד יִפְקֹד of you and *take you up from this land* to the land that He swore to Abraham, Isaac and Jacob": And Joseph made the children of Israel swear saying "God will surely take account פָּקֹד יִפְקֹד of you and *you shall take up my bones* from here." (emphasis added)

The neatness of the language is noteworthy. God's taking account of the people will lead God to take *them up*, especially because God made a past promise to the patriarchs to do so. That oath to the patriarchs now leads Joseph to make Israel mimic that oath by swearing to take up his bones just as, and when, God takes the people up. The key repetitive phrase in both verses is an emphatic "surely take account of." The context can only suggest an act of memory, or perhaps two acts, on God's part. God remembers the promise to the patriarchs and remembers that their descendants are living in Egypt. God's remembering will trigger the people's remembering to take the bones of Joseph with them. Joseph's prediction is fulfilled in Exodus. God indeed remembers the people once they begin to languish in Egypt and uses the same verb to do so in both Exodus 3:16 and 4:31.[15] God also holds the people to account over several generations, especially in the famous statement of accountability, "visiting the iniquities of the fathers on the children," found in Exodus 20:5, 34:7, Numbers 14:18, and Deuteronomy 5:9. Divine punishment usually results.

Thus we have God's positive remembering of the people in fulfillment of a divine promise as well as God's punishment of the people in consequence of their expected failures. In fact, two possible definitions for פקד include being remembered for good or for bad. Eising defines פקד as "pay heed."[16] Martin Buber captures the various nuances of these definitions in his own: "accounting and recounting, of taking into account, of giving an account of – hence also God's authority that orders human fate, his supplying in need, his deliverance from oppression, but also his taskmasterly activity of balancing deed and consequence."[17] Such an accounting of Israel necessarily requires that God review the people's actions not only in the present but in the past.

With these different notions of the word in mind, let us turn to how פקד is deployed in Numbers. The most straightforward meaning of the verb as it is used in the beginning chapters means "record." For instance, in chapter 1, Moses, Aaron, and representatives of each of the twelve tribes record Israelite men from the age of twenty and up who can bear arms. The men are categorized by tribe and by clan, in their ancestral houses. The narrator concludes each numbering with an identical formula: "and those enrolled." The JPS translation chooses "enrolled," which implies the result of the recording – after being counted, one is now enrolled on the list, thus in the army. In chapter 1 alone a form of the root is used at least twenty times. The word emphasizes just how precisely regulated the people Israel are at the outset of Numbers. The military dimension suggests that it is time for each individual to stand up and be counted – to commit himself entirely to God's plan.

Within chapter 1 the Levites are the only exception to this record keeping. They are exempt from military service. Instead, Moses is ordered to put them in charge of the tabernacle in a different verbal form of the same root, the causative: הפקד. It cannot be a coincidence that the very same root, having already been used so much in Numbers 1, is now used again for the Levites by actualizing a different meaning of the verb, yet one closely interconnected in consequence of its use in the preceding verses. In keeping the tabernacle – that is, watching over it, guarding it, packing and unpacking, arranging its implements – the Levites mimic God's watching over the people Israel so thoroughly counted just moments before.

In chapter 2 the repeated and dense use of "record" and "enrolled" continue. This time, locations of each tribe in the camp are also recorded. At the end of the census, each and every male Israelite is located in a specific place, belonging to a specific tribe, and included in a numerical calculation of that tribe. Each Israelite matters. Each Israelite's place is clear.

The priestly hierarchy and the various roles assigned to priests and Levites are the subjects of chapters 3 and 4. We observe פקד to mean both "to be responsible for" and "to record" throughout the two chapters. For instance, Aaron and his sons are responsible for their priesthood (Num. 3:10) and Eleazar is responsible for the Levites (3:32). He is also responsible for the sacred objects and furnishings of the tabernacle (4:16). On the other hand, Moses is instructed to count the Levites just as he counted the Israelites (4:34–49). To count a Levite makes him accountable to Aaron and his sons. By extrapolation, the linkage of the two meanings holds true for all of Israel. The best way for Moses and the priests to be in charge of Levites and the children of Israel is to count and account for them. Ultimately, they are accountable to God. This implies that God is required to keep track of them as well. To do so, God subjects all of their actions, present and past, to review. Thus God must remember precisely as we observed God doing in the other books of Moses.

Numbers 14 confirms the argument. The Israelites are counted in order to be held responsible for their actions by God. Even though outside the purview of the first ten chapters, chapter 14 holds the key to the meaning of the repetitive use of פקד. It is the failure to stand up and be counted in chapter 14 that renders the entire counting system null and void, or so God temporarily concludes. The people refuse to conquer the land. In consequence, God destroys them but will save their children. All those who were counted in the opening chapters וכל פקדיכם will fall in the wilderness (14:29). The divine punishment suggestively plays on a pervasive dread in the ancient world of being counted, because the counted one would then be more vulnerable to death.[18] But the use of the specific term פקד in Numbers 14 for that counting suggests that God would never have ceased protecting Israel, not only throughout the wilderness but especially once settled in the promised land, if only Israel had fulfilled its side of the agreement. But because Israel failed to do so, those counted so optimistically and so carefully at the outset are destroyed. As we will see in chapter 6, God destroys them by ceasing to keep track of them. They no longer matter. Therefore their physical location within the camp no longer matters. They can, and will, be abandoned to the obscurity of wilderness.

However, פקד is dominant one last time, in Numbers 26. The new generation is counted and enrolled in the second census.[19] The relationship has been preserved and continues through a new counting and holding to account. In sum, the purposeful use of the term פקד in Numbers 1–4, 14, and 26 emphasizes its importance to the book. Each example sheds light on its interaction with remembering. Under the priestly system, God remembers Israelites through counting, recording, and holding them to account. But when Israel comes to remember Egypt in distorted fashion, God will punish the people by losing track of them.

~ The priestly uses of memory

But before the events of chapters 11–14 make that tragic result necessary, God attempts to motivate the Israelites, once counted, to fulfill the divine plan by telling Israel what to remember. In so doing, God and the priestly editors do nothing less than exploit memory to compel acquiescence from the Israelites, to control them and, more benignly, to celebrate with them. Let us look at several examples of the use of memory in these chapters. God begins by reminding Moses of the liberation of Israel from Egypt. This occurs in the midst of announcing the special role of the Levites as a substitute for the first-born Israelites. "For every first born is mine – at the time that I struck down every first born in the land of Egypt I consecrated to me all the first born of Israel from man to beast – mine they will be, I am Yhwh" (Num. 3:13). God reiterates the claim almost word for word in 8:16–17. God's liberation of the people from Egypt justifies the subsequent demands made by God, Moses, and the priests of both Levite and Israelite over time. By sparing Israel, God enables the people to serve Him. To commemorate that liberation, Numbers announces the first wilderness observance of the Passover after Egypt in chapter 9:1–3, implementing the decree of yearly celebration.

זכר – memory – first appears in Numbers 5. Not surprisingly, it is used for ritual purposes as the priests maintain order through regulating a marital crisis. The case of the jealous husband with plenty of suspicion but without any proof is resolved when he brings his suspected wife to the priest along with an offering.[20] Numbers 5:15 describes the offering as a "meal offering of jealousy, a meal offering of remembrance (מנחת זכרון) which recalls wrongdoing (מזכרת עון)." Numbers 5:18 repeats the term (מנחת הזכרון) while adding the definite article. It is unclear precisely what a meal offering of remembrance might be, but the whole procedure is meant to expose the wrongdoing so that punishment is inevitable.[21] If the woman is guilty, the community will have the opportunity to learn of the fact quickly after the priest brings her forward to stand before Yhwh. If guilty, she will become an "imprecation among your people" (5:21), to which pronouncement she must utter an amen (5:22). A guilty verdict will certainly be spread among the people as well as the fact that the woman has been subjected to her husband's control, control reinforced by the priest's technical efficiency. But what if she is innocent? Unfortunately, she will still be punished by the public humiliation.[22] I would suggest that the entire narrative of the procedure is meant to serve, at the expense of the woman, as an unmistakable deterrence to a future audience. The detailed description of the ordeal's procedures suggest that what is being remembered in the meal-offering of remembrance is the humiliating procedure itself. The use of different forms of זכר in the procedure suggests a priest, fully in charge of regulating such a private matter, doing so through the use of memory in a ritual context to deter, warn, and firmly control the community.

זכר is absent in chapter 7, but a communal *act* of memory is evident in the recording of tribal gifts upon the completion of the tabernacle. In fact, the entire chapter could be considered a communal archive. The contributions of each tribe of Israel are listed in precise and repetitious detail. Pierre Nora describes such an orderly inventory with its meticulous recording of events as a signature act of memory.[23] The chapter's tone is wonderfully celebratory, especially in contrast to chapter 5. The biblical archive captures the people's willing assent and enthusiastic support of the building of the tabernacle – shrine to God's presence and ongoing protection of them – for all time. The record of the gift-giving marks a crucial priestly milestone in the life of the nation. That note of celebration muffles the more ominous note of priestly control sounded in chapter 5.

The sense of celebratory, harmonic order so tangible in chapter 7 culminates in chapter 9's representation of the daily cloud and nightly fire that cover the tabernacle. Verse 16 emphasizes the continuing presence of this favorable sign of divine accompaniment: "It was always so." The decision to make or break camp does not depend on human considerations – a convenient spot, with a good water supply, or the length of travel or time of day – but rests solely on God's discretion:

> And at such times as the cloud stayed from evening until morning, when the cloud lifted in the morning they would march on. Day or night, whenever the cloud lifted, they would march on. Whether it was two days or a month or a year – however long the cloud lingered over the Tabernacle – the Israelites remained in camp and did not set out; only when it lifted did they set out. By order of YHWH they made camp and by order of YHWH they set out. They would keep the charge of YHWH at the bidding of YHWH through the hand of Moses. (Num. 9:21–23)

No better picture exists of the ideal relations among the people, God, and Moses as conveyed by the first ten chapters than in this precise recital of camping and marching through the wilderness as orchestrated by God.

The use of memory as a means of unifying the people and of creating order through mechanisms of social control culminates in another celebratory moment: the making and blowing of the trumpets in chapter 10. The event encapsulates the vision projected in chapters 1–10 and more than any other sets up the stark contrast created by the events of chapter 11. Yet before turning to the trumpets, let me briefly digress to identify the distinct priestly language and forms of these first ten chapters.

⤳ *Priestly language and forms*

The first ten chapters convey and reinforce this priestly vision of the wilderness period in highly repetitive and formulaic language. Such language embodies a depiction of the world as predictable and stable, creating a "narrative order of varied repetition."[24] We have already seen numerous examples of such repetition in the first 10 chapters, for instance, in the use of the term פקד. The repeated formula "YHWH commanded" followed by "so they did" provides another example of priestly repetition. The formula attests to a people in harmony with God and Moses. Joseph Blenkinsopp labels the phrase "an execution formula" that is typical of priestly materials.[25] It can be found in chapters 2, 3, 5, 8, and 9 of Numbers. Sean McEvenue argues that execution formulas communicate "a general sense of order and purpose born of the constant recurrence of God's word followed by its fulfillment."[26] That order is reinforced through the use of repetition and formulaic phrases, the chief stylistic devices employed by priestly writers.

The preference for repetition reaches its culmination in "panel writing." McEvenue defines panel writing as the structuring of a series of events repetitively. Each is held together by the use of the same formulas and form.[27] Chapter 7 of Numbers, the repetitive giving of the gifts from each tribe to the tabernacle, immediately comes to mind as a parade example of panel writing, as does the beginning of the march in chapter 10:13–28.

Further examples typical of priestly materials as cited by McEvenue, and in ample evidence in Numbers 1–10, include the careful enumeration of tribes, a stress on lists, and the exact identification of those involved in a narrative and where they are situated. The genealogies of the tribes represent P's concern for purity, symmetry, legitimacy and order.[28] Chapter 2 illustrates McEvenue's description of a priestly style in its reassuring conclusion that all is well: "The Israelites did accordingly, just as YHWH has commanded Moses, so they camped by their standards and so they traveled, each with his clan according to his ancestral house" (Num. 2:34).

∽ *Priestly structure*

The content and style of the various priestly materials examined thus far can be understood to coalesce into an edited unit of materials that Jacob Milgram has called a "chiasm."[29] Nowhere is the priestly pleasure in structure more prevalent than in the use of a chiasm to organize whole sections of material. Such a chiasmic structure makes the inner coherence of chapters 1–10 transparent as follows:

A Chapters 1 and 2 — the numbering of the tribes, their placement and the order of the march during the journey

B Chapter 3 — the introduction of the Levitical class and their roles

C Chapter 4 — focus on the tabernacle – revising the roles of the Kohatites in subordination to the sons of Aaron when transporting the tabernacle.

X Chapters 5 and 6 — regulations requiring priestly monitoring, which include the Sotah ritual and the initiation of the Nazirite. These chapters culminate in the priestly blessing.

C′ Chapter 7 — focus on the tabernacle – the tribal gifts given to the tabernacle when Moses finished anointing and consecrating it

B′ Chapter 8 — the consecration of the Levites

A′ Chapters 9 and 10 — the cloud and trumpets trigger the tribal march through the wilderness, *precisely in the order laid out in the beginning.*[30]

The "X" of the above structure draws attention to the highly technical, even esoteric knowledge held only by the priests. It also confirms that leaders buttress their authority by asserting their unique access to technical but necessary knowledge needed by the wider community.[31]

Such a precise structuring of the priestly materials represents a carefully thought-out vision for communal Israel. We have seen what Robert Alter describes as P's "magisterial formulation, everything is ordered, set in its appointed place, and contained within a symmetrical frame."[32] Menachem Haran suggests that this priestly vision of Israel in the wilderness camp is nothing short of utopian:

P describes a situation that is utopian and idealistic to the extent of being schematic (a situation which the priestly authors believed to have existed within the people of Israel from the moment they stood at the foot of Mount Sinai until their arrival in the Promised Land.) The utopian, imaginary prospect of the tribes of Israel assembled in right-angle formation around a lavishly adorned tabernacle enthralls P's authors from a distance in time and space, and against this backdrop they give full expression – so full as to make the prospect at times unrealistic – to their legal aspirations and theological concepts.[33]

The content, language, and structure of Numbers 1–10 convey this priestly description of the people in an ideal state. These chapters also illustrate how the turn to the past and the use of memory are inextricably linked to the justification and continuity of that state. One final example will suffice.

∼ *The blowing of the trumpets*

Numbers 10 neatly captures the use of memory as a tool of priestly control. I refer to the instructions for the creation and blowing of silver trumpets, legislation that serves as the culmination of the priestly texts of the first ten chapters.

> Have two silver trumpets made; make them of hammered work. They shall serve you to summon the community and to set the divisions in motion. When both are blown in long blasts, the whole community shall assemble before you at the entrance of the Tent of Meeting; and if only one is blown, the chieftains, heads of Israel's contingents, shall assemble before you. But when you sound short blasts, the divisions encamped on the east shall move forward; and when you sound short blasts a second time, those encamped on the south shall move forward. Thus short blasts shall be blown for setting them in motion, while to convoke the congregation you shall blow long blasts, not short ones. The trumpets shall be blown by Aaron's sons, the priests; they shall be for you as a law for the ages throughout your generations. (Num. 10:2–8, JPS trans.)

The blowing of trumpets and more significantly, the status accorded the priests who blow them, is formalized as continuing through time, expressed in the key phrase: "they shall be for you as a law for the ages throughout your generations" (Num. 10:8), or והיו לכם לחקת עולם לדרתיכם.[34] This phrase not only legitimates priestly control but suggests the priestly assumption that the memory of those trumpets first blown in the wilderness will ensure priestly authority over time by granting their leadership continuing legitimacy.

Indeed, the silver trumpets not only are blown to initiate the marches through the wilderness but are intended for continued use in the promised land. Immediately after instructing Moses on the proper signals to initiate the Israelite movement in the wilderness, God goes on to explicitly command the future use of those same trumpets once the people are in the land:

> When you are at war *in your land* against an aggressor who attacks you, you shall sound short blasts on the trumpets that you may be remembered (ונזכרתם) before YHWH your God and be delivered from your enemies. And on your joyous occasions – your fixed festivals and new moon days – you shall sound the trumpets over your burnt offerings and over your sacrifices of well-being. (Num. 10:9–10a, JPS trans., emphasis added)

The passage creates both the *content* of the memory – the blowing of trumpets to initiate the movement of the wilderness camp – and the conditions under which those memories will be *retrieved* – during times of war or of festivals in the land.[35] The passage assumes memory's content can be easily provided – the settled nation will remember past marches through the wilderness – while exhibiting the appropriation of memory for national purposes, which correspond to a priestly agenda.[36] Rooting the blowing of trumpets in the wilderness past would give legitimacy to their use in motivating future generations to unite and go out to battle or to submit to the priestly regulations for festivals.

Thus the blowing of the trumpets links an act envisioned in the future with a past imagined in a highly specific way, sometimes referred to as "an invented tradition." Hobsbawm describes invention traditions thus:

> They normally attempt to establish continuity with a suitable historical past. ... They are responses to novel situations which take the form of reference to old situations, or which establish their own past by quasi-obligatory repetitions.[37]

Invented traditions have as their goal the establishment of social cohesion and the legitimization of institutions.[38] The blowing of trumpets accomplishes those goals, legitimizing as it does priestly institutions and the preservation of priestly status and authority. Social cohesion is reinforced in the repeated calls to "the community" or "all the community." If a different signal is blown, then only the chieftains of the community need gather. Yet only the sons of Aaron are allowed to blow the trumpets. The community is divided among the people, their leaders, and the priests, reinforcing a clear hierarchy of authority. The blowing of the trumpets publicly reinforces "the arrangements of society."[39] It is that hierarchy and those arrangements that the memory of the trumpets blown by the sons of Aaron is meant to uphold.

Finally, the tradition of blowing the trumpets illustrates memory's crucial theological purpose for the priests – to strengthen the relationship between God and the people by providing a mnemonic device for God to remember divine obligations. The passage concludes: "And they shall serve you as a memorial (לזכרון) before your God; I, YHWH, your God" (Num. 10:10b). The trumpets remind God of Israel, while the sacrifices that accompany the blowing of the trumpets express the people's gratitude for the constancy of that divine presence, sealing their relationship. Memory becomes the fitting means of preserving the harmonious interaction between God, the remembering deliverer, and the people, celebrants of divine protection.[40]

Several assumptions of the priestly understanding of memory are illustrated in this passage. Priestly ritual and national celebration come together in the use of זכר. Specific memories can be legislated and used to unify the nation. At the same time, through a ritual such as the blowing of the trumpets, both the priestly hierarchy and priestly theological claims are reinforced. Memory has become the key to ensuring God's relationship in perpetuity to the people Israel under the authority of the priesthood. In their entirety, chapters 1–10 appear to confirm an argument made by Bernard Lewis:

> Those who are in power control to a very large extent the presentation of the past, and seek to make sure that it is presented in such a way as to buttress and legitimize their own authority, and to affirm the rights and merits of the group which they lead.[41]

And yet, in a shockingly abrupt departure from the tones of the opening chapters, such a claim, along with its promise of success, is proven in need of considerable revision. Without warning, the events of chapter 11 irretrievably shatter the ideal portrait so carefully drawn until that point. It opens with the very first utterance of the populace:

The people took to complaining bitterly in the ears of YHWH. And YHWH heard and was incensed: a fire of YHWH broke out against them, consuming the edges of the camp. (Num. 11:1)

The jarring shift in tone in Numbers 11 signals the unraveling of the tightly structured narrative until that point. Indeed, a narrative incoherence threatens, set off by the complaints of the people. Memories of Egypt rapidly follow.[42] Subsequent events challenge the ready appropriation of the past, throwing into serious doubt the extent to which memory should be considered, if at all, a viable means of ensuring Israel's future.

∾ Variations on a theme: the subversions of memory

At first the people's complaints lead to a divine attack along the borders of this carefully regulated camp. Yet within minutes (and verses) the results spread throughout the entire camp: "Moses heard the people weeping, every clan apart, each person at the entrance of his tent. And YHWH was very angry, and in the eyes of Moses it was displeasing" (Num. 11:10). The tightly configured camp, unified in a common goal, the thousands camping and marching by their standards, is now replaced by an image of a splintered people, each person at his own tent. Their memories have literally stopped the people in their tracks. Absent is the harmonious flow from God's commands to the words of Moses to the people's eager, compliant agreement. A radically different depiction of the period in the wilderness is put forward, again corresponding to a view of memory, but this time as a relentless, brutal cause of subversion that wreaks havoc among the Israelites.

The events of chapter 11 initiate and develop this alternative view. Not surprisingly, a scholarly consensus identifies Numbers 11 as containing nonpriestly materials.[43] Outside of Deuteronomy, the nonpriestly sources of the Pentateuch have been most clearly identified with the remarkable stories of the founding families in Genesis. In the Genesis narratives individual characters take center stage. For instance, Jacob stands out in vivid, realistic fashion. Elsewhere I have argued that the biblical writer uses the ways in which Jacob remembers his past to characterize him successfully. What and who Jacob remembers colors his character, as the case may be, bitter, mournful, or vengeful.[44] It is possible that a nonpriestly writer has again used memory in chapter 11 of Numbers. But this time, it is not individual but collective memory, used to characterize not Jacob but his alternative appellation: Israel. As the people Israel remember Egypt, they become increasingly recalcitrant and unruly.

Friedman highlights the extent to which nonpriestly accounts (which he labels JE) are concerned predominantly with the human dimension. In particular, J examines the shortcomings of the people as well as their collective responsibility. Friedman notes that over the course of its narrative, there is in J "a narrowing of apparent divine control of events coupled with an inverse increase in the human share."[45] This seems a particularly apt description of Numbers 11, where human complaint and rebellion become the prevailing picture of the people in the wilderness period and God, at least temporarily, acts impulsively. That picture preserves an account of the people's failure to meet God's requests of them, unanticipated in the chapters leading up to it. In fact, chapter 11 is at an enormous remove from the narrative that precedes it, suggesting that it indeed originates in a different source.

I do not claim that all the diverse materials and genres of chapters 11–25 originate in the same source; far from it. Numbers' middle section contains a collection of materials, including priestly traditions, that range over several hundred years. But I do want to claim that the radically different understanding of memory and its consequences first articulated in chapter 11 serves, through its narrated ramifications, to organize and shape the middle section of Numbers into its own bounded unit. This unit is noticeably distinct from chapters 1–10. At present I will examine Numbers 11–14. In chapters 5 and 6, I examine strategies of deterrence found in Numbers 15–25 that are a direct response to the subversions of memory first set in motion by the events of chapter 11.

Chapter 11 introduces and goes on to illustrate three assumptions of this strikingly different conception of memory. First, countermemory challenges and even overwhelms official memory. The people refashion Egypt into the object of their desire. These countermemories are rooted in bodily sensations and uttered out loud in words of vociferous complaint. In consequence, the second assumption of this alternative conception of memory pinpoints its inevitable connection to unfettered speech. As the necessary conveyor of collective memory, speech is as pernicious and uncontrollable as memory itself. Finally, if left unchecked, the sort of subversive memory illustrated in Numbers 11 knows no bounds, but will quickly spread and destabilize the entire community, ending in an explosive, full-scale attack on the authority of Moses and, ultimately, of God. I take up each assumption in turn.

As they weep, the Israelites utter the words that most clearly contradict the version of Egypt repeatedly narrated prior to this point. They moan:

> Who will feed us meat? We remember the fish that we ate in Egypt for free, the cucumbers, and the melons, and the leeks, and the onions and the garlic. And now our gullets are dried up. There is nothing at all except for this manna (in front of) our eyes. (Num. 11:4b–6)[46]

The foodstuffs they remember – leeks, onions, etc. – apparently reflect the actual diet of Egypt.[47] They are desiring, almost tasting, the real food of Egypt versus this unchanging, even though miraculous stuff, manna. Yet in so doing, they forget other aspects of their lives in Egypt. Forgotten is Pharoah's enslavement of them, the slaying of first-born Israelites, and the other oppressions suffered in Egypt; the wonders wrought by God to free the people, the journey safely through the sea to Mt. Sinai, and the granting of a covenant. All are pushed aside by the desire for food. Thus *bodily* memory – primarily of being fed or feeding – overpowers the more abstract memories that precede chapter 11, stories of historical events and of God's saving acts. Their counter memories operate to push "elements to the fore that are, or tend to be, forgotten in the official memory . . . explicitly contradict[ing] another memory."[48]

As remembered by the people, this alternative version of the past has become "an absence and an object of desire that had to be earnestly sought, its remains recovered."[49] The Egyptian past sought by the people at this juncture is a particularly infantile one. In a discussion of the bodily cravings that pervade chapter 11, Ilana Pardes quotes Nehama Leibowitz, who draws attention to the infantile cravings of the people: "Egypt is an eternal refrain in their mouths. . . . They yearned for 'Egypt' as a babe for its mother's breasts."[50] Memories of oral gratification dominate. In fact, Pardes suggests that the imagery of the promised land, a land flowing with milk and honey (suggesting breast milk) is meant by Moses precisely as a counter to the cravings for Egypt. Yet Moses' promises fail to convince. The people "persist in evoking life by the Nile, where they were nurtured by another mother, whose fleshpots seem to them more tangible than Canaan's milk and honey."[51] The force and consequence of these bodily cravings suggests a type of memory far outside the realm of invented traditions, certainly outside the realm of easy manipulation. Ignoring the massive determining power of this type of memory is dangerous. Richard Terdiman observes: "The pasts we carry but do not entirely cognize regularly rise to colonize our present."[52] As subsequent events confirm, Terdiman's description aptly captures the narrative depiction of the Israelite failure to grab hold of God's plans, "colonized" in the present and obstructed in their future by their past in Egypt.

In attempting to recover that past by conjuring up Egyptian delicacies, the people commit the egregious error of failing to distinguish between the food of Egypt and the manna they so disparage. God is the source of the manna. That the people still desire Egyptian food is an indication of their blindness to God's acts on their behalf. By rejecting God's food, do they also reject God? God interprets their complaint precisely in these terms: "for you have rejected YHWH who is among you" (Num. 11:20). Ominously, God goes even further, making explicit the conclusion of their desire for Egyptian food. They must think they were better off there. God frames this furious rebuke of the people by amplifying their remembering with words they did not yet say: "For it was better for us in Egypt" (11:18) and "Oh, why did we ever leave Egypt" (11:20).

This connection between the food of Egypt and the manna was first created in the book of Exodus shortly after the liberation from Egypt. The episodes in Exodus and those in Numbers are considered by many to be doublets. It is worthwhile to digress briefly to discover the extent to which these episodes are parallel and the extent to which they are distinct. For it is in their differences that the unique perspective that I am claiming for Numbers comes most into focus.

In Exodus 15:24–25, soon after witnessing God's glorious division of the Reed Sea so that the people Israel could escape while their Egyptian pursuers drown, the people begin to complain about the lack of water. Strikingly, God responds to their complaint by providing them what they need without comment. They next complain in an even higher decibel in Exodus 16, introducing a theme that becomes dominant in Numbers: that Egypt provided them flesh and bread to the point of satiation. Therefore they should have remained there. Again, God's response is free of condemnation or indictment. God gives them quail and then manna. Only after someone violated the injunction against gathering manna on Shabbat does God finally react angrily. Yet what is striking in God's response to that violation is the lack of punishment. Rather, God takes the opportunity to teach the people: "See that YHWH has given you the Sabbath; therefore He gives you on the sixth day food for two days. Let everyone remain where he is; let no one leave his place on the seventh day" (Exod. 16:29). Calm and instruction prevail in these episodes of complaint.

Now let us return to Numbers 11 and the present episode of manna and quails. To begin, both the episode in Exodus and that in Numbers occur after a three-day march – the first from the sea and the second from Sinai. In addition, the foodstuffs provided by God – quail and manna – are the same. Yet the two episodes are also noticeably distinct from one another. As put by Milgrom, they are "variants of the same tradition. But they cannot be equated."[53] In fact, in Numbers the consequences of complaint are distinct enough to justify a claim that we are now in a different narrative arena heading toward a catastrophe that was unthinkable in Exodus. For in Numbers God strikes out against the people in a lethal fashion. Consider the episode of the quails. In Exodus God provides quails without comment. In Numbers the provision of quails leads to widespread death. The difference of course has to do with Sinai. The events in Exodus occur before the people take upon themselves God's covenant. But once that occurs, God reads their disobedience in a completely different light.

In sum, while Egypt is the source of the people's disobedience in both Exodus and Numbers, it is only in Numbers that desire for Egypt leads to their downfall. In fact, the reference to Egypt in Exodus is passed over by God, Moses, and the narrator, but in Numbers the downfall of an entire generation begins after one single countermemory of Egypt.

This countermemory of the people in Numbers 11 and its ramifications mark a stark contrast not only to the episode in Exodus but to the ideal state of the people Israel depicted just before in Numbers 1–10. Suddenly, in Numbers 11 the people behave as a collection of former slaves against whom Moses must now struggle in order to forge them into a nation. Their very first question – "*who* will feed us?" – in fact suggests the extent of their growing alienation from the leadership of Moses and of God. They are quickly deteriorating into a mob, portrayed in as human, and menacing, a manner as possible.

~ *Memory and the deleterious nature of speech*

The reader can almost hear how loudly the people utter their memories of appetites satisfied or deprived. Speech becomes the necessary and, at points in our narrative, lethal weapon of memory. Just as the utterances of the people unleash the change in their fortunes, words will hold an equally important influence over the fate of Miriam and Aaron, enveloping them in the same negative light. Following upon the heels of God's anger in chapter 11, verse one of chapter 12 begins, "And Miriam and Aaron spoke against Moses." The contentious issue they raise even concerns speech. They assert their status as partners in conversation with God: "for hasn't YHWH spoken through us as well?" (Num. 12:2).[54] God's response suggests a sense of divine irony: "Hear then my words" (Num. 12:6), as if to say, if you really want to hear my words, I'll grant you that wish, but you will mightily regret it! God punishes Miriam for the words she utters against Moses (sparing the high priest Aaron), differentiating Moses from Miriam and Aaron by announcing: "Mouth to mouth I speak with him" (Num. 12:8). God fittingly emphasizes the very instrument of speech, the mouth. The chapter, then, is a short treatise on speech, illustrating its explosive and dangerous power if used unwisely or carelessly. The attack on Moses by his very own family, just after the disturbing events of chapter 11, suggests that the carefully crafted narrative in the opening chapters of the book – of the special relation of Moses and God as together they lead the willing people Israel to the promised land – is being challenged and dismantled piece by piece.

The culmination of the use of words as weapons of subversion, even more destructive than those murmured by the people or by Miriam and Aaron, comes about in the episode of the spies. Their words upon the return from scouting the promised land are given a special label, דבה (translated as "calumnies" in the JPS version). The spies spread evil reports (דבת הארץ) of the land among the people in Numbers 13:32. God's punishment of the spies identifies this evil report precisely as the reason they will die:

> And the men whom Moses sent to scout the land and returned and caused the entire community to complain against him by spreading an evil report about the land – those men – the spreaders of the evil report of the land – a displeasing one – died in a plague before YHWH. (Num. 14:36–37)

דבה is the same word used in Genesis 37:2 to describe the negative reports Joseph brings his father concerning his brothers. The allusion to Genesis through this rather unusual term suggests that just as that report led to a disaster for Joseph, as he is kidnaped by his brothers and sold into Egyptian service, so too the negative reports of the spies lead to the punishment of these people, with the startling difference that they *want to be returned* to that very same Egypt that they now remember so favorably.

The people's collective response to the spies in chapter 14 further magnifies the cascade of words, this time of unceasing complaint, that permeates the camp. At the same time their words also confirm God's anticipatory identification (in Num. 11) of their flirtation with the idea of returning to Egypt:

> *All the children of Israel* complained against Moses and against Aaron and *all the community* said to them: if only we had died in the land of Egypt or in this wilderness if only had we died. Why is Y H W H taking us to this land to fall by the sword? Our wives and our children will become spoil – wouldn't it be better for us to return to Egypt? And they said to each other, let's head back and return to Egypt. (Num. 14:2–4, emphasis added)

The response is uttered in unison by the entire people, as emphasized by the beginning "all the children of Israel" and then the additional "all the community." Paradoxically, their complaining does in fact unite the people – "they said to each other" – but on behalf of a project far different from that envisioned in the opening chapters. In unison they turn their thoughts back to Egypt. In response to the most serious crisis of confidence since the people left Egypt, they want to undo their steps and immediately return to an Egypt that has become a consuming object of desire.

God responds to the outburst of complaint and countermemory in a flourish of divine words, exercising a rhetorical power meant finally to silence the people. God makes absolutely explicit the memory of the Exodus that He expected them to possess: God's signs and wonders. That they fail to remember events in this way leads to their punishment:

> None of the men who have seen my Presence and my signs which I did in Egypt and in the Wilderness yet tried me these ten times and did not hearken to my voice shall see the land which I swore to their fathers. None of those who spurn me shall see it. (Num. 14:22–23)

Milgrom points out how the notion of "measure for measure" operates in God's punishment of the people. All those who remembered Egypt in the distorted ways recorded in this section of Numbers, turning their past lives there into the object of their desires, shall be condemned to retreat, retracing the steps that earlier led them away from Egypt.[55] God orders the condemned generation: "Tomorrow turn and march into the Wilderness by way of the Sea of Reeds" (Num. 14:25). Only those unencumbered by the failure to remember God's version of events will be allowed entry to the promised land.

Finally, a treatise on speech requires its own lexicon. Beginning in chapter 11, one can observe precisely such a lexicon for a specific subcategory of speech: complaint. Together the variety of words capture and convey the insidious quality of the uttered memories that permeate and dominate the narrative of this period in Israel's history. Moses (and the audience) is subject to a litany of misery: complaint, quarrel, crying out, yelling, and weeping. The most common form of complaint – מלינים – is rendered in English as murmuring. The noun form תלונות, complaint, is also used. In fact, in chapter 14 alone, a form of לוֹן, murmur, occurs six times. This lexicon of complaint comes to a climax in chapter 14:27 as God asks:

> Till when for this evil community, that they stir up murmuring against me? The murmuring of the Children of Israel that they murmur against me, I have heard.[56]

The complaints and those who utter them are emphasized through the simple devices of repetition and framing: murmuring/the complaints of the children of Israel/repeated murmuring.

∼ Memory and authority

Both the Israelite countermemories and the speeches in which they are embedded are portrayed as destabilizing and uncontainable, even affecting the carefully constructed hierarchy headed by Moses and God. This is especially evident in chapter 11. The atmosphere in the camp created by the weeping of the people in longing for Egypt rapidly spreads to Moses, leading him to question his own authority and even God's judgment. Ultimately, the complaints of the people, coupled with those of Moses, even affect God, who lashes out at the people.

After hearing the people weep, Moses asks God:

> Why have you dealt ill with your servant, and why have I not found favor in your eyes to place the burden of all this people upon me? Did I conceive all this people, did I bear them, that you should say to me "Carry them in your bosom as a nursemaid carries the suckling to the land that You have promised on oath to their fathers?" Where am I to get meat to give to all this people when they cry before me saying "give us meat that we may eat"? I am unable alone to carry all this people for it is too heavy for me. (Num. 11:11–14)

Moses launches his most serious reproach against God since first appointed leader. He even dares to redefine the call by God as a punishment rather than an honor. He would like to disavow his responsibility for the people, an obligation that binds him to the people in the same way that a nurse is bound to a child. The wet-nurse image angrily conjured up by Moses fittingly corresponds to the depiction, just moments before, of the insatiable appetite and ravenous hunger of the people. Such appetites demand the feeding that Moses wants to withhold. He is simply not up to the task. The people's misplaced remembering has led him, at least temporarily, to relinquish his long-standing and essential role as their protector against God's rages.[57]

The destabilizing memory of Egypt also infects God, triggering divine anger until it reaches an impulsive crescendo of destruction. God starts promisingly enough by commanding the people, via Moses, to purify themselves, reminiscent of the events leading up to the moment of divine revelation at Sinai in the book of Exodus. God immediately interrupts those preparations by rebuking them for their whining. He then ominously informs the people that their wish for meat will be granted:

> YHWH will give you meat and you shall eat. You shall eat not one day, nor two, nor even five days or ten or twenty but a whole month, until it comes out of your nostrils and becomes loathsome to you. (Num. 11:18b–20a)

Though not exactly a favorable response, there is no indication that the punishment will be anything worse than an eventual weariness with the diet of desired meat. God even defines the giving of meat as a sign of His infinite power, asking: "Is there a limit to the power of YHWH?" (Num. 11:23). A wind sweeps quail into the wilderness camp in fulfillment of God's promise. There is so much quail that it covers the entire area two cubits deep. The incident should now be concluded as an illustration of divine beneficence and forbearance in providing so much meat to the camp. However, at the sight of the people's eager gathering and then tasting of the meat, God unpredictably strikes out:

> The meat was still between their teeth, nor yet chewed, when the anger of YHWH blazed forth among the people and YHWH struck the people a very severe blow. (Num. 11:33)

The story of the quails brilliantly illustrates the insidious effects of the people's memories of Egypt, effects that spread throughout the camp, sparing no one, not even God. The people's memories, at first triggering disquiet only among themselves, rapidly spread that disquiet to Moses and, ultimately, to God, resulting in a rash, indiscriminate burst of destruction. Fittingly, just as these subversive memories strike the entire community, so too does God's punishment.

The series of events triggered by chapter 11 raise the question whether the people's memories of Egyptian delicacies can be destroyed or at least silenced and replaced by God's plans for Israel. The condemnation of the entire generation in chapter 14 suggests the starkest of conclusions. The only way to stifle memories of Egyptian delicacies is to kill off those who hold them. This far bleaker understanding of memory highlights the extent to which memory, especially bodily memory, defies appropriation. As succinctly put by Richard Terdiman, memory is not only capable of sustaining cultural hegemony, but equally capable of subverting it.[58]

∿ *Through an editor's lens: Egypt or the promised land*

The discussion of chapters 10 and 11 highlights two very different conceptions of memory and its usefulness. Each is embedded in a series of stories and events strikingly distinct from one another. Yet they are also undeniably juxtaposed. Following one another in narrative sequence, these opposing views literally share connecting textual space. Observing the way in which memory and countermemory may oppose each other, Nathan Wachtel proposes a possible explanation of such an occurrence, an explanation with political overtones:

several memories coexist and even oppose each other, memories that are the objects of struggles, strategies and power relations: sometimes official, dominant memories upheld by institutions; sometimes latent, secret recollections, those of the dominated groups.[59]

Numbers confirms this description. Memory (the official version) and countermemory (that of the dominated group) exert an almost tangible force on collective arrangements as embedded and opposed to each other in chapters 1–10 and 11–25. In the first instance, memory is a reliable, pliable tool of nation building, recording the story of God's liberation of the people from Egypt, who, in response, exhibit loyal and unified obedience to God's commands through Moses. Memory can be legislated for all time, providing the means of instruction and the justification for communal celebration. In each and every instance, memory is an unquestioned instrument in the hands of an authority it upholds. In contrast, a different type of memory unsettles what appeared until that point to be unshakable. It is an unpredictable and uncontainable force, triggered by bodily appetites and spread by means of speech, that impedes the entire journey and leads to debilitating attacks on the authority of Moses and of God, with lethal results. Yet the fascinating result of the edited version of Numbers is the striking preservation of both views. Memory needs to be understood as both reliable *and* explosive.

When read as part of the larger narrative fabric of the wilderness journey, the celebratory blowing of the trumpets followed by weeping for Egyptian delicacies intricately fit together. Of course one notices the abrupt shifting of scene and tone in chapter 11. We are drawn to observe each narrative moment separately and understand what underlies the imagined hopes and uncertainties of the wilderness journey. I have gone out of my way to try to do so. Such conflicting images characterize ancient Israel's record of the past in general. "In many respects, the religious culture of ancient Israel is characterized by a perpetual negotiation with its memories and representations of the past."[60] But after reading chapters 10 and 11 as distinct from one another, it is time to examine the effect of their having been placed in sequential order. Read together, the result is a far more comprehensive and richer view of memory. Read together, the result becomes a nuanced examination of the hazards of relying on memory in shaping a usable past.

Why would the editors of Numbers be interested in creating such a sustained reflection on memory? What interests are being served and to what end?[61] In the opening chapters of the present work I proposed that the editing of Numbers most likely originated in a priestly context, probably over an extended period of time. If we add the additional evidence of this chapter, those priestly interests and concerns are apparent not only in the editors but in the priestly materials of Numbers 1–10 that came into their hands. My understanding of the editors and their project versus the earlier priestly texts has, as already mentioned, been influenced by the proposals of Israel Knohl.

Even though I referred to Knohl's argument in an earlier chapter, because it is pertinent to the current discussion of the juxtapositions of Numbers 10 and 11, I will briefly highlight what I consider to be relevant at this juncture. A group of priests whom he designated as members of a Holiness School emerged out of an earlier priestly group, edited the materials of that earlier group, and ultimately edited the final form of the Torah. Recall that Knohl sketched a scenario for the context of that editing. The broader interests of HS rested on the building of a more inclusive community of priests and Israelites. To fulfill such a vision, HS familiarized itself with the popular traditions and depictions of the children of Israel as represented in nonpriestly materials as well as the traditions already known to it from priestly scrolls. While HS wanted to ensure the viability of a priestly class, it needed to identify the real and concrete obstacles in its way. It could do this in effect by turning to the nonpriestly sources such as Numbers 11, which attempted to understand the human dimension of Israelite experience in all its unpredictability. In using that material HS could add an alternative understanding and critique of the people to the priestly preoccupations. The combination of these diverse biblical traditions would subject the aims of an earlier priestly vision to a reality that had to be confronted and understood before the editors could hope to fulfill that vision.[62] The final form of Numbers exemplifies such a project.

The combined biblical sources, consisting of layers of priestly materials ranging over a long period of time and nonpriestly sources, create the larger, edited story of the wilderness period. Memory is crucial to that story. Perhaps warily, even reluctantly, the editors of Numbers conclude that memory is absolutely necessary to their chief goal: rebuilding and shaping the nation through the appropriation and editing of its traditions. However, by preserving the tale of the murmuring generation and its memories of Egypt at the very core of the narrative, the editors have warned their audience against too simple a reliance on collective memory. In so doing they reveal a shrewd understanding not only of memory but of those who remember.

Thus an interaction between sources has been created that focuses on the positive and negative aspects not only of memory but of the people Israel. A well-known precedent for a dialogue between sources can be found in the opening chapters of Genesis. There the priestly and nonpriestly sources are preserved in a fundamental debate over the nature of God's involvement with the earth creatures, the relation between male and female, even humanity's ultimate status on earth. The editing of Numbers creates a similar dialogue. The priestly depiction of the wilderness period as a time of order and stability for the people in their relationship to each other and to God would be immensely appealing and reassuring to a later audience. Yet the redactors use the nonpriestly materials to test that vision with an emphatically different perception of humans and their very real limitations. P's utopian, idealist, and ultimately hopeful vision of Israel is not, on its own, sufficiently realistic. The later priestly editors allow the nonpriestly sources of chapter 11 to complicate matters. The chief point of their project is that neither perspective, that of chapter 10 nor of chapter 11, works on its own. If the first is too unrealistic, the second is too bleak. Both are needed and both are used, woven into the larger fabric of the journey.

Paradoxically, it is the tale of Israel's collective turn to the Egyptian past that creates the opportunity for the priestly appropriation of the nonpriestly materials. Because of its harshly realistic and stark tone, chapter 11 provides the editors far more dramatic material than that of the opening chapters. The rebellion in the wilderness becomes a cautionary tale, used to persuade a much later audience to submit to priestly authority based not only on visionary promises but on a palpable sense of crisis and danger. Chapter 11 is the pivot on which the argument turns. As put by Stephen Owen:

> In the encounter with the past there is usually some fragment that mediates between past and present, a cracked lens that both reveals and conceals. These fragments appear in many forms: fragments of discourse, fragments of memory, fragments of some artifact surviving in the world. And since the fragment always stands between us and the past, it is worth reflecting on what kind of category it is and how it "means."[63]

The memories of Egyptian delicacies and the catastrophe they unleash are one such fragment, used by the editors as a cautionary tale and strong critique of Israel's waywardness. The placement of chapter 11 allows the editor to acknowledge the truly problematic aspects of collective memory and its implications in assessing Israel's past failures. Only then can he rely on memory to shape the whole of the wilderness journey on behalf of future generations. He has no better alternative. But it is to a far more developed conception of memory that he can turn in the later sections of Numbers.

Finally, and most crucially, if read together, chapters 10 and 11 create a dramatic and stark choice for Israel – a point intended for each generation. The people repeatedly face nothing less than either life in the land promised them by God after having liberated them from Egypt or death in the anonymity of the wilderness. Numbers 10, with its depiction of a harmonious present linked to a secure future, leads directly into the retrogressions of the past found in chapter 11. That past, a version of Egypt they cannot forget, dooms an entire generation. Only their children, a new generation, led by new leaders, can implement God's plans, but only in the future. To do so, they must reject the seductions of Egypt, *again and again, in every generation.* This extraordinarily rich use of the past is thus polemical in the extreme.

Yet choosing correctly depends in large part on the view of Egypt held by the people. As the site of oppression and of God's liberating acts, Egypt should obligate the people in the present to live a future life in accord with God's plans for them. This is the assumption of the first section of Numbers. The people take unfamiliar steps forward in an unfamiliar terrain toward the one site worth possessing: the promised land. The path is dedicated to a new life as God, Moses, and the priests lead them. The food and water found on the way are the signs of divine providence. God, the guide through the wilderness, is also the predominant speaker. The realm of this section is the ideal, as the people live up to the demands placed on them.

Yet Egypt renders God's aims in the present impossible. Egypt comes to represent a series of opposite images.[64] Along the Egyptian axis are the voices of the people, through their complaints and the recounting of their old life. This is an axis of the concretely real and known: familiar food, familiar conditions, and even a familiar relationship of ruler and oppressed. The people carry the vestiges of their lives in Egypt into the wilderness. To destroy Egypt, God must destroy the generation. Thus the axis of Egypt becomes the arena of death, as the people, now doomed to retrace their steps, end in unmarked graves in the wilderness. This dichotomy is embedded in the larger narrative as illustrated by the following:

Retreat	Going forward
The past	The future
The popular voice	The voice of God and Moses
Egypt as the desired object	The promised land
Abrogates obligations to God	Under obligation to God
The familiar, old life	An unfamiliar, new life of Israelite law and practice
Slavery	Liberation
Egyptian delicacies	Manna
Punishment	Reward
Retracing of steps	Reaching the borders of Canaan
Death in unmarked graves	Life for the new generation

The two opposing series create an impassable divide between the Egyptian past and the promised future in the new land. They also highlight the gap between an ideal, near abstract vision of what should be and an unflinchingly honest depiction of how actual humans are likely to behave. Only a later hand, with access to both traditions, could organize the tales of the wilderness in order to develop and highlight those distinctions, preserving a record of the wilderness period as both ideal and its opposite, unrelentingly harsh and disappointing. Yet it does not stop there. As we will see, the editors of Numbers use those distinctions creatively and strategically to chart a way out of the wilderness.

∼ Conclusion

The wilderness suggests a vista of wide open territory, free from unwelcome reminders of past lives and sorrows, a territory wonderfully situated for a newly forming, newly hopeful people. Recently liberated from oppression, in the wilderness Israel could shape itself into God's people, in the image offered by Moses and Aaron. They are close – very close – to accepting that vision, becoming that people. Overflowing with gifts for the tabernacle, contentedly following the pillars of fire and of smoke, listening to the sons of Aaron blow the trumpets. Suddenly, memories of their former lives, tastes and smells of Egyptian delicacies, haunt and overcome them. Cries and longings lead to rebellion and death. The rest of Numbers suggests that the visionary promise of its opening can come into being only by forcing an entire generation to watch the destruction of its elders, slowly but relentlessly over forty years. To give birth to new possibilities, Israel must reject its past. But such a rejection is exceedingly difficult, even after disappointment replaces desire. In the cries of Reuben and Gad, Moses hears the futility of using the past at all. But they reassure him. They have in fact learned the lessons of their parents. So too do the editors hear memories and longings that worry them. They too face the futility of relying on the past. Yet they reach the same conclusion as Moses. They accept the necessary and inevitable use of memory in fulfilling their most pressing agenda: shaping the story of the past in such a way as to lead the present audience forward into its future.

FIVE

Crisis and Commemoration: The Use of Ritual Objects

> The ritual construction of authority is a stabilization of power and therein a specific augmentation of power.[1]

In the midst of a discussion looking back at the biblical period when kings ruled Israel, the rabbis of the Talmud raised the following question:

> Was, however, the anointing oil in existence [in the days of Jehoahaz]? Surely it was taught: At the time when the Holy Ark was hidden away there were also hidden the anointing oil, the jar of manna, Aaron's staff with its almonds and blossoms, and the coffer which the Philistines had sent to Israel as a gift.... And who hid them? It was Josiah, King of Judah. (Talmud Bavli: Horayoth 12a)

Were they ever found? Indeed, what was the fate of the many objects mentioned in the bible from the period of the First Temple and even earlier? As attested in the rabbis' discussion, the question did not have a clear answer. Speculation and uncertainty surrounded the subsequent history of many objects mentioned in the early texts of Israel. What the rabbis did possess, however, were the biblical stories of their formation. We possess those same stories.

In particular, the story of Aaron's staff, with its almonds and blossoms, is of direct interest to the present discussion as it is the last of three objects that figure in a series of dramatic crises at the core of the Book of Numbers. The tale of the flowering staff (Num. 17:16–26) immediately follows the story of Korah's hammered fire pans, turned into plating on the front of the altar (Num. 17:1–5). That story is itself preceded by the command to place tassels (צִיצִת) on the edges of a garment (Num. 15:37–41) issued following the debacle of the spies. The interconnections between each crisis as well as the use made of each object to reinforce a priestly agenda for Israel form the subject of the present chapter.[2]

Let me begin by placing this chapter's focus in the broader context of the priestly redaction of Numbers. In chapter 1 I identified the rather complex notions of tradition and memory suggested by the highly selective editing of the narrative of the wilderness past. That chapter lays the foundation for understanding the priestly task: to shape the disparate materials from the past that came into priestly hands in such a way as to promote their vision for the proper conduct and leadership of Israel in the future. Subsequent chapters illustrate the ways in which the editors went about crafting a persuasive argument. In chapter 2 I examined the process by which they used editorial interventions such as juxtaposition and the weaving together of diverse materials in order to develop their argument that Israel leave Egypt and the wilderness past behind in order to inherit the land under priestly authority. In chapter 3 I analyzed the evidence for the identity of the editors as priestly as well as proposing a historical context for that editing. In chapter 4 I elucidated the attempts of the priestly editors both to reflect on the nature of memory and to control it as they shaped the journey through the wilderness. In the present chapter we will see how the priestly shaping of tradition and memory come together in the commemorative use of the three ritual objects under scrutiny, a use dictated both by the symbolism of each object and by their careful placement in sequence within the larger narrative.[3]

Each object does nothing less than defuse the mutiny faced by Moses and Aaron in the middle section of Numbers, chapters 11–17, as they struggle with a people who repeatedly reject God's plans for them. The tassels, plating, and staff are designed to remind the people of God and the commandments, leading to the proper conduct and the proper deference to God's chosen leaders. Yet the tales in which they are created also illustrate the limitations of the priestly editing of Numbers. For the stories of crisis and commemoration paradoxically keep the option of dissent alive. Those used as examples of how not to behave – the spies, Korah, and his band – are given central positions within the narrative. Two of the objects that remind us of their stories – the plating and the flowering staff – are even placed at the very center of the camp, in the tabernacle, while the third object, the tassels, are worn on every male Israelite body.

The objects are thus linked to the most central and holy site in the camp, the tabernacle. In fact, the three objects, and the stories in which they are embedded, explicitly add the problem of holiness to the list of priestly concerns. Numbers 15 and its instructions that the people Israel wear tassels on their garments encourages, and even commands, the entire people to be holy. The charge of Korah the Levite that follows in Numbers 16 picks up on that aspiration as he articulates a central dilemma for the line of Aaron concerning the prerogatives of priestly holiness for his descendants versus the cultivation of holiness both within the rest of the Levitical class and the entire people Israel. According to Korah, "all the community are holy, all of them" (Num. 16:3). The scenes that follow explore the tense ramifications of that dilemma, giving us access to the editors' thinking and strategies as well as the limits of their control over texts that come into their hands. In spite of those limits, the priestly editors succeed in using the tales of crisis and commemoration to advance their vision of a future in the promised land.

Thus the stage has been set for a series of dramatic struggles and aspirations of the different interests in the wilderness – those of the people, the priests, and the Levites. In this chapter I define the increasingly high-stake series of confrontations as "social dramas," a phrase associated with the work of Victor Turner. When social arrangements within a community result in conflict, a social drama usually ensues. Such a drama provides a means of resolving the conflict it dramatizes. I suggest that the events of Numbers 15–17 can be clarified, and their meaning discerned, through Turner's model. Of course, his model only provides one perspective from which to select and organize data; recognizing such a limitation, in what follows I nonetheless turn to this model and hope that the results of my analysis justify the choice. Let me begin by identifying those elements of Turner's theory that shape the present argument.

∼ The social drama

Turner begins his description of the social drama by assuming the "propensity of social groups toward conflict."[4] In response to the threat or presence of conflict, a group will impose hierarchical arrangements on itself. Such arrangements are invariably challenged by dissatisfied members of the group, usually accompanied by significant tension and, at times, violence. In consequence, the majority, or at least those in power, will seek some vehicle for the expression, regulation, and resolution of such tense conflict either in a one-time drama or, more commonly, in cyclical, perhaps yearly, performances. Turner defines such "public episodes of tensional irruption" as social drama.[5] Social dramas are in large measure "political processes, that is, they involve competition for scarce ends – power, dignity, prestige, honor, purity."[6] Social drama strikes me as a particularly apt frame in which to interpret the crises in Numbers, one of the more political books of the bible, especially due to its depiction of the repeated attacks on the hierarchical arrangement within the wilderness camp. Those who edited the work as they did aimed to reinforce the leadership of Moses and Aaron. They used the episodes of rebellion and dissent to do so.

Thus a social drama seeks to resolve the inherent oppositions and struggles within a self-defined community. It is "an arena in which purely social conflicts are worked out."[7] Turner identifies four stages in the unfolding drama that allow such a resolution to occur. These stages include the initial *breach*. A breach in social relationships threatens a change in the stability of the community.[8] Therefore a breach requires urgent resolution, leading to a state of *crisis*. Turner defines a crisis as "one of those turning points or moments of danger and suspense, when a true state of affairs is revealed, when it is least easy to don masks or pretend that there is nothing rotten in the village."[9] The crisis then demands *redressive action* of some sort. Redress consists of "pragmatic techniques and symbolic actions."[10] We will observe both in our reading of the rebellion within the camp. If that redressive action succeeds, then the drama concludes with the *reintegration* of all the participants within the community. Turner ended up modifying that last term, suggesting the "*recognition of schism*" as a possible alternative. In other words, Turner revised his model to acknowledge that social dramas do not necessarily restore the status quo. In fact, some conflicts or tensions endure.[11] Turner's four stages provide a useful structure in which to delineate the unfolding events in each discrete episode examined in the current rereading of Numbers and to observe the connections of the various dramas with one another. In addition to its usefulness as a descriptive framework, I argue that the enactment of social drama within the narrative of Numbers 15–17 does in fact become the chief means through which priestly authority is reasserted after the rebellions within the wilderness camp threaten the very continuation of the newly formed people Israel.

Turner does not define a social drama in exclusively ritual terms, although it may contain ritual dimensions. In fact, social dramas are triggered by a variety of issues, including matters of political or social import. The biblical examples illustrate the interactions among the social, the ritual, and the political. Ritual dimensions include the involvement of ritual functionaries (priests and Levites) in the drama. The location of each drama is often in or near the sanctuary, the primary ritual space of the wilderness camp. The objects produced at the end of each drama are used either as part of ritual practice or exhibited in ritual settings. Yet, as we shall see, the ritual and the political are strongly interconnected. And these dramas have serious implications for the social harmony of the wilderness camp. Thus the social drama touches on communal arrangements in the broadest sense. Note that Turner captures that larger perspective in using the term "drama" instead of "ritual." "This form was essentially dramatic. My metaphor and model here was a human esthetic form, a product of culture."[12] In consequence, when analyzing social dramas within the biblical narrative, I address all three dimensions – the ritual, the social, and the political – as well as how they overlap.

In each example I begin by paying attention to the larger narrative context that leads to the social drama. In discussing the drama itself, I refer, when appropriate, to the stages outlined by Turner, identify the argument made by the drama, and, especially, consider how it is described and embedded within the biblical text.[13] To do so I will break down the social drama. Turner invites such detailed analysis: "When the interests and attitudes of groups and individuals stood in obvious opposition, social dramas did seem to me to constitute isolable and minutely describable units of social process."[14]

Yet in such a detailed analysis, point of view can be a notoriously problematic variable. Renato Rosaldo has gently chided Turner and others for assuming that their point of view as observers would be sufficient in accounting for the meaning of the social drama to the participants themselves. Rosaldo asks:

> In their own narratives do the protagonists think of events as having climaxes, turning points, or crises? . . . Do Turner and the protagonist agree about what constitutes the social drama's chain of events? . . . The protagonists interpret the central incidents so differently that the notion of a unified social drama

seems, at best, problematic. . . . When the social analyst and the protagonist use culturally divergent forms of narrative analysis, the problems of point of view become both clearer and more complex.[15]

In response to this critique, I would offer the argument that point of view is precisely what I am interested in observing, but it is a point of view that is preserved in a written text thousands of years old, obviously denying the observer direct access to the participants. Therefore I have to rely on evidence provided by the text, such as the precise language used by those involved in the drama. I can also observe the spatial positioning of the players in the performance. Catherine Bell reminds us: "Through a series of physical movements, ritual practices spatially and temporally construct an environment organized according to schemes of privileged opposition."[16] As we will have reason to observe, the choreography of Korah's rebellion confirms Bell's insight as well as providing information about the point of view of the rebels toward the leadership in the camp.

And to get at the point of view of the leaders, I will pay close attention to Turner's final phase, the end of the drama and its aftermath. The results provide insight into the interests not only of Moses and Aaron but of the priestly editors whom I assume to be aligned with them. We can get at the motives of the editors by identifying what the outcome of the social drama has explained, justified, and/or legitimated. Has a particular authority been inscribed or, just as often, reinscribed? Has a course of action been delegitimated? In answering those questions I can begin to discern the interests of the priestly editors, those who placed these dramas in a particular sequence at a particular moment in the narrative of the journey with particular purposes in mind.

The creation of a highly symbolic object at drama's end is integral to those priestly purposes. Cumulatively, the three objects under scrutiny – the tassels, plating, and flowering rod – bring about the restoration of equilibrium in the camp. At the same time they commemorate the antagonists, though in negative fashion. Each object also reminds the children of Israel to avoid the egregious errors of their parents. In so doing each contributes to the fixing and exploitation of the collective memory of the wilderness journey. To substantiate these claims, we must decipher the symbolism or meaning of each object. The preceding story provides the *context*. Turner concisely expresses the connection: "antecedent circumstances . . . help to determine the meaning of the symbols."[17] Max Black also identifies the importance of context. He assumes that an object may in fact be "designed to reproduce as faithfully as possible in some new medium the structure or web of relationships in an original."[18] To a great extent the present work agrees with their assumptions. I will pay careful attention to the "antecedent circumstances." Those circumstances produce the conditions that require the social drama in the first place and to a large degree determine the type of object that is formed at its end.

However, fixing a specific meaning for each object is often difficult and perhaps even unadvisable. E. H. Gombrich reminds us that sustained reflection of an object rewards the viewer with an appreciation of its rich and varied meaning:

> The symbol that presents to us a revelation cannot be said to have one identifiable meaning assigned to its distinctive features. All its aspects are felt to be charged with a plenitude of meanings that can never be exhaustively learned, but must be found in the very process of contemplation it is designed to engender.[19]

In the biblical case, each object represents a critique or punishment of the offending party, reinforcing the hierarchy of Moses and Aaron and aiding in the restoration of order. At the same time each object manages to remind us not only of those who were punished but of the alternative possibilities they represent, alternatives that might still influence the people Israel.

A last caveat, already hinted at above, is in order before turning to each of the objects and the social dramas that created them. Though Turner observed social dramas in real time out in the field, I of course do not. The social dramas of the bible unfold on a written page, thousands of years after their enactment (if ever performed). While many anthropologists *may* choose to treat rituals and social dramas as "analogous to culturally produced texts," I have no choice but to do so.[20] Jameson explains why it is that many anthropologists treat such a performance as a "decipherable text."[21] "We textualize...not because rites are intrinsically like texts, but because we approach both looking for meaning as something that can be deciphered, decoded, or interpreted."[22] Out of necessity, the present attempt reads the social dramas in the wilderness exactly as suggested by Jameson, as written texts to be deciphered and interpreted. One advantage of such an approach lies in its correspondence to the reception of the stories of Numbers in its later audience. They did not observe the social dramas of the scouts or of the Levites in a present moment but heard them recounted as stories from a time in the wilderness past. It was in written form (and oral recitation) that the social drama would engage and perhaps persuade its audience. It is in that written form that such a drama will now be considered.

∼ "A reminder for the children of Israel . . . ": the tassels, plating, and Aaron's flowering staff

> But your carcasses shall fall in this wilderness, while your children roam the wilderness forty years, thus they shall bear your faithlessness until your carcasses are at an end in the wilderness; according to the number of the days that you scouted the land, forty days, (for each) day a year you shall bear your iniquities forty years and shall know my opposition. I YHWH have spoken if I do not do this to all this wicked community banded together against me – in this very wilderness they will come to an end, there they will die. (Num 14:32–35)[23]

In one furious outburst, God condemns the entire generation liberated from Egypt to death in the wilderness. It is up to the children to fulfill the promises made to the patriarchs long ago. God's punishment of the angry and mutinous Israelites in Numbers 14 triggers even further challenges, no less angry and no less mutinous. First comes the collapse of the people's commitment to conquer the land on hearing the report of the spies, only to be followed after an interlude of calm by an unmistakable challenge to the very hierarchy established to ensure the safety and continuation of the holy community once settled. Thus the story of the spies in chapters 13 and 14 is purposefully linked to the rebellions of Korah, Dathan, and Abiram in chapters 16 and 17. Without doubt, the challenge, and subsequent condemnation, of the entire generation in Numbers 14 provides the breach in social relationships that triggers all three social dramas under consideration.

Phillip Budd deduces evidence for the interconnections among these chapters by first noting their correlation with chapters 1–4 of Numbers. He notes that Numbers 1–2 are concerned with the constitution of the Israelite community that is dismantled by the events of Numbers 13–14, events that illustrate Israel's failure to be that community. Likewise, Numbers 3–4, the creation of the priestly hierarchy, correlate with the Levitical failure to accept that hierarchy in Numbers 16–17.[24] Budd's observation provides the logic of connection to the earlier chapters of Numbers. A coherent thematic presentation of the events of the journey is being edited together piece by piece. I would add further evidence for the skillful priestly editing of Numbers in the careful placement of the stories of rebellion in specific narrative space, the middle of the book, in specific narrative time, the middle of the journey, and in the specific sequence of the objects themselves.

∽ The tassels

Following the order of the episodes in which the three objects under discussion are created, we begin with the tassels. Chapter 15 of Numbers, which concludes with the tassels, opens with legislation that seems rather out of place, especially if one considers the drama of the scouts in chapter 13, God's dramatic condemnation of the people in chapter 14, and the tense rebellion about to occur in chapter 16. In fact, I would pinpoint the social drama that leads to the creation of the tassels as originating not in chapter 15 but earlier, in chapter 13. Nonetheless, I will work backward, and begin in Numbers 15 as the immediate context for the creation of the tassels. I intend to illustrate the way in which the events of this chapter interact with the deeper crisis embroiling the wilderness camp.

As if nothing is amiss, in Numbers 15:1–21 God patiently instructs the people via Moses regarding the quantity of items to be sacrificed once they settle in the land. Details abound of amounts of flour, oil, and wine. Yet the connection with the preceding narrative is clear. Following the condemnation of those liberated from Egypt, Numbers 15 reassures the people that in fact the next generation shall inherit the land as God promised. Providing instructions that can be completed only after they arrive in the land confirms God's promise.[25] The scene has suddenly shifted from the wilderness camp and its pervasive imagery of actual and anticipated death to an atmosphere of order, control, and even pleasing odors in which God will delight once the new generation inhabits the land. The image of the people entering that land, given them by God, is stated in 15:2 and repeated in 15:18. Once in the land, both citizen and outsider fall under these new injunctions (15:15). Introducing "citizen" emphasizes a change in setting because only in the land could "citizen" make sense as a category of affiliation. Furthermore, this concern with anticipating and ensuring the future is emphasized through the use of לדרתיכם – "throughout your generations"– repeated five times in the chapter. Thus the content of Numbers 15, which appears at first glance to be out of place, nonetheless has a logical connection with the earlier crisis and serves as a reassuring response, directed at the next generation, to God's condemnation of its parents. Such a connection testifies to creative and skillful editing.

In Numbers 15:22–31, the narrator introduces inadvertent versus intentional wrongdoing. In so doing, he continues to anticipate future situations once in the land, but now he also glances behind him at the intentional collective wrongdoing of chapter 14.[26] As a result of the events of Numbers 14, now in Numbers 15 if the *entire community* inadvertently commits wrongdoing, sacrifices will provide the necessary remedy throughout the generations:

> The priest shall make expiation for all the community of the children of Israel and they shall be forgiven; for it was an error, and they have brought their offering, an offering by fire to YHWH and their sin offering before the presence of YHWH on account of their error. (Num. 15.25)

In the aftermath of the collective crisis brought about by the spies, a reference to the entire community appears necessary. Now the community can be reassured that a process is in place for inadvertent wrongdoing on behalf of their descendants. God does not carelessly condemn and is willing to forgive. The text goes on to include individual errors, if also committed inadvertently, in the expiation process.

Nonetheless, as already illustrated by the events of chapter 14, 15:30–31 states that intentional wrongdoing will be severely punished. But now it is only an individual, not the entire community, who may be defined as an intentional wrongdoer. The individual violator will be punished with excommunication. A story follows about an individual who violates the Sabbath in the wilderness by gathering wood on the seventh day. Such a violation results in death by stoning, obviously a penalty even more severe than excommunication.[27] Suddenly, we are back in an atmosphere of crisis, forcibly removed from the impartial tone of legislation and from the orderly future that legislation conjures up for Israel in the land. Visions of the future are abruptly replaced by a community stoning an individual in the present time of the wilderness. A breach in social relations has certainly occurred, as evidenced by the violator being permanently separated from the community, removed outside the borders of the camp, and killed.

The stoning of the individual (a miniature social drama though not the focus of discussion) leads directly into the regulation of the tassels. This final regulation again focuses the reader on the future. The tassels are designed to protect the entire people from intentional acts of wrongdoing, especially considering the fate of the Sabbath gatherer. Could there be other alternatives to repeating his fate in the future, especially for those envisioned so hopefully living in the land? Could some strategy remind the people of these injunctions and protect them? That concern provides the immediate context for the law of the tassels, which ends the chapter.[28]

> And YHWH spoke to Moses saying: Speak to the children of Israel and say to them: make for themselves tassels on the corners of their garments throughout their generations (לדרתם); and place on the corner tassel a cord of blue. And it will be for you a tassel that you may see it and remember all the commandments of YHWH and do them and not *scout* (ולא תתרו) *after your hearts and after your eyes which you whore after*. So that you remember and do all my commandments and *be holy* to your God. I YHWH your God who brought you out from the land of Egypt to be your God, I YHWH your God. (Num. 15:37–41, emphasis added)

The verses are meant not only for those present in the wilderness camp but for all future generations, linking this piece of legislation with the focus on the future in the rest of Numbers 15. As I argued above, the regulation also aims to protect the people from intentional wrongdoing, thereby minimizing the potential for the death penalty. These verses assume that if the Israelites were left to follow the dictates of their own hearts and eyes, they would easily commit the kind of behavior that would trigger a recurrence of God's wrath. Therefore they require protection from themselves (and God's anger). Observance of the Lord's commandments provides such a safeguard. But how can they keep the commandments in front of them? The verses offer a simple mnemonic device. Looking at the tassels functions "just as a person ties a knot on his garment to remember something."[29]

Thus, the verses aim to promote a type of recall that leads to right action. Not only that, but the tassels aim to remind the people of a specific memory both as motivation and as a source of obligation – God's taking them out of Egypt. Yet, lurking in the very language of the legislation is the reminder of wrong actions, born out of a different kind of memory of Egypt. For the language of this command points directly back to the story of the scouts and the people's angry insistence on returning to Egypt, an all too recent and terrifying crisis within the camp.[30] The key sentence for the allusion is verse 39: "And it will be for you a tassel that you may see it (וראיתם אתו) and remember all the commandments of YHWH and do them and not scout (ולא תתרו) after your hearts and after your eyes which you whore after." The three significant words are seeing, scouting, and whoring. In particular, "to scout out" appears so frequently in the story of the scouts and its aftermath, and so rarely anywhere else in the Torah, as to suggest a purposeful allusion to chapter 13.[31] Thus I now turn to the social drama triggered by the report of the scouts, because it is the context for the creation of the tassels. First I examine the episode's highly specific use of language as evidence of its link to the creation of the tassels. Next I briefly describe the social breach brought about by the scouts, the palpable crisis and the redressive action that is delayed until the creation of the tassels. The tassels are the means through which that crisis, one so severe as to threaten the very future of the people Israel, is seemingly resolved.

~ To scout the land

Scouting out, לתור, can be considered a key word – or *Leitwort* – in the story of the scouts. Already in the first verse of chapter 13 God commands Moses to select men to scout out – ויתרו – the land.[32] Moses repeats the command in 13:17 to scout out the land. He adds "seeing" to the order in 13:18. In 13:21 the spies fulfill his order and go up to scout the land. Verse 13:25 states that they have returned from their expedition: מתור הארץ.

By this point, scouting – לתור – is the chief action associated with the men sent on the mission. In verses 32–33, the climax of the chapter, the spies themselves use and combine scouting and seeing, לתור and ראינו.

> So they spread an unfavorable report of the land which they scouted (תרו) to the children of Israel saying "the land which we passed through to scout out (לתור) is a land that eats her inhabitants and all the people we saw (ראינו) in its midst are of great size and there we saw the nephilim, children of Anak from the nephilim, and we were in our eyes like grasshoppers and thus we were in their eyes." (Num. 13:32–33)

The link between scouting and seeing lies in what their eyes fail to see – that God has sent them ahead to scout the land so that they bring back a favorable report of a goodly land. Therefore they leave out of their report the assurance that with God's aid they can indeed conquer the land. In fact, they are convinced they cannot. For the scouts are guilty of the wrong kind of seeing, shaped entirely by their fears. Relying on their eyes, they see only giants. Listening to their hearts, they register only terror. The command of the tassels – warning the Israelites not to follow after their hearts and eyes – is based on the failures of the eyes and hearts of the scouts who seriously mislead the people.[33]

Of course their punishment in chapter 14 confirms the mistaken sight of the scouts. They are killed off. The people, caught in the subversive force of the scouts' report and infected by their fears of the land, immediately and nostalgically remember Egypt. A breach in social relations has widened. Their lack of faith leads to the crisis of God's condemnation. As dictated by the concept of measure for measure, their failure to remember *the sight* of God's signs, wonders, and glory leads in turn to their *not seeing* the promised land. In Numbers 14:33 God defines the people's failure, leading to their condemnation, as זנותיכם – their whoring after – the last of the terms in the tassel commandment. In God's sentencing of them to forty years of wandering, it is as if the people themselves scouted out the land, for they will be destined to wander in years what the scouts wandered in days: "according to the number of the days that you scouted the land" (Num. 14:34). Thus God's condemnation of the people charges them with a failure to *see* correctly, *whoring* and *scouting* – precisely the words brought together in the tassels law of chapter 15 in verse 39. That the two passages share such specific language firmly establishes the link between the disastrous story of the scouts and the formation of the tassels.

Baruch Levine points out that law and story are frequently connected in the Torah. Usually, it is a specific narrative situation that prompts subsequent legislation.[34] The present example is no exception. The wrong type of seeing as the Israelites scout out the land leads to whoring after their own eyes and heart, and ultimately to distorted memories of Egypt. The tassels underline the importance, even urgency, of learning to see and remember correctly. The very structure of verses 38–41 in chapter 15 makes the point. The right kind of remembering brackets and protects against the wrong kind of seeing. Only after the command to make tassels, to see them and remember God's commandments, comes the warning not to follow after their own hearts and eyes, which alludes so directly to the story of the scouts. Hearing those allusions the reader conjures up the fiasco of the scouts and the atmosphere of crisis recounted in the preceding two chapters. Then comes a reiteration to recall and observe the divine commands as well as God's liberation of them from Egypt. The result of remembering correctly is to be holy to God, its reverse (i.e., doubting God, longing for Egypt), punishment. Both kinds of remembering are acknowledged here with the command to distinguish between them. These verses exemplify the use of memory as a warning and tool of instruction while nonetheless acknowledging its deleterious effects by alluding to the social drama of the scouts, the people's distorted memories of Egypt, and God's punishing fury.

◇ On the edges of the garment

Having identified the associative connections in the language that link the social drama of the scouts and the tassels, I want to highlight the meaning of tassels as the mnemonic object chosen to resolve the crisis and prevent its renewal. It is the placement of the tassels along the edges of every Israelite garment that provides the key. Mary Douglas offers a theoretical explanation for the aptness of the choice of a tasseled garment designated to be worn on the human body. According to Douglas, the body, with its own clearly marked borders (along with its vulnerable openings), is often used or manipulated to represent a bounded system, including society as a whole.[35] If a society is threatened in some way – certainly the situation of Israel after the report of the scouts – then the body, symbol of the larger society, faces that same threat even more directly and needs protection. The tasseled garment provides such protection.

Douglas describes the importance of boundaries and margins for a society:

> The idea of society is a powerful image. It is potent in its own right to control or to stir men to action. This image has form; it has external boundaries, margins, internal structure. Its outlines contain power to reward conformity and repulse attack.[36]

The events within the wilderness camp that lead up to the calamitous report of the scouts confirm her argument. The dissent begins, interestingly enough, *precisely at the edge of the Wilderness camp* in chapter 11, echoing Douglas's general point that a threat to a society is often illustrated by an attack on its margins. God initially reacts to the people's complaints by send-ing a ravaging fire to consume the outskirts of the camp, repulsing attack at the site it began (see Num. 11:1). Thus, God's first attack on the wilderness camp begins at its borders (figuratively but also literally, at the beginning of a new narrative section of Numbers in which the crisis erupts). Another type of attack at the margins immediately follows the first – this time within the social hierarchy of the organized camp. The lusting of the "riffraff" – those whose status is peripheral within the camp – triggers the more widespread popular discontent, stirring up memories of Egyptian delicacies. (One rab-binic interpretation picks up on the image of the riffraff as a "border" group by locating them physically at the edges of the camp.)[37]

That food triggers the complaint is telling. The body is most vulnera-ble, again according to Douglas, precisely where foreign objects – such as food – may enter it.[38] Craving the leeks and melons of Egypt implicates each Israelite body, leading to a discontent that grows until it reaches dangerous proportions in the incident of the scouts. As a result of such misdirected desires, God extinguishes the individual and collective body. Finally, the scouts themselves are actual border-crossers, traveling into and out of the promised land.

The command to place tassels along the edges of a garment, and then to wear that garment daily, enacts a symbolic protective response to the many assaults on the communal borders just described. Shoring up the edges of the camp and reasserting order depends on the self-control of each individual within its borders. The tassels provide a psychological hedge, protecting each member of the new generation from his own impulses by reminding him of the lethal mistakes of the preceding generation. The wearing and seeing of the tassels are meant to do nothing less than transform the people. If successful, over time those very same tassels will preserve this transformed community. Frank Gorman hints at ritual's ability to preserve "the established order, by preventing the inbreaking of chaos."[39] The "inbreaking of chaos" beautifully captures the swift and threatening flow of rebellion against the established order, which the threads of the ציצה are designed to ward off.

∾ "Be holy to your God"

The phrase "You shall be holy to your God" (Num. 15:40) introduces the final, and perhaps the most important, concern of the legislation – the status of each and every Israelite. In fact the phrase leads directly into the next narrative of crisis and commemoration – that of Korah. Because Korah begins his rebellion by claiming that the entire people are holy, it is pertinent to consider how the law of the tassels bequeaths holiness to all of Israel.

Attached to the tassel is a cord of blue. Milgrom points out the significance of the cord's color. It is an ancient sign of royalty. He goes on to argue, based on rabbinic sources, that the tassels ציצית were considered a mixture of wool and linen known as שעטנז. The mixture is normally prohibited to the actual Israelite but allowed on the tassels in imitation of the turban of the high priest and other priestly clothing. According to Milgrom: "It is a conscious attempt to encourage all Israel to aspire to a degree of holiness comparable to that of the priests."[40] In addition, the ancient Near Eastern context illustrates that the ציצית are considered an extension of their owner's authority. Milgrom sums up the evidence: "It was worn by those who counted; it was the identification tag of nobility."[41]

All these elements – the royal color of the cord, the rare mixture of linens, and the fact that the wearer has a certain authority – suggests that in wearing the ציצית the average Israelite obtains a higher status. The command itself explicitly reinforces this: "you shall be holy to your God" (Num. 15:40b). Thus, not only the priests but all the people are holy. Israel Knohl claims the connection between the command to be holy and the cord of blue attached to the ציצית is quite intentional. He writes:

> According to HS, which presents the holy life as the task and mission of the entire community, all Israel must wear this holy sign at all times. Just as in the headpiece, the gold frontlet (ציץ) tied with a cord of blue designates the anointed priest as "holy to God" ... so too the fringes (ציצית) which also contain a blue cord, testify to Israel's mission to be consecrated unto their God.[42]

On the face of it, the concept that all of Israel is holy would appear to unify the people and resolve the atmosphere of crisis brought about by the scouts. Instead, the claim that all of Israel is holy triggers yet another social drama, as threatening and as violent as that of the scouts. Thus the final stage of Turner's social drama – reintegration – is delayed by another crisis and social drama.

Before moving on to the next crisis, let us pause and consider the first three stages of Turner's social drama that are present in this first example. They offer a very suggestive lens through which to look at the episode of the scouts. Through the spreading of their report, the scouts trigger a clear breach in social relationships among the entire people with a resulting challenge to the leadership of Moses and God, producing the most serious crisis yet in the wilderness. Such a crisis demands some kind of immediate redressive action. God provides that action by punishing those involved and condemning the entire generation in Numbers 14. Yet in its essence God's punishment does not resolve the situation or reintegrate those who followed the scouts. On the contrary, they are permanently excised. Thus resolution is still necessary on behalf of those who remain and is attempted through the creation and legislation of the tassels in chapter 15, a chapter whose general tone ensures the children of the condemned generation a more secure future in the promised land. The language of the tassels passage weaves together the different events of chapters 13–15 into a larger whole. The tassels, placed on the body, remind the children of Israel of the type of behavior that will prevent catastrophe. In behaving rightly the people Israel shall be holy and ensure their own future.

Yet the appealing egalitarian law of the tassels is immediately made problematic by the rebellious Korah in his challenge to the very basis of the priestly hierarchy. In his careful exploitation of the rhetoric of holiness found in Numbers 15:40, Korah claims the motivation for his rebellion. It seems that at times ritual may work against itself, producing unintended consequences. This may be one such time. As argued by Catherine Bell: "Ritual can be a strategic way to traditionalize – but it can also challenge and renegotiate the very basis of tradition."[43] The tassels produce this double-edged result. They are introduced at the end of Numbers 15 to urgently reimpose order in the camp, legislating an action for all time and guarding the people against the catastrophic results of following their own inclinations. Yet the promise of holiness embodied by the tassels brings Israel back to the abyss. Knohl suggests that the redactors of Numbers intentionally linked the tassels legislation and Korah's rebellious challenge. He proposes that the editors, "by placing the fringes passage directly before the passage of the chieftains' complaint may have sought to provide a background for the plaint."[44] I now turn to that plaint, its background, and the violent social drama that results.

∼ The plating

In the opening of chapter 16, Korah and his band attack Moses and Aaron with the following charge:

> You have gone too far since all the community, *everyone, are holy* and in their midst is YHWH. Why then do you raise yourselves above the congregation of YHWH? (Num. 16:3)

Korah makes a simple claim. Each and every Israelite is holy. In fact, it is precisely this claim that most needs elaboration. It would seem, then, that Korah is an important spokesperson in the camp, who is making a timely and reasonable query. Yet his sudden appearance in the narrative and his bald grasping after power suggest the opposite. Still, he is not immediately dismissed out of hand. In fact, the crisis he sparks allows for an elaboration of the question of holiness. It will be resolved (though only partially) by the formation of the plating on the altar in chapter 17.

Who, then, is Korah? He is introduced with a lineage that signals his importance to the story while providing the background for his challenge to Moses and Aaron. Korah is described as the "son of Yitzhar, son of Kohat, son of Levi" (Num. 16:1). Korah is a Levite, belonging to a group that is introduced simultaneously in Numbers as a distinct entity and as subordinate to Aaron and his sons. This priestly arrangement is unique to Numbers. In other biblical texts the Levites are simply priests.[45] To understand the special situation of the Levites in the book of Numbers – the context in which to make sense of Korah's rebellion – one must digress to their introduction and subsequent subordination in the work's opening chapters.

The role of the Levites is elaborated at greatest length in Numbers 3 but only after an act of memory on the part of the narrator. He begins by recording the line of Aaron, along with an aside about Aaron's two eldest sons, Nadav and Avihu: "But Nadav and Avihu died before the Presence of YHWH, when they offered alien fire – אש זרה – before YHWH in the wilderness of Sinai" (Num. 3:4a). The verse refers to an incident in chapter 10 of Leviticus. The episode of Nadav and Avihu, to which I will return, has a good deal of influence on the creation of a Levitical class in contradistinction to the sons of Aaron and subsequently, on the story of Korah.

Next God commands Moses to advance the tribe of Levi – Korah's tribe – but only to serve Aaron the priest and the community by performing the work of the tabernacle. The Levites thus serve as intermediaries between the priesthood and the people. God ends the command with a warning that anyone who comes too close, presumably to the inner sanctum of the sanctuary, the exclusive domain of the priest, faces death: "The stranger (outsider, encroacher) – הזר – who comes close shall be put to death" (Num. 3:10, repeated again in 3:38). The outsider – הזר – directly echoes the term used just above for the strange fire אש זרה of Nadav and Avihu. The encroachment of Nadav and Avihu, which led to their deaths, is associated through allusion with the possibility of a recurrence of that kind of incident. The Levites, themselves unable to enter the inner sanctum, therefore in the category of outsider, are singled out to guard the holy site. They are neither one nor the other, neither priest nor Israelite. Their indeterminate status poses special dangers for them.

Immediately following God's warning, the link between the Levites and the deaths of Aaron's first born is made explicit. The Levites do indeed substitute for the first born, not only of Aaron but of every Israelite. God explains the reasoning behind the creation of a Levitical class:

> And I behold take the Levites from the midst of the children of Israel in place of every first issue of the womb from the children of Israel, and the Levites shall be mine. For every first born is mine – from the day I struck every first born in the land of Egypt I consecrated to me all the first born in Israel from human to beast – Mine they shall be, I YHWH. (Num. 3:12–13)

Thus chapter 3 of Numbers develops a suggestive association between the actual deaths of the first-born Egyptians, the actual deaths of the first-born sons of Aaron, and the clearly stated desire to prevent such deaths among the first-born Israelites through the substitution of the Levitical class. Twice more chapter 3 refers to the Levitical substitution: "Record every first-born male of the children of Israel from the age of a month and upward and make a numbering of their names; and take the Levites for me, I YHWH, in place of every first born from the children of Israel" (Num. 3:40–41). God immediately repeats the command to Moses in verse 45: "Take the Levites in place of every first born from the children of Israel . . . and the Levites shall be mine, I YHWH."

The linking of the events of the Exodus story with the deaths of Nadav and Avihu, along with the almost urgent insistence in Numbers that the Levites will substitute for the first-born Israelites, points to a paradox in the deaths of Aaron's first born. The Passover story celebrates God's overturning of the peril of Pharoah's decree against the Israelite males by taking the Israelites out of Egypt. That Nadav and Avihu escape Pharoah only to be struck down by God is indeed a strange and troubling aspect of their story. The subsequent mention of Nadav and Avihu both in Numbers 3 and later in the census of chapter 26:61 hints at the unresolved anxiety concerning their deaths. I suggest that the function of the tribe of Levi is reimagined, according to Numbers, to remove the threat of any further deaths among the first-born Israelites, *including, in particular, the first-born priests.* Thus the creation of the Levitical class responds to the strange deaths of Nadav and Avihu and is designed to protect both priests and Israelites. But how will the Levites protect themselves?

Chapter 3 next records the lineage of the Levites along with the responsibilities of each subgroup. The three sons of Levi include Gershon, Kohath, and Merari. The middle son, Kohath, is of particular interest because Kohath's son, Izhar, fathers Korah, providing the most direct association of these chapters with Korah's later appearance in Numbers 16. A brief chart will illustrate that the connection between Korah the Levite and Aaron, high priest, is a familial one. I list only the relevant information.

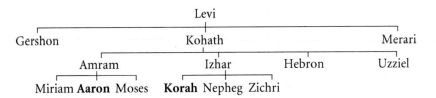

Thus Korah, Aaron, and Moses are first cousins, of the same generation.[46] The oldest son of Amram (who is the oldest son of Kohath), namely, Aaron, holds the high priesthood. Korah, also an oldest son, must serve his cousin. The possibility for rivalry exists from the outset. Magonet points out that their status as first cousins is significant: "Perhaps it was that proximity, and the lack of power that Korah had, that led him to attempt his rebellion."[47]

Chapter 3 describes the responsibilities of the Kohatite subgroup: "Their duties included the ark, and the table and the lampstand and the altars and the *implements of holiness –* כלי הקדש *–* that were used with them and the screen and all the service connected with these" (Num. 3:31, emphasis added). The Kohatites are responsible for the consecrated objects of the tabernacle, therefore in daily contact with holiness. Moreover, the objects for which they are responsible are found inside the tabernacle in a restricted, and possibly dangerous, zone of holiness. In contrast, the two other subgroups of Levites are somewhat removed from danger, handling the outside of the tabernacle: the outer hanging cloths and the outer structure.

Yet in spite of their responsibility for the sacred objects, the distance in status between the priests and Korah's subgroup, the Kohatites, is explicitly established in chapter 4 with an immediate revision of the tasks assigned to them in chapter 3. Chapter 4 begins by repeating that the Kohatites are assigned the *most* sacred objects, the holiest of the holy (emphasized by the repetition of the word holy), קדש הקדשים, the most dangerous to handle. It is in fact a considerable honor to be assigned the objects of the inner sanctum. Yet the Kohatite responsibilities are immediately curtailed. Before the Kohatites can carry them, Aaron and his sons must handle and cover the objects.

> When Aaron and his sons have finished covering the sacred objects and all the furnishings of the sacred objects at the breaking of camp, *only then* shall the Kohathites come and lift them, so that they do not come in contact with the sacred objects and die.... Do not let the group of Kohathite clans be cut off from the Levites. Do this with them, that they may live and not die when they approach the most sacred objects: let Aaron and his sons go in and assign each of them to his duties and to his load. But let not [the Kohatites] go inside and witness the dismantling of the sanctuary, lest they die. (Num. 4:15a,18–20, JPS trans., emphasis added)

While the text suggests that the Kohatites are limited in their duties by the desire to protect them from the harm of seeing the holiest objects of the sanctuary, in practice the restriction publicly acknowledges the lower status of the Kohatites. It forces them to step aside.[48] They must wait outside while the priests handle the objects. Only after the priests are done can the Kohatites enter the inner sanctum, and then only under the direction of Aaron and his sons. These verses reinforce the established hierarchy, strengthening the barrier between the holiness of priest and anyone else, including a Levite. Such a limitation on the Kohatite certainly creates a further cause of resentment, expressed and exploited by Korah. As Magonet observes of the Kohatites:

> Within the hierarchy of gradations of holiness, and hence power and danger, they are at the very edge of the innermost ring – and yet not quite there,

and subservient to Aaron's sons. The logic of this structure is clear, given its premises, but the possibilities for discontent are also evident, even at this stage.[49]

The dangers inherent in their new assignments explicitly include not only the Kohatites but, as of Numbers 8, all the Levites. This chapter highlights the risks for the Levites at the moment they become ritually qualified to serve. Several intriguing phrases suggest the underlying, but rather pronounced, view of the Levites as a sacrificial offering, emphasizing the dangers of their indeterminate status. The crucial verses in support of such a claim, even if only metaphorical, are the following:

> You shall bring (והקרבת) the Levites before the tent of meeting and you shall assemble all the community of the children of Israel and you shall bring the Levites close before YHWH and the children of Israel shall lay their hands on the Levites and Aaron shall offer the Levites as an elevation offering (תנופה) before YHWH on behalf of the children of Israel that they may perform the service of YHWH. (Num. 8:9–11)

Three terms stand out in these verses: bringing close, the laying of hands on the Levites, and the elevation offering. Each term is integrally related to the sacrificial procedures involving animals and grain offerings detailed in Leviticus. Among its other meanings, "bringing close" refers to the offering of an animal for sacrifice. It is the term used when Nadav and Avihu offer strange fire before God as remembered in Numbers 3:4. The Israelites lay their hands on the Levites in an easily identifiable gesture typical of animal sacrifice. Are the Levites to be designated as Israel's sacrifice?[50] The final term, elevation offering – תנופה – is certainly a most intriguing appellation for the Levites, repeated at least three more times in these verses. Milgrom, in an excursus on the ritual of תנופה, lists the variety of times the ritual is mentioned elsewhere in the bible. Breasts or thighs of an animal sacrifice can be elevated. So can bread offerings, barley, or wheat. Even certain materials of the tabernacle can be lifted high.[51] But the only humans mentioned in such a sacrificial context are the Levites. Of course, "elevation" is a paradoxical term considering the dangers attached to their new position. Treating the Levites like a sacrificial object humbles them in exactly the way Victor Turner has proposed in his observations of the dramas attached to changes in leadership. Turner points out that a candidate is often humbled by a "structural inferior" (in our case, by the Israelites) before being

elevated to a new status. Such a humbling exemplifies the power of structural inferiors in a rite of temporary status reversal.[52] In Numbers 8 the
Israelites are indeed temporarily powerful, even indispensable. It is the laying on of hands by the Israelites, combined with the elevation offering of the
Levites performed by Aaron (note that both priest and Israelite are involved),
that transfer the Levites from the ranks of the Israelites to become God's
property.[53]

At the end of the ritual in chapter 8:15, God defines the Levites once more
as a תנופה, an elevation offering. Just as in the earlier chapters, God again
links the substitution of the Levites for the Israelite first born with the slaying
of the first-born Egyptians in verses 16–17.

> For they have been given to me from among the children of Israel: instead
> of the first issue of the womb, of all the first-born children of Israel I took
> them to me. For mine are all first born of the children of Israel, of human
> and of beast; on the day I struck down all the first born in the land of Egypt
> I consecrated them to me. (Num. 8:16–17)

It should be clear by now that the slaying of the Egyptian first born, the
deaths of Nadav and Avihu, and the potential killing of first-born Israelites
provide the context for, and trigger the introduction of, the elevation of the
Levites in a new role in these early chapters of Numbers.

The ceremony ritually qualifying the Levites confirms Mary Douglas's
observation that a change in status for a particular group or individual,
separating them from others within society, will invariably be achieved in
stages. In the biblical example, the Levites are first singled out in the opening
chapters of Numbers. The ceremony documented in chapter 8 then seals
their new position and status within the group. Douglas writes: "The danger
is controlled by ritual which precisely separates him from his old status,
segregates him for a time and then publicly declares his entry to his new
status."[54] Yet it is precisely the new status of the Levites that poses the most
dangers for them. As the language of chapter 8 proclaims, they are now
established permanently in-between, between priest and Israelite, between
holy and profane. God says: "You shall stand the Levites before Aaron and
before his children and elevate them as an elevation offering to YHWH and
you shall separate the Levites from among the children of Israel" (Num. 8:13–
14). The Levites certainly avert future problems for the others by becoming
intermediaries. But it is clear they do so as a sacrifice – an elevation offering,

תנופה, before God. Milgrom describes the risk in their situation: "what if the [Levitical] guards fail in their responsibility and encroachment takes place? Will the entire community of Israel be exposed to God's unbounded wrath? ... the answer is no; only the guards bear the brunt of divine anger."[55]

The dangers of being killed are now greater for the Levites than for any one else in the camp – as the language of sacrifice bluntly suggests. Yet their new and dangerous status does not protect the Levites from humiliation or prevent causes for resentment. They must repeatedly step aside for their cousins, the priests. Thus the seeds have been planted for conflicts over questions of hierarchy, status, and the prerogatives of holiness – issues Korah skillfully exploits in his rebellion but that are, in any case, in need of further clarification.[56] Of course, it is Korah who exposes the Levites to the most danger as he dismantles the lines carefully drawn around them by Moses and God. Thus I have gone into a rather lengthy but necessary detour in order to provide the narrative context for the social drama about to unfold in Numbers 16.

∼ "And Korah took..."

The very first verb of chapter 16:1a – "and Korah took – ויקח" raises an immediate question. The verse does not tell us what he took. Only the story in its entirety explains this grasping after an unnamed target. As Magonet points out, the omission of an object of the verb has triggered endless commentary. He himself suggests that Korah wants to take the power of the priesthood from Aaron, reflecting "his own desire and ambition to be the priest, and himself *take* the censer, the fire and the incense, and stand before the Lord."[57] Yet Korah's personal bid for power, his rivalry with his cousin, is only part of the larger concerns raised by his rebellion. Korah fans the lack of clarity and discontent over the prerogatives of holiness, including those of each and every Israelite. In this way, he joins those who came before him in challenging Moses. Thus Korah's grasping after power forms a pattern with the prior events that together lead to the disastrous condemnation and punishment of the wilderness generation. Ultimately, Korah's ruinous taking triggers another kind of taking – as Eleazar, son of Aaron, takes the firepans of Korah and his rebels to create the second of the three sacred objects under discussion: plating on the altar.

After reminding us of Korah's Levitical lineage, chapter 16:1 identifies the other rebels who join him. These include Dathan, Abiram, and On, all descendants of Reuben, along with 250 other Israelites. As Nehama Leibowitz aptly describes them, these include:

> Reubenites aggrieved at being deprived of the firstborn right, the Israelite firstborn annoyed at forfeiting the priesthood in favor of the Levites, and Levites such as Korah who were annoyed at the entrusting of the priesthood to the sons of Aaron.[58]

In other words, the shifts in status – the substitution of the Levites for first-born Israelites as described in chapters 3 and 4 (i.e., including the Reubenites) as well as the subservience of Levite to priest (Korah and other Kohatites) – have provided ample sources of resentment. Thus we have not only a clear religious context for the rebellion but a politically charged one as well. At stake is the entire leadership structure of Israel.

Because the Reubenites are specifically mentioned along with Korah, it has been argued that the rebellion is a highly conflated and edited version of at least two or more distinct traditions.[59] If Knohl is correct, then the character of Korah the Levite, along with his fire pan – the main focus of the present argument – is not even introduced until the late stages of editing.[60] I do not dispute such an argument. As a reader of biblical texts, I am alert to and interested in each piece of text and fragment of tradition. In this instance, that would include each main player in the revolt. But I am also interested in, and will direct the bulk of my comments to, the rebellion's final form in which this motley crew join forces to attack Moses and Aaron.

The coherence of the final edited layer comes into view when attention is directed at the specific details found in the narrative of chapter 16. To begin, there is in fact a connection between the Reubenites and Korah. According to a map of the wilderness encampment, the Kohatites, of which Korah is a member, camp next to the Reubenites.[61] They would have ample opportunity to share grievances with one another. Second, the careful use of language, exemplified, as we will see, in the use of key words, at least two pairs of opposing terms, and frequent use of allusion, weaves the separate fragments of rebellion into a whole cloth. Add to this use of language a precise rendering of the spatial movements of the rebels and of Moses, and the connection of each discrete act of rebellion to the other comes into sharper focus, further strengthening the coherence and logic of the final form. Finally, that coherence is evident not only in the fragments of rebellion edited together, but in the rebellion's placement within the larger narrative. Korah and the Reubenites join a short list of provocative figures that precede them only by a chapter in challenging Moses and Aaron, pushing the ruling authority of the camp almost to the breaking point.

∼ *Korah's rebellion*

After the introduction of the players, the second verse of chapter 16 describes Korah's move as he and 250 followers rise up, וַיָּקֻמוּ, against Moses. After Korah and his band attack, Moses falls – וַיִּפֹּל – on his face. The vicissitudes of revolt are beautifully and immediately captured in this image of rising and falling in an encounter "between opposed orders."[62] Korah and the others go on to rebuke Aaron and Moses in 16:3: "You have gone too far since all the community, *everyone, are holy* and in their midst is YHWH." This main charge continues to capture the spatial imagery that is so striking a part of the narration. Korah and the rebels would expand the perimeters of holiness *throughout the camp* in direct defiance of the priestly vision of God's tabernacle residing in the very center of the camp with God's presence settled upon it. The rebels then conjure up another image of movement, claiming that Moses and Aaron have raised themselves above the others (תִּתְנַשְּׂאוּ). The word choice not only picks up on the chieftains of the community, נְשִׂיאֵי עֵדָה, – who join Korah (16:2) but hints at the other forms and meanings of the root.[63] "To raise up" refers directly back to the hierarchy established in the earlier chapters, as it is the Levites, especially the Kohatites, who must "carry" the tabernacle and its furnishings (the verb is from the same root). Note, for instance, Numbers 4:15. The verb appears precisely at the moment the Kohatites must step aside for the priests:

> When Aaron and his sons have finished covering the sacred objects and all the furnishings of the sacred objects at the breaking of camp, only then shall the Kohatites come and lift them (לָשֵׂאת). (JPS trans.)

Thus, through the deft use of the root, both chieftains and Levites are implicated in the revolt. In a mere three verses, the text of Korah's rebellion has already provided a rich lexicon of conflict and spatial imagery and a clear indication of the actors in the drama.

Moses responds to Korah's challenge in language not only laced with irony but perhaps unintended ambiguity, because his words also allude to yet another earlier event, the elaborate ceremony of bringing the Levites close to God as an elevation offering in Numbers 8.

> And he said to Korah and to all his company saying "morning and YHWH will make known who is His and who is holy and will bring close יהקריב to Him the one he has chosen to bring close to him." (Num. 16:5)

In other words, Moses quickly identifies this new breach in relations and the resulting crisis. He wastes no time but immediately conceives a redressive action, Turner's third stage. By wanting to redress the crisis as quickly as he can, he raises the stakes by making clear that the issue is not merely a challenge to the leadership of Aaron and Moses but direct access to God. Moses responds to Korah's claim that the entire community is holy by assuring him that he is wrong. God has chosen one man only. Yet in spite of Moses' ready retort, it is not quite that straightforward. Remember that in Numbers 3 and 4 the Kohatites *are* closely associated with the holy through their responsibilities for the holy implements. And in chapter 8 the entire class of Levites are in fact brought close to the Lord who climactically announces that He has taken them to Himself. After declaring the unique status of the Levites earlier, will God now minimize their importance? It would seem that Korah is on firm footing here.

∼ *Redressive action: the contest of the fire pans*

Responding then to what some might consider a legitimate demand, Moses finds a way to make God's choice absolutely clear. He enacts a social drama by devising a highly public contest. He orders Korah and all his company to take their fire pans, מחתות, put fire in them, place incense on the fire, and appear before God the following day. Moses confidently assumes that God will intervene by choosing who is most holy, decisively putting down Korah's challenge. Perhaps inadvertently, Turner captures the emotional tone of the whole undertaking. Turner suggests that "both pragmatic techniques and symbolic action reach their fullest expression ... [because] the group ... is here at its most 'self-conscious' and may attain the clarity of someone fighting in a corner for his life."[64] Korah and his band are in fact fighting for their life. But so is Moses. By means of the fire pans Moses hopes the "actual relations of command and obedience . . . [will be] justified."[65] Thus the fire pan becomes the means through which the crisis in leadership will be resolved. The fire pan is the crucial and significant prop in the narrative, as evidenced in the repeated reference to it in subsequent verses – at least eight more times before the end of the episode.

For good measure, Moses finishes his instructions with a retort that echoes Korah's initial charge against him: "You have taken on too much, children of Levi!" (Num. 16:7). As if only now reminded of the rest of the Levites, Moses turns and rebukes all of them. The very fact that God chose them to perform the duties of the tabernacle should be sufficient reward. Moses succinctly states the challenge that has not yet been expressed by Korah but that Moses clearly observes as the real issue. "Do you also seek the priesthood?" (Num. 16:10b).[66] His introduction of this unspoken issue makes sense only in the context of the earlier chapters. The establishment of a clear hierarchy in those chapters has laid the groundwork of resentment and discontent now so dangerously out in the open.

∼ Space and the vicissitudes of rebellion

Moses next turns his attention to the other challengers, Dathan and Abiram, whose joint rejection of his request provides the clearest example of the distorted remembering of Egypt found in Numbers. They describe that land in words reserved exclusively for the promised land. In unison they announce:

> We will not come up (לא נעלה). Is it not enough that you brought us up (העליתנו) from a land flowing with milk and honey to have us die in the wilderness? (Num. 16:12–13)

Again, the careful, at times ironic, use of language in the story is evident. The refusal of Dathan and Abiram to go to Moses aptly illustrates their rejection of his authority. Their refusal confirms an insight of Mary Douglas:

> individual actors are aware of a greater or smaller range of inclusiveness. In these situations, they behave as if moving in patterned positions in relation to others, and as if choosing between possible patterns of relationships.[67]

Their refusal to come up is precisely the point. They are refusing not only to come up to Moses but to go up to the promised land. Instead, they use the term for "going up" to describe the liberation from Egypt as a kind of punishment, taking them away from their preferred home. The term נעלה – going up – continues the lexical pairing of words described above. Now, instead of "rising and falling" (Korah against Moses and Aaron) we have "going up" and, as we will see, "going down." By not going up to Moses, Dathan and Abiram trigger the need for yet another redressive action, this time in the dramatic manner of their punishment. They will fall deep indeed, swallowed by the earth itself as they descend into the shadowy underworld of Sheol.

～ *At the threshold of the tent*

Two sites within the camp are crucial for the events of the rebellion. The actions of Korah take place at the tent of meeting (the tabernacle), while those involving Dathan and Abiram occur at their tents. At both sites the highly charged drama unfolds at the threshold of the tent, a powerfully symbolic space that represents the drive of Korah, Dathan, and Abiram to transgress and cross the hierarchical boundaries imposed on the camp.

To begin, in 16:18 Korah and his band gather at the opening of the tent of meeting with their fire pans precisely at the site where the Levites should be standing guard against the crossing over of others, as explicitly spelled out by God. Apparently, the Levites have rejected and relinquished that role. As Korah and his band stand at the threshold of the tent of meeting, God angrily orders Moses and Aaron: "Separate yourselves from among this community and I will consume them in an instant" (Num. 16:21). Just before, in verse 9, Moses reminded Korah that God had separated out the Levites from the people, distinguishing them with the special tasks of the tabernacle. In wanting to separate Moses and Aaron from everyone else, God is willing to erase the separate status of the Levites, with grave implications for the rest of Israel. Yet Moses and Aaron refuse: "They fell on their faces and said: O God, God of the spirits of all flesh, when one man sins, will you be furious with all the community?" (Num. 16:22). The contrast between Korah's rising up and their repeated falling conveys a central message of the story. His is an arrogant attempt to grab the leadership while they remain submissive and humble before the God of Israel. By rising up against the established lines of authority, not only does Korah challenge Moses and Aaron, but he directly challenges God.

In response to the pleas of Moses that God spare the people, God orders the entire congregation to withdraw from Dathan, Abiram, and Korah. The reader should no longer be surprised that the verb used by God to order the withdrawal is precisely that uttered before by Dathan and Abiram. We have repeatedly seen the careful use of repetitive words to weave together this rebellion.

Note that until now the main action has occurred at the threshold to the tabernacle, the site of the conflict between Levite and priest. This main action is quite public, as one would expect for a social drama that aims for ultimate resolution and reintegration. Clifford Geertz identifies the way in which a physical site, in this instance the tabernacle, could be considered a stage upon which "exemplary dramas of ascendancy and subordination were over and over again played out.... [these areas] clarify the specific meaning of various sorts of spaces themselves and the relationship that obtained among them."[68] In other words, the tabernacle, with its carefully structured sections that allow only some to enter, embodies the very hierarchies Korah seeks to overturn. That Korah's conflict happens at the threshold of the tabernacle appears almost overdetermined.

But Moses also faces a secular/political challenge from Dathan and Abiram that is also expressed in the careful use of space. Moses must leave the sacred arena of the tabernacle, in the very midst of the confrontation between priest and Levite, in order to deal with the challenge of Dathan and Abiram. Now it is Moses who rises up – ‏וַיָּקָם‎ – and goes to the tents of the two men to face off against them after they refuse to come to him. The conflict with Dathan and Abiram involves questions of a different type of leadership, this time among the Israelites in the camp itself. Again Geertz is helpful in observing that "the various regions are stages or arenas, on which the head-on status encounters, which form the substance of political life, are punctiliously played out."[69] As Moses moves between the sacred and the secular, he is followed by a procession of the people who intently witness the unfolding crisis. That move actually encircles both sacred tabernacle and the tents of Dathan and Abiram, cementing the link between the different revolts. "Whereas circumambulation usually sanctifies or protects the place bounded by its circumference, a procession normally links different spatial orders, for instance, *civic and sacred* or urban and rural space."[70]

As he confronts Dathan and Abiram, Moses warns the people to flee from their tents. They do so in yet another form of the by now familiar "going up" – וַיֵּעָלוּ – in Numbers 16:27, reinforcing both the isolation of the rebels from the community and illustrating to the rebels, and perhaps to the reader, the lack of support among the Israelites for the rebellion.

Yet again the action takes place at the threshold. Van Gennep suggests that the threshold not only symbolizes an attack on borders but reinforces a seeking after a new status, precisely the goal of Dathan and Abiram.[71] They seek a change in the status of the leaders of Israel as well as Israel's very destination. But such a change in status carries enormous risks. Grimes emphasizes the dangers contained at the threshold in his description of the ritual use of the portal, suggestive, in this instance, of the opening of a tent:

> Since a portal often separates a sacred precinct from a profane one or a regulated from an unregulated zone, it is both a termination and beginning point. As a structure that is both inside and outside the same zone, it is a site of considerable ambivalence, attracting dangerous as well as beneficent forces.[72]

Dathan and Abiram are indeed recipients of such a dangerous force. Standing in the portal, they disappear. They die by uncommon means, swallowed by the earth as they stand in front of their open tents. God punishes their violation of the boundaries of authority with another violation. Buried alive, they "go down" in an image that cements the link between their refusal to go up, both to Moses and to the Land, and their punishment. Once Israel witnesses their fate, they flee in all directions, no longer united by rebellion.[73]

Only then does the text tell us what happened to the 250 followers of Korah. In the briefest of notices, 16:35 announces that they are consumed by a divine fire. Note that the verse does not mention the death of Korah. Only chapter 17: 5 includes Korah in the fate of his band. But only chapter 26:10 announces the manner of his death:

> And the earth opened her mouth and swallowed them and Korah, when the fire consumed the 250, and they became a warning sign. (Num. 26:10)

In other words, Numbers 26 conflates the two different scenes of death. Korah is explicitly included only much later.

In his discussion of the social drama, Turner quotes W. H. Auden's notion of society as continuously "flowing," as a "dangerous tide . . . that never stops or dies . . . and held one moment burns the hand."[74] That poetic image strikes me as a particularly apt way in which to capture the power of Korah's rebellion and its fiery aftermath in the unfolding narrative of the wilderness journey. In a society caught in a literal flux between a condemned generation about to die and its children, all assumptions and arrangements are thrown into question. The very leadership of the camp – both political and religious – would naturally experience the brunt of such turbulence. Only a social drama such as that of Korah's rebellion could possibly do justice to the severity of the tensions of that moment in Israel's journey through the wilderness. Yet if Turner is correct, the aftermath of Korah's social drama must then restore stability. And in the view of the priestly editors, only a certain type of resultant stability and order would be legitimate and desirable. The aftermath of rebellion in the wilderness must unquestionably establish the priestly authority for all time. The means that ensure the priestly success, as we shall see, rest with the fire pans of Korah and his band.

∼ The fire pans

The fire pans of the rebels survive the fire to be used to commemorate the events of Korah's rebellion. As I shall illustrate, the fire pans, once hammered into plating, represent the complicated web of relationships between priest and Levite – the prior narrative context and fuel of social drama described above. The physical location of the plating, inside the tabernacle, and its function as a covering are significant elements in the resolution of that crisis. However, the creation of plating out of the fire pans also exemplifies the paradox of relying on a symbolic object. Each object retains the potential to transmit more than a single message. The fire pans are no exception.

Mentioned repeatedly in the story, the fire pans are an almost overdetermined choice of symbolic object. Moses first refers to them in 16:6 as crucial props in the test to illustrate God's choice. In 16:17 Moses gives Korah precise instructions regarding them:

> Each man take his fire pan and put on them incense and come close before YHWH – each and his fire pan – 250 fire pans and you and Aaron – each with his fire pan. And they took each man his fire pan, placing on them fire and putting incense on them, and stood at the opening of the Tent of Meeting as did Moses and Aaron. (Num. 16:17–18)

In two verses, the firepans are mentioned five times. They are now inextricably identified with those holding them: the 250, Korah, and Aaron. The fact that the firepans are actually hand-held strengthens the close identification between figure and object.[75]

The language of this instruction sounds strangely familiar and in fact contains an unmistakable allusion to Nadav and Abihu. Leviticus 10:1 opens: "And the children of Aaron, Nadav and Avihu, *took each his fire pan and placing in them fire, put incense on it* and brought near before the presence of YHWH alien fire." In Numbers 16:18, except for the mention of the "alien fire," the actions of Korah and his men are remarkably close to those of Nadav and Avihu: "And they *took each man his fire pan, placing in them fire, and putting incense on them.*" It appears then that in the book of Numbers the story of Nadav and Avihu not only provides the context for the assignment of responsibility to the Levites in chapter 3 of Numbers, but also forms the background for the rebellion of Korah and his band. The earlier story even shapes the punishment of Korah's followers. The description of their deaths seems strangely familiar: "And a fire went forth from YHWH and consumed the 250 men who brought near the incense" (Num. 16:35). That imagery is nearly identical in its phrasing to that found in the deaths of Nadav and Avihu: "And a fire went forth from YHWH and consumed them" (Lev. 10:2).[76] Thus the 250 die in a manner similar to that of Nadav and Avihu.

An explanation for the explicit linkage between the fire pans and deaths of Nadav and Avihu and the followers of Korah is perhaps first suggested by Moses himself in Leviticus as he silences Aaron in the immediate aftermath of the deaths of his sons: "This is what YHWH said, saying: through those near to me I show Myself holy and before all the people I am accorded honor" (Lev. 10:3). The text omits God's reaction. Rather, it is Moses who suggests that in their deaths, Nadav and Avihu have as much access to God's holiness as possible – though at the price of their lives. All who come too close, seeking holiness, are in mortal danger. According to the logic of the allusion, those who come too close must include the 250 followers of Korah. Seeking holiness can be a dangerous venture. If Nadav and Avihu, priests after all, experience such lethal consequences when they overstep, then how much more so if one is a Levite. The social drama of Korah's rebellion establishes a warning against the attempt to usurp the prerogatives of priestly holiness. In fact, by transgressing boundaries and triggering such a crisis, Korah reinforces the need for the newly created, clearly demarcated, but still fragile hierarchy of priest–Levite–Israelite, each assigned a separate zone, perhaps even a separate gradation of holiness. The fire pans are the means of restoring that hierarchy. Yet, paradoxically, once they are hammered into plating, the fire pans that warn against the dangers of unprotected access to the holy allow Korah to come closer to his goal.

∼ Plating on the altar

How can we first detect, and then understand, the meanings attached to the particular object formed at the end of Korah's rebellion? Why plating on the altar? In Leviticus 10:3 Moses sums up the deaths of Nadav and Avihu in one phrase: "through those near to me I show Myself holy." God expresses a similar sentiment in nearly identical language in the opening of chapter 17 when instructing Moses to order Eleazar, son of Aaron, to remove the fire pans of Korah and turn them into plating for the altar:

> [Remove] the fire pans of these sinners at the cost of their lives – and let them be made into hammered sheets, plating for the altar – for they have come near before YHWH and they have become holy – and they will be a sign to the children of Israel. (Num. 17:3)

The fire pans – so closely associated until this point with Korah and his band – have become holy because they were touched by divine fire. Haran explains:

> And Eleazar was given this command only because the censers of Korah's company had become "holy," i.e. impregnated with contagious holiness by their contact with the fire that "came forth from the Lord" (a similar "contagious" holiness, passed by contact to other objects, is attributed by P, as is well known, to the Tabernacle and all its appurtenances).... the only possible way of disposing of them was to add them to the bronze plating of the outer altar.[77]

In his death, Korah, of the Kohatites, leaves behind an object that obtains the holiness that eluded him during his lifetime.

Indeed, the transformed fire pan is not only sacred but meant to survive. The plating has become a commemorative object (זכרון):

> A reminder to the children of Israel so that no outsider (איש זר) not from the seed of Aaron, shall come near to offer incense before YHWH and will not be like Korah and his band. (Num. 17:5)

The plating reminds us of Korah the Levite, who dramatically illustrates the result of encroachment. Korah's story makes clear that while the Levites must protect the tabernacle, they are not holy. Even though the Levite enjoys some prerogatives in his new status, he is an outsider, an איש זר. However, Korah's legacy is still more complicated.

∾ Inside the tabernacle

Turned into plating, the fire pans are placed in front of the altar, at the very center of the cultic activity of sacrifice. These transformed fire pans, so closely associated with the events of the recent rebellion, remind the children of Israel of Korah and his men. Thus Korah, even if only in memory, resides in the tabernacle. Yet even in death, Korah and his men do not come too close. After all, the plating rests not in the inner Holy of Holies, but on the altar, located in the outer area of the tabernacle. That the plating manages to convey this message by its placement rests on its function as an analogue for the original. Remember Max Black's description of an analogue: "some material object ... designed to reproduce as faithfully as possible in some new medium the structure or web of relationships in an original."[78] The injunction in Numbers 4 that the Kohatites remain outside the inner sanctum and avoid directly approaching the most sacred objects is echoed and even duplicated in the very placement of the plating. Just as Korah can come only so close, but no closer, as dictated by the "structure or web of relationships" in the Levitical treatise, so too his transformed fire pan can be placed only on the altar in the *outer* court.

In addition, consider their function as plating. The fire pans provide cover, separating and protecting the inner from the outer. The protective layering duplicates the position of the actual Levite, who stands at the entrance of the tent, between inner and outer. Yet because a covering is the most exposed, it can be thought to be the most vulnerable to the vagaries of wear, precisely the situation of the Levites.

Finally, one must note that the plating covers the altar. There are several pieces of furniture within the tabernacle that could be candidates for additional plating. These include the lampstand, the table for the bread, and the sacred utensils. That the plating covers the altar – the site of numerous future sacrifices – rather than any of the other furnishings of the tabernacle reinforces by close proximity the Levitical role as a kind of sacrificial substitute for the rest of Israel as established in Numbers 8.

In front of the altar, the fire pans of Korah and his band are easily and frequently seen. This explains their apt use as a memorial. Like the tassels before them, the plating relies on memory to instruct and warn the people, hoping to contain and even resolve the deleterious effects of yet another crisis. Illustrating the consequences of such a bald grasping after power, the plating reminds the people that they must again choose. Proper memory, of Korah's failure and punishment, restores order. Improper memory, of Korah's audacity and daring, subverts it. Yet by representing the tale of Korah in a symbol placed at the very center of the camp, in the tabernacle where it can be easily seen, the plating reminds the people in the years to come not only of the misdeeds of Korah but of his entire story, including his cry: "For all the people are holy" – still after all an unresolved aspiration of Israel.

At this juncture let me briefly review the correspondences between Korah's rebellion and Turner's notion of a social drama. The breach in relationship, embodied in the assault on Moses and Aaron, sparks a crisis severe enough that Moses loses no time in trying to stop it through the public contest over the firepans, clearly a redressive action. The deaths of Dathan and Abiram as well as the burning of the rebels and the hammering of their fire pans into plating restores a certain amount of equilibrium. These events strengthen the established hierarchy. The conclusion of Korah's rebellion clearly establishes Aaron's primacy. Yet it is not enough. Remember Turner's theory considers two possible outcomes for a social drama: reintegration and the restoration of calm versus a recognition of schism. Both possibilities are still in play in the aftermath of Korah's rebellion. After witnessing the deaths of the rebels and the hammering of their fire pans into plating, with one voice the children of Israel cry out against Moses and Aaron: "You two have brought death upon the people of YHWH" (Num. 17:6).

∾ *Aaron's fire pan*

The people's shocked and indignant reaction to the end of Korah's rebellion triggers one last use of the fire pan, but now in the hands of Aaron. As the people continue to complain even after the dramatic deaths of the rebels,

God orders Moses and Aaron to separate themselves from the people yet again (using a different term for the command): "remove yourselves from this community" (Num. 17:10). God uses a verb that sounds similiar in sound to the verb used just verses before when God instructs Eleazar "to remove" the fire pans of Korah (Num. 17:2). The language of the story, so strikingly precise, weaves the entire drama – including its aftermath – together. The similarity in the sounds suggests that because the fire pans removed from the ashes have failed to protect the people from their own folly, now Moses must remove himself from them.

God strikes out with a plague against the complainers (Num. 17:11). The plague alludes yet again to Numbers 8, this time verse 19.[79] In chapter 8 God warns that a plague will break out among the Israelites if they approach the sanctuary. To protect them from such an eventuality, the Levites must step forward to serve in the tabernacle on their behalf. In fact, this particular term for plague is restricted in the book of Numbers to these two places.[80] The reference to the earlier warning suggests that the original role envisioned for the Levites, to protect the people from the plague, has failed. Now in chapter 17 only Aaron is capable of providing such protection.

But how? Aaron takes his fire pan, already identified with its use in the test against Korah. The use of the fire pan instead of any other object to stop the plague can hardly be coincidental. Indeed, offering incense outside the sacred precincts is an unprecedented act.[81] The fire pan has become *the* central object of the story, resulting in an evolution of its function. At the outset it is identified with the audacious rebels. In the end, in the hands of Aaron it has become an object of possible salvation. Perhaps the same incense that caused destruction when used by an unauthorized person, Korah, will remind God (and convince Israel) when used by an authorized person, Aaron, that the proper hierarchy has been restored and therefore destruction should be averted.[82] Finally, Aaron returns to Moses, at the opening of the tent of the meeting (the very site of Korah's challenge) after stopping the plague. Both the challenge to the status quo and the attack against Moses and Aaron have ceased where they began, at the opening of the tent. Yet apparently God remains uncertain of the efficacy of the fire pans. For after the plague, God instructs Moses to enact a new drama, the third in the series but the first initiated by God. God will also create the final object under consideration – the flowering staff of Aaron.

∿ Aaron's flowering staff

The creation of Aaron's flowering staff concludes chapter 17. The story that necessitates its formation is the briefest of the three. Thus this discussion is correspondingly brief. Much of the context for the creation of this object has already been discussed in the rebellion of Korah, namely, the status of the Levites versus the sons of Aaron. The breach and crisis have already happened. The instructions concerning the staff should be considered the final and most successful redressive action of our examples, especially as it not only restores but strengthens the status quo. By the end of this episode, both the community and the Levites recognize and accept the need for the hierarchy set up by Moses and God: sons of Aaron–Levites–Israelites.

In a different approach to the continuing problem of leadership within the camp, God devises a nonviolent test that ends in the creation of a rather sanguine symbol (in contrast to the plating with its reminder of sacrifice, violence, and dramatic death). Immediately after Aaron stops the plague against Israel, God orders Moses to command the chiefs of each tribe to give him a staff.[83] In Numbers 17:18 God orders Moses to write the name of Aaron on the staff of Levi – thereby setting Aaron at the head of the surviving Levites, now that Korah and the other rebels are dead.[84] The Levites may be subordinate to the priests, made painstakingly explicit in the aftermath of the rebellion, but they will now be confirmed as holding a higher status than the Israelites! This brief story aims at nothing less than the reconciliation of the sons of Aaron with their cousins, all of whom belong to the tribe of Levi. It does so through a quiet public test free of the atmosphere of crisis we have seen until now.

After gathering the staffs of each of the twelve tribes, Moses is instructed to place them inside the tent of meeting in front of the pact. Milgrom identifies the pact as synonymous with the ark, which rests in the Holy of Holies.[85] Therefore, unlike the plating, these new objects are placed, at least temporarily, in the holiest zone out of sight of Israel. God explains the purpose of the test: "And it shall be the man whom I will choose – his staff will flower and I will rid myself of the complaints of the children of Israel which they complain against you" (Num. 17:20). God's singling out of one man echoes Moses' earlier, angry announcement to Korah that God will choose whom God wants – namely, Aaron. Yet now it is emphasized that Aaron represents the tribe of Levi.

By also referring to the complaints of the people, God makes clear that the background that leads up to the current test includes not only Korah's rebellion but the entire series of complaints begun in chapter 11 and continuing until this very moment, even after Korah's death. In other words, all of Israel is implicated in this contest and therefore all of Israel must witness this final redressive action. God sets out to restore calm within the entire camp while also reconciling Aaron and the Levites in front of the people.

Not only does the staff of Levi, with Aaron's name on it, flower the next morning, but it produces blossoms and ripe almonds. Moses brings all twelve staffs, including that of Aaron now representing the Levites, out of the tabernacle and presents them to the people, because the power of the object works to restore stability only if seen by the entire people. "Moses then brought out all the staffs from before YHWH to all the Israelites and they saw and took each his staff" (Num. 17:24). The abundance of physical growth vividly represents God's point. In spite of the devastations of Korah's rebellion and the plague that just hit Israel, from this moment on the house of Levi will be a growing and productive house. It will have a long and successful future. After the deaths of so many – Nadav, Avihu, Korah and his crowd (sons and cousin of Aaron) – the remainder of the tribe of Levi will not only survive but flourish. They will be fertile – implied in the choice of object. As the extension of the male holding it, the staff is a phallic symbol par excellence.[86]

Due to the contrast between their flowering staff and the other eleven staffs, the entire tribe of Levi will outrank the rest of the Israelites. Thus the test itself resolves the inherent tensions between Levite and Cohen. They are now united as God's choice. They also share the distinction of being set apart from the rest of Israel. This message is breathtakingly condensed yet effectively and powerfully expressed through the image of the flowering staff.

The flowering staff also serves another function. It reminds the people to put aside their resentments, lest they die. After having shown the people the result of the test, Moses is again instructed by God: "return the staff of Aaron before the Pact for safekeeping as a sign to the rebellious children so that their complaints cease against me so that they do not die" (Num. 17:25). Note that while the plating was called both a sign and a memorial (see 17:3 and 17:5), the flowering staff is called simply a sign. Nonetheless, as a sign, Aaron's flowering staff functions, just as the plating before it, as a reminder to Israel to accept the current arrangements, "so that their complaints cease." Finally, just as the tassels and the plating are meant to endure over time, so too is the staff of Aaron, as indicated by the use of the term "safekeeping." Why must the sign be kept safe? Implied in this provision is the assumption that the people will need to be reminded continually to choose the right kind of memory. Viewing the flowering staff only once will hardly be sufficient. The sign must be kept safe, as it will be needed over and over. Even this late in the narrative, after all that the people have witnessed and experienced, God still assumes their continued stubborn resistance to the divine plans for them.

The drama that produces the flowering of one staff out of twelve is truncated. Perhaps it is best understood as the final component in the drama of Korah's rebellion. Surely, it succeeds in restoring a sense of stability in the priestly hierarchy of priest and Levite. Yet the people's response is puzzling. After seeing the flowering rod returned to a place of safekeeping in the tabernacle, they cry out: "Lo, we perish. We are lost, all of us, we are lost. All who come too close to the Tabernacle of YHWH will die – are we doomed to perish?" (Num, 17:27–28). The answer to their cry comes in what follows, a return to legislation after the narrative of rebellion. Chapter 18 lays out the solution to the dangers of the tabernacle's presence in the midst of Israel, but the solution is precisely that first proposed by God back in Numbers 3, 4, and 8. The Levites will shield the people Israel from coming too close, thereby preventing their unnecessary deaths. So it is that after a period of crisis, in chapter 18 the Levites finally accept their subordinate role vis-à-vis the priests. In return for such protection the Israelites compensate both priest and Levites. Apparently, calm has been restored.

∾ Conclusion

Turner's concept of "social drama" has shaped this reading of the three crises that erupt in the middle of the wilderness journey. What has the reliance on the social drama provided for an understanding of the priestly editing of Numbers? Certainly, the four stages of the drama create an apt structure in which to observe and make sense of the unfolding biblical narrative. The drama's emphasis on the social conflicts within a community corresponds to the atmosphere of the highly charged political, and ultimately lethal, confrontations that occur during the wilderness journey. Turner captures the intensity of such an atmosphere as well as the usefulness of the social drama in understanding and responding to it. His model is "agonistic, rife with problem and conflict . . . it is that which is not yet settled, concluded and known . . . it is what terrifies in the breach and crisis phrases of a social drama."[87]

As we have had reason to observe, the stages of the drama do not just describe its course but influence its content. As such, the types of action necessary to resolve the crisis in these episodes could be used by the later biblical editors to further their priestly agenda. In particular, the last two stages of Turner's model are especially pertinent to the strategy of the priestly editors. Remember that to be effective, the third stage, that of redressive action, requires a public act of some sort. In our examples, God and Moses set into action the public performance of tests and punishment. The subsequent fate of the dissenters serves as a powerful deterrence for the Israelite audience, an audience that includes all subsequent generations. Ultimately, the fourth stage of the social drama persuades the audience to adhere to a particular set of arrangements and leaders.

Thus the social drama becomes the means through which stability and order are restored after chaos. The three episodes contain the predictable discontent and resentment that inevitably follow God's condemnation of an entire generation in Numbers 14. Tension erupts and gets expressed. It will also be regulated and exploited. For after allowing for the release of tension, the social dramas in Numbers reinscribe and strengthen certain political arrangements of leadership and authority over against the challenges of those others who seek power. Of course the main point for the priestly editors is that the social drama is not a one-time occurrence in the wilderness past. The persuasive power of the social drama recurs in the rereading of the narrative over time. The record of dissent and resolution provides an important release in the ongoing life of the community in which it is recited and received. Bell argues that the effect of rereading past events in the present produces "a strategic reproduction of the past in such a way as to maximize its domination of the present, usually by particular authorities defined as the sole guardians of the past and the experts on ritual."[88] Certainly, the priests were considered the experts on ritual. But in Numbers they also set out to be the sole guardians of the past in their editing of the tales of crisis and commemoration. The objects formed at the end of each tale contribute mightily to that priestly guardianship of the past.

Reading the tales of the three objects in chronological order reveals an internal logic to their placement that emphasizes their strategic use in the hands of the priests. Think of the images of the stories as they unfold. We can imagine an Israelite wearing tassels on the edges of his garment, protecting his body (and the body Israel) from harm. Yet this image is superseded by that of bodies being buried alive or incinerated, a shocking picture indeed. Yet this shock is replaced with a picture of fertility, a rejuvenated and flourishing body represented by the blossoming of a flower. In other words, these strangely juxtaposed images have suggested the type of deterrence and persuasion necessary to overcome the discontent and disobedience of Israel. If the commandment to wear tassels is not sufficient, then the catastrophic result of disobedience must be. In consequence Israel recommits itself to the divine plan and a fertile and promising future. That final image of the restoration of harmony adds a further positive incentive for the people Israel to adhere to the priestly vision of the community.

In addition to their order, the objects contribute to the priestly argument in Numbers by providing a strategic response to the ever-present threat of memory's elusiveness and distortions. The tassels, plating, and staff do nothing less than channel and contain memory's negative effects by reminding Israel of the catastrophes that would occur if Egypt, rather than the promised land, would again become the desire of the people. Each object concretizes and reinforces the purposes of God and of Moses. And each reminds the people of the punishments that led to their formation. Distinguishing between the consequences of acceptable versus dangerous memory, the objects provide permanent instruction for the people Israel about the proper contents of memory. The tassels instruct the people to remember the commandments of the Lord so that they shall be holy. The plating reminds the Levites and Israelites of the priestly hierarchy in the camp with its attendant zones of holiness, still relevant in the land. Aaron's flowering staff reconciles priest and Levite while attempting to stop the people from engaging in the dissent of their predecessors. If they achieve their mnemonic purposes, the objects would result in nothing less than the continued life of Israel as a holy people under the close guidance of the priests.

In spite of this optimistic hope, the narrative of the wilderness remains unflinchingly realistic in the struggle for each and every Israelite. The objects incorporate reminders of the enormous challenges facing Moses and Aaron, of the likelihood of failure. The people never cease to complain. Hovering in the shadows of words of warning and reproof is the reminder of all those who failed and perished along the way: the scouts, Korah and his band, and, ultimately, the entire generation that left Egypt only to be discarded in the obscurity of the wilderness, leaving behind them the tassels, plating, and staff. Poignantly, these mnemonic objects are almost all that remain of an entire generation. In the end, the objects reflect the unresolved struggle of Israel with God and with itself.

Thus the social dramas and their objects do not entirely eradicate discord within the camp. It continues, even preventing Moses and Aaron from reaching the promised land. In consequence, even more drastic measures are necessary. They are to be found in the reports of a generation dying off in the wilderness. Death transforms the desert landscape into a foreboding and desolate territory, the very antitype of the promised land.

SIX

Falling in the Wilderness: The Politics of Death and Burial

...collective memory serves as an excellent instrument of power.[1]

Mortal remains are never a matter of indifference where bonds of love and kinship exist.[2]

In his mythic poem מתי מדבר, the modern Hebrew poet Hayyim Nahman Bialik imagines the entire biblical generation that has been liberated from Egypt lying exposed in the wilderness. In the opening stanza, they are first spotted sprawled across the ground:

Their faces are tough and tanned,...
Their foreheads are stubborn and bold, defying the wrath of the heavens.

Bialik vacillates between depicting them as dead or merely at rest:

...the mighty phalanx awakes.
They suddenly rouse themselves, the stalwart men of war,
lightening ablaze in their eyes, their faces aflame, hands on swords.

Whether dead or merely sleeping, the wilderness encompasses them in anonymity, shielding them from the outside observer:

No one on earth knows the site, nor knows of their rise, or their fall.
Heaps of hills piled up by the storm enclose and encircle them.

In an epigraph to his poem Bialik alludes to a talmudic legend that pictures this same generation alive and at rest. In the legend, an Arab merchant leads Rabbah b. Bar Hana through the desert to find the generation. Rabbah b.

Bar Hana describes what he saw: "They looked as if in a state of exhilaration. They slept on their backs: the knee of one of them was raised."[3]

Why do both poet and rabbinic legend render the wilderness generation merely at rest rather than dead? There can be no mistaking the description in the original biblical text. God's condemnation of the generation includes an explicit sentence of death:

Say to them: "As I live," says YHWH, "I will do to you just as you have urged Me. In this very wilderness shall your carcasses fall." (Num. 14:28–29a)[4]

What is more, the narrative in Numbers that begins in chapter 11 and concludes at the end of chapter 26 describes the variety of deaths that result from those divine words of condemnation in abundant and graphic detail. How, then, could later readers of the biblical story ignore the explicit certainty of death and imagine the generation in a merely somnolent state, exposed to sun and wind?

Bialik hints at a solution to this apparent contradiction in the last lines of his first stanza. Conceiving the generation as lying exposed to the elements, the poet writes:

Only the scars on seared faces . . .
the chipping of arrow and javelin, the carved hilts of the sword remain,
like inscriptions on tombstones.

In referring to inscriptions and tombstones for the dead, Bialik makes apparent the gap found in the biblical account. While Numbers narrates the variety of ways in which the people die, it records the burial of members of the generation only once, with extreme brevity (Num. 11:34). The subsequent lack of specificity when it comes to the location of their graves, or even if they were in fact buried, is especially startling when contrasted to the introduction of that very same generation at the opening of Numbers. Those who were so meticulously accounted for at the outset are now left in their deaths unmarked, and perhaps unburied, somewhere in the wilderness. By depicting those unburied bodies as exposed to the desert and to later human sightings, Bialik's poem and the rabbinic legend raise the horrifying question of what became of them, highlighting the strangeness of their fate.[5]

In this chapter, I analyze that fate by tracing the contours of the wilderness generation's final days as reported in the biblical text. The written record contains evidence of careful design and coherence. I assume such design to be an exegetical and, in fact, polemical, act on the part of the editors who shape the various reports of death within the larger narrative into a rather unusual type of commemoration, one highly critical of those commemorated. My reading focuses on the results of that editorial/exegetical project.[6] I conclude that the biblical record not only reports on the punishment of the generation, but itself constitutes an essential aspect of that punishment.

I begin by placing God's punishment of the generation in the larger context of the middle chapters of Numbers, 11–26. Only in context will the content of divine punishment make sense. The language and logic of destruction are used with great precision in the biblical account. As a result of that destruction, by the end of Numbers the wilderness has been transformed into a symbolic space, the premier site of death, juxtaposed in the starkest of terms with its counterpart, the land promised Israel by God.

Between a discussion of the language and logic of destruction and the transformation of the wilderness into a symbolic space lies the core of the present chapter: the reports of death as well as the treatment of the dead. Unlike many passages in other biblical books that are focused on the experiences of the elite to the exclusion of the ordinary Israelite, in Numbers both the generation condemned to die in the wilderness and those that will inherit the land receive a great deal of attention. Those who will enter the land are the intended targets of the priestly persuasion we have observed thus far. But to be effective, the priestly editors begin by intensely focusing on their parents, the generation liberated from Egypt. That focus begins at the very beginning of Numbers with the precise counting of Israelite men, the naming of their tribes, and the placement of each tribe around the tabernacle in the wilderness camp. The reports of the obliteration of those so carefully numbered and placed at the outset provide an uncanny counterpart to the earlier narrative. Because their deaths are a crucial component in God's punishment (and in the editor's strategy), I shall examine the way in which they have been exploited.

Death is used for political purposes, much as the tales of crisis and commemoration discussed in the preceding chapter. In fact the biblical record confirms an argument put forward in the recent work of the Italian critic Armando Petrucci that the recording of death is essentially a political practice: "the funerary use of writing is an important element in the 'politics of death' every organized culture sets up and administers so that it may stand out as itself."[7]

In the ancient world out of which Israel emerged, the politics of death includes not only reports of death but also how such criteria as one's status and/or wealth at the time of death might dictate the type of treatment received. Treatment of the dead extends to burial practices. Status would influence the location of burial, the type of burial, and whether there is a tomb.[8] I intend to argue that in Numbers the status of the leaders and that of the generation as those condemned by God is highly determinative of the treatment of the dead, including the written reports of death and of the disposition of the remains. In addition, to support my argument that these reports are not only sharply political but, in fact, would be considered devastating by an ancient audience, I will sketch the larger cultural context out of which the reported fate of the dead might be evaluated. In the end I hope to make clear the extent to which the editors of the text have organized the record of the dead in as stark and terrifying a way as possible to persuade the readers of their time (their persistent concern throughout) to choose the life offered them in the land under divinely ordained priestly supervision rather than risk the fate of those who died in the obscurity and anonymity of the wilderness.

The context of death: the subversions of memory

At the start of chapter 11 of Numbers, the people liberated from Egypt begin to complain, and then begin to die. Their behavior reaches a crisis in chapter 14, sparking God's explicit and blanket condemnation of the entire generation. By the end of chapter 25 of Numbers, not one member of the generation, save Caleb, Joshua, and Moses, remains. The fact of the generation's impending obliteration and its fulfillment introduces a disturbing tension throughout a series of episodes that only the climactic verses of the census found in Numbers 26:64–65a quell:

> Among these [the descendants of those who left Egypt] there was not one of those enrolled by Moses and Aaron the priest when they enrolled the Israelites in the wilderness of Sinai. For YHWH had said of them: "They shall surely die in the wilderness."[9]

A focus on the future can occur only after the disturbing record of the older generation's demise is complete.

As we have seen, the demise of the generation begins in chapter 11 at precisely the moment in the narrative when memory is introduced as a subversive and destructive force. Let me briefly review the description of the events that follow as they provide the necessary context for the subsequent treatment of the generation once dead. Coming after the carefully orchestrated chapters that depict the harmonious relationship among God as guide, Moses as His prophet, and the people as willing followers, chapter 11 abruptly disrupts all that preceded it.[10] At this juncture in the journey, the actual voices of the populace are heard for the first time. They are voices raised in unceasing complaint. They begin with a catalog of the Egyptian delicacies they remember from their days as slaves in Egypt. Such memories infect the morale of the camp to such an extent that, a few chapters later, when the scouts return with a negative report of the land, the people immediately, and unanimously, decide to retrace their steps. Instead of guiding God's army on its way to conquering the land, Israel's leaders helplessly watch as the people's highly selective memories of Egypt lead to the collapse of divine plans.

In fact God attributes the behavior of the wilderness generation precisely to this selective rendering of their past. Their longing for Egypt and their refusal to conquer the land are inextricably linked. They fail to see that they have rejected the only life available to them. Their misapprehension of this simple fact is nowhere more apparent than in their plan to return to Egypt. The editors shape the narrative of the deaths of the generation that follows in order to set the record straight, fully exploiting God's punishment of the generation to ensure that the new generation avoids the mistakes of its elders. By telling the tale a certain way, future misfortune, even catastrophe, may be avoided.

The language and peculiar logic of death

In sheer volume and variety the imagery employed to describe the killing of the Israelites from chapter 11 through chapter 25 constitutes a grim eruption of death. The catalog of death in these chapters includes different kinds of plague, God's consuming fire, excommunication, stoning, being engulfed by the earth, and lethal poisoning by snakes. The manner of death, at least in some cases, serves as fitting punishment for particular lapses on the part of the people.

For instance, being consumed (the stem אכל also forms the verb "to eat"), usually by divine fire, plays a prominent role in the deaths of the wilderness generation. God chooses this method at the very opening of the section narrating the deterioration of the people's relationship with God, a deterioration triggered at first by a vague complaint that quickly develops into specific memories of Egyptian fish and leeks. God hears the people as they begin to complain and, according to 11:1, becomes incensed. Reacting immediately, He unleashes a consuming fire that attacks the edge of the wilderness camp. References to eating continue throughout chapter 11 as the people first remember eating certain foods in Egypt and then actually begin to eat quail in the present episode (eating is repeated a significant number of times). Thus, Israel's longing to eat the wrong kinds of food fuels God's consuming wrath. That wrath continues in 12:12 as a form of אכל next describes God's punishment of Miriam. She is struck by a skin affliction. While spared death at that point, Miriam is described by a horrified Aaron as someone whose flesh has been "half eaten away." The spies use the verb in 13:32 to describe the promised land as a land that devours or eats its inhabitants. God then uses a consuming fire to punish the rebellious followers of Korah in 16:35: "And a fire went forth from YHWH and consumed the 250." In 17:10, in reaction to yet another provocation of the people, God orders Moses and Aaron "to remove yourselves from the midst of this community and I will consume them in an instant." Even though the verb used in 17:10 is not from the same root, it is similar in sound to the dominant root, especially since it is used in the first-person singular.[11] The combined effect of these verses conveys a terrifying process of destruction.

The repeated use of אכל in each of these episodes (or its oral equivalent) imposes its own narrative and theological order. In response to the people's desire to eat of Egypt's delicacies, their death by consumption makes a peculiar, logical sense. "Eating" as a form of death, actual or threatened, represents a fine example of the biblical concept of punishment "measure for measure." Obsessed by their cravings for the remembered food of Egypt, the people trigger a series of episodes in which they are consumed by the fire of the Lord or fear being consumed by the devouring land.[12]

Chapter 11 contains a second example of this principle of measure for measure. After granting the people their wish to eat meat as they did in

Egypt, God is infuriated by the sight of the meat in their mouths and kills them off with a plague: "The meat was still between their teeth, nor yet chewed, when the anger of YHWH blazed forth against the people and YHWH struck the people with a very great plague" (Num. 11:33). The Hebrew noun used for the plague is מכה, rather than the more common מגפה (the latter term is used in chapters 14, 17, and 25, other instances of Israelite death). Within Numbers, until 11:33 the verbal form of מכה is reserved exclusively for the Egyptians (3:13 and 8:17) and surfaces again in reference to the death of the Egyptian firstborn (33:4). Chapters 3:13 and 8:17 even contain identical phrasing, referring to the time when God "*smote* every firstborn in the land of Egypt." After Numbers 11:33, the verbal form of the root is used again in reference to the Israelites in Numbers 14:12 when God wishes to strike them down after they reject God's plans to conquer the land and instead want to return to Egypt. Those who then try unsuccessfully to go forward are struck a lethal blow in 14:45. The use of the word in this context appears to be quite precise. In consequence of their lusting after Egyptian delicacies and their plans to return to Egypt, the people suffer the same form of death as that of the Egyptians.[13]

Even in the midst of a narrative already replete with the imagery of death, chapter 14 stands out as the intensification and fullest expression of the terrifying reality that death pervades the camp. Just as in chapter 11, death's form is determined by the logic of measure for measure. With its very first words, the chapter explodes with the people's complaint:

> The whole community broke into loud cries, and the people wept that night. All the Israelites railed against Moses and against Aaron, and all the congregation said to them, "If only we had died in the land of Egypt, or if only we might die in this wilderness! Why is YHWH taking us to this land to fall by the sword? [לנפל בחרב]" (Num. 14:1–3)

God explicitly uses the principle of measure for measure in the divine response.

> As I live ... I will do to you just as you have urged Me. In this very wilderness your carcasses shall fall [יפלו פגריכם].... Your children who you said would be carried off – these will I allow to enter; they shall know the land that you have rejected.... You shall bear your punishment for forty years, corresponding to the number of days – forty days – that you scouted the land; a year for each day. (Num. 14:28–29, 31, 34)

Note that in verse 29 God uses the very term – fall – that the people first use in verse 3 of the same chapter as they express the fear that they shall fall by the enemy's sword. The manner in which the people die illustrates the extent to which the story of their failures in life shape their punishment. They shall fall, but only through God's abandonment of them. Their children will be carried off by God, but to a life in the land they themselves will never see. The length of years left to them parallels the length of the scouting mission that led to such disaster in the first place.[14]

Measure for measure

In a fitting, even brilliant, use of this biblical concept of measure for measure, the editors take God's logic even further and employ memory itself as a device to punish the wilderness generation, guaranteeing that its acts of memory will now dictate its end. Having selectively edited their memories of Egypt, forgetting the oppression and slavery while remembering Egyptian delicacies, the people in turn are subject to actual editing, punished by the erasure of their memory from the text. Instead of a record of their lives during the subsequent years of wandering, their legacy is dominated by a fragmented catalog of death and its aftermath – especially their abandonment to the oblivion of the wilderness. The reports of their deaths, as we shall see below, appear especially harsh when contrasted to the reports of their leaders' deaths during the same period. As a matter of fact, even dissenters such as Dathan and Abiram receive far more elaborate and detailed death reports than those accorded the people.[15]

If one agrees with Armando Petrucci, as I do, that in most cultures, "writing the dead" invariably constitutes a political act, then the reports of death and the fate of the wilderness generation in Numbers should be considered acutely political. The politics of death in Numbers adds to the persistent political strife already depicted in the wilderness narrative – the struggles between holy and profane, popular versus divine leadership, even the contents of the collective memory. But reports on death also become a crucial tool in the resolution of many of these issues. As Petrucci has argued, writing about the dead should be understood as "a practice of the living addressed to other living beings ... aimed at ... recording the power and social presence of [a particular] group."[16] Thus, the record itself acts to resolve the politics that imbue Numbers, ensuring that those in charge (Moses and Aaron, representing the priestly power structure) will remain so.

The crafting of a death report aims to implement that political agenda. Variables subject to calculation might include the presence or absence of a commemorative record (as put by Petrucci, the right to a written death is not automatic), the length and content of the report, whether the deceased is named, and, as we will see, the presence or absence of a grave site. Grave sites usually create a division of territory between the living and the dead.[17] This is certainly true of the biblical record. In what follows I will comment more specifically on the division of the land between the living and the dead, a division in the context of Numbers between wilderness and promised land. But before doing so, I begin by examining the differences in the content and length of different death reports. Each reflect the status of the dying person. God's appointed – Miriam, Aaron, and Moses – versus those rejected by God – the dissenters and the people – are treated quite differently in the biblical record. In addition, within the death reports of the three siblings, there are striking and politically meaningful variations, including those influenced by the politics of gender. An examination of the details highlights those differences. I begin with the dissenters, move on to the leaders, and then devote the rest of the chapter to the wilderness generation itself.

The manner in which the dissenters die, in an unusual or extraordinary fashion, is meant to convey a lesson to the people. The case of Dathan and Abiram provides the most explicit example of the political exploitation of such deaths to restore the hierarchy of power in the camp. After openly challenging the leadership of Moses, these two, along with their families, will die in as public and dramatic a fashion as Moses can devise and the writer can imaginatively depict. Moses asks God to illustrate, through the imposition of unusual death, the depth of divine support of his leadership.

Now Dathan and Abiram had come out and they stood at the entrance of their tents, with their wives, their children, and their little ones. Moses said: By this you shall know that it was YHWH who sent me to do all these things; that they are not of my own devising: if these men die as all men do, if their lot be the common lot of all humankind, it was not YHWH who sent me. But if YHWH brings about something unheard of, so that the *ground opens its mouth and swallows them up with all that belongs to them,* and *they go down alive to*

Sheol, you shall know that these men have spurned YHWH. Scarcely had he finished speaking all these words when the ground burst asunder under them and the *earth opened its mouth and swallowed them up* with their households, all Korah's people and all their possessions. They went *down alive into Sheol, with all that belonged to them*; the earth covered them and they perished from the midst of the assembly. (Num. 16:27b-33, emphasis added, based on the JPS trans.)

The dissenters stand at the threshold of their tents, unknowingly signaling their imminent exit from the tents of Israel. Not content merely with the fact that they will die, Moses explicitly makes the form of their deaths part of the confrontation. In so doing, he exploits the opportunity to "score points" with the watching Israelites and reinforce his authority. Note that just as Moses finishes speaking, almost simultaneously, without a pause, God acts to fulfill his request by having the earth swallow the dissenters alive. The fulfillment of Moses' precise instructions is conveyed by the repetition of key phrases, which I have italicized. There can be no mistaking God's support of Moses. Finally, the episode neatly fits into the larger narrative context of the stories of complaint. The imagery of the earth's open mouth swallowing Dathan and Abiram at this point appears overly determined, picking up as it does on the motif of consumption cited above.[18]

In another example of the exploitation of death for political purposes, God orders the impalement of the idolaters in 25:4: "Take all the heads of the people and impale them before YHWH, facing the sun, so that the wrath of YHWH may turn away from Israel." God decrees a sentence of death so rare that it appears nowhere else in Numbers. In fact, there is no record of its implementation in chapter 25. The threat of impalement nonetheless suggests the common element contained in each report. Those punished for dissent or idolatry must die in a highly unusual fashion in order to draw public attention to their deaths ("facing the sun," i.e., in broad daylight). The reporting or, in the present case, even the threat of their deaths aims to perpetuate the power of God and the divinely appointed leaders while thoroughly extinguishing the dangerous breach represented by the rebels and the idolaters.[19]

In contrast, the three leaders – Miriam, Aaron, and Moses – die naturally and undramatically, though the deaths of the brothers are explicitly depicted as the result of divine punishment. As will soon become apparent, the reports of their deaths also contrast with those of the people. Finally, the reporting on their deaths picks up on, and perpetuates, the tensions between them due to their different roles while alive. The deaths of Miriam and Aaron are reported within verses of each other in Numbers 20.[20] God's decree against Moses also occurs in that same chapter, but the report of his actual death is delayed until the end of Deuteronomy. Yet the narration of Moses' death further magnifies the political forces at work in reporting on death in the wilderness, including the perpetuation of the hierarchy among the three siblings. Thus, I include the report of Moses' death, found at the end of Deuteronomy, in the following discussion.[21]

The report of Miriam's death, contained in one terse phrase, opens the chapter: "And the children of Israel, the entire community, arrived at the wilderness of Zin on the first new moon and the people stayed at Kadesh and Miriam died there and she was buried there" (Num. 20:1).[22] In spite of its brevity, when contrasted to the death reports of the dissenters and of the people, the details of Miriam's death – its date on the first new moon, the place of her burial, especially the notice that she is buried – suggest that she is a leader of significant import in the Torah. The very emphasis on such details conveys a sense of uncomplicated dignity suitable for a leader of Israel.[23] In addition, the three references to the people in the report ("the children of Israel," "the entire community," "the people") suggest that she dies not alone but in the midst of the people with whom she once celebrated the crossing of the sea. Finally, Miriam's death is obviously linked to that of her brothers, securing her stature as a leader in Israel. The three are joined together as each of them die on the last three stops of the journey.[24]

Immediately after Miriam's death, perhaps even as a result of it, the people gather again to complain. In a state of utter exhaustion, exasperation or both, Moses and Aaron act in such a way as to cause God to exclude these two from the land.[25] The chapter continues with the narrative of Aaron's death. The report is far more elaborate than the terse announcement of the prophetess's death. That fact suggests that while the text grants both Aaron and Miriam qualitatively more respectful accounts than those granted the people or the dissenters, when compared with each other, the politics of gender appear to have had a hand in the brevity of Miriam's death report versus that of Aaron. On the other hand, one should note that God's punishment of the two men contrasts with the onset of Miriam's death. Her death is not associated with divine punishment.

The narrative of Aaron's death has much to accomplish on a political level. The question of priestly succession is paramount. But so, too, must Aaron's status be preserved, especially at the moment of his death. Just as with Miriam, the site of his death is named. He will die on Mount Hor on the boundary of the land of Edom. In noticeable contrast to the brief mention of Kadesh at the time of Miriam's death, the name of the present site is repeated four times – in Numbers 20:22, 23, 25, and 27 – as if to imprint it in the collective memory. Its repetition in the recounting of the journey in Numbers 33:38 confirms that point (Miriam's death at Kadesh is not repeated in the itinerary). As he ascends the mountain to die, Aaron is accompanied by his brother and son while explicitly followed visually by the entire people: "and they went up to Mount Hor in the sight of all the congregation" (Num. 20:27). Finally, in the only report of its kind in Numbers, the people mourn Aaron for a period of thirty days. Together, these three elements – a named site of death, an escort, and communal mourning – accord Aaron a dignified, honorable death:

> Moses stripped Aaron of his vestments and put them on his son Eleazar, and Aaron died there on the summit of the mountain. And Moses and Eleazar came down from the mountain, and the whole community saw that Aaron had perished and all the house of Israel wept for Aaron thirty days. (Num. 20:28–29)

The priestly succession is accomplished. Poignantly, in order to take on the role of high priest, signified by the wearing of his father's clothing, Eleazar must first witness his father's death.

The report of the death of Moses begins in the midst of his steady retelling of the tale of the wilderness journey in the Book of Deuteronomy. In that retelling, Moses offers his audience, and the reader, a particular view of past events narrated as a firsthand account in the Book of Numbers. He informs Joshua in "the sight of all Israel" that Joshua will be the one to lead the people into the land (Deut. 31:7). Moses then resumes the telling of his tale, envisioning that future time in the land. He is interrupted by God precisely, perhaps even ironically, at the point that Moses anticipates the people crossing the Jordan. God reminds Moses that he will not accompany them in that crossing.

Instead God demands that Moses now transfer his authority to a leader of the next generation. "YHWH said to Moses: The time is drawing near for you to die. Call Joshua and present yourselves in the tent of meeting that I may instruct him" (Deut. 31:14). Yet just moments before, Moses had already publicly announced the succession. Why must he take further action? Politically, it is crucial to establish that Joshua is God's choice as well as that of Moses. Unlike the straightforward genealogical basis for priestly succession, the selection of Joshua as a political/military leader must rely on God's particular command. Thus, Joshua gains legitimacy and status through his association not only with Moses but also with God. The transfer of actual power occurs in the tent of meeting, associated in the minds of the people with God's many interactions with Moses.[26]

Joshua's succession appears to have that of Eleazar in mind. If Aaron publicly transfers priestly authority to his son, then Moses must publicly transfer political power to Joshua. Joshua becomes a necessary counterweight to Eleazar within the community.[27] The priest must not be allowed to gain complete rule over the people but must share power with Joshua. But as I pointed out in chapter 3, at least in Numbers Moses orders Joshua to turn publicly to Eleazar for advice. Thus, the beginning of each death report replicates the political competition of the previous generation and hints at the unresolved and tense struggle that briefly erupted between Moses and Aaron (e.g., Num. 12) that could continue in the next generation and beyond.

Joshua's succession and the death of Moses are not narrated in direct sequence or at one moment in time. The report is scattered through several passages at the end of Deuteronomy (including 31:14–15, 23; 32:48–52, and 34:1–12), in contrast to the rather compact narrative of Aaron's death. This far lengthier report overshadows that of Aaron, clearly establishing Moses as the unquestioned leader of the period.[28] I would suggest that this might be an example of a tradition that has too much authority for the priestly editors to excise from their account. The separation of the succession from his actual death allows Moses to die alone, excepting the presence of God. This time, no escort accompanies Moses up the mountain. Only the reader can observe his lonely ascent. The intimacy between God and Moses must not be intruded upon by the presence of a third party, even Joshua.

The final scene, Deuteronomy 34:1–12, which concludes not only the life of Moses but that of the book with which he is associated, marks the death of Moses as unique, ensuring that he remain the unparalleled leader of Israel for all time. As the reader eavesdrops, God identifies the land for Moses and reminds him that it is indeed the land promised to the patriarchs. God repeats again, "I have let you see it with your own eyes but *there* you shall not cross." I have reproduced the exact word order of the Hebrew here to illustrate the emphasis on "there." Why does God repeat the statement of punishment? Indeed, these are God's final words to Moses. Why end the story this way? God's final words create an atmosphere of pathos, of tragic and mournful incompleteness. If one assumes that death reports contain a political agenda of some sort, then God's final words appear intended to remind the reader that not even Moses escapes divine punishment and reproach, even, or especially, at the moment of his death.

Yet God's next action partially resolves the tension between the desire to retain Moses' character as a member of the Israelite community, subject to the same laws and punishments, and the desire to elevate his stature as God's most cherished prophet. Following those harsh final words, God personally buries Moses. Of course, in contrast to both Miriam and Aaron, the site of the grave remains anonymous. That anonymity prevents the people from developing any special attachment to an area connected to Moses. He must not be worshiped instead of God. The people mourn Moses for thirty days, precisely the amount given to the mourning of Aaron. Finally, Moses receives a summary of his career denied his brother Aaron: "Never again did there arise in Israel a prophet like Moses" (Deut. 34:10). The report secures Moses' reputation and supreme status.

The content and length of these three death reports reinforce the hierarchical arrangement among the siblings uneasily settled in Numbers 12. Moses remains God's unique prophet, while Aaron and Miriam are subordinate. Even so, the dignified and detailed reports of death and the mention of burials stand in stark contrast to the fate of the rest of their generation. Such differential treatment reinforces and permanently seals the position of the leaders established during their lifetimes versus those of the people who repeatedly challenged them. Such treatment reinforces the political/religious ideology of the text and the social prestige of the family of Miriam, Aaron, and Moses.[29]

In fact, the amount of textual space devoted to the deaths of Aaron, Moses, and even the rebels allows for an elaboration of detail and attention missing in the reports of the average Israelite death. For instance, unlike the leaders or, for that matter, the rebels who are named at the moment of death, ordinary Israelites go unnamed when they die. In reports devoid of individuality, not even their tribal names are mentioned (in marked contrast to the detailed listing of tribal names in the opening of Numbers). Thus, a distinction has been created between those who are named at the moment of their deaths – either out of honor or as a warning – versus the vast number of those condemned by God who die in anonymity, fated to oblivion.

In another noticeable and, I would argue, purposeful contrast to the reports we have seen thus far, the majority of reports of the people's deaths are strikingly brief. In a report typical of the narration of Israelite death, the narrator announces the fate of the failed conquerors among the people – those who died in a shattering blow – in a dry statement of the bare facts, in less than a complete verse, in 14:45b. Subsequent reports share the same narrated brevity, the same dry tone, without mention of burial or collective response until the entire wilderness generation is gone. In chapter 21, after further complaints about the food found in the wilderness, God sends poisonous serpents to kill off the people "somewhere along the way." Following the already staggering number of Israelite dead, the narrator recounts these new deaths in a manner that borders on the perfunctory: "And YHWH sent the seraph serpents against the people and they bit the people and there died many people of Israel" (Num. 21:6). Chapter 25 concludes the chain of death in an equally brief announcement, amounting to one verse: "Those who died of the plague numbered twenty-four thousand" (Num. 25:9). I would suggest that the brevity of these reports indicates more than indifference to the deaths of the Israelites but forms part of their punishment. They are summarily and pointedly dismissed after failing to fulfill God's plans for them.

The disposition of remains

What happens to the thousands of Israelites killed off in the wilderness? The final example of differential treatment of the dead in Numbers concerns the disposition of the remains of the generation versus those of their leaders. A majority of the people are left behind without mention of burial or marker, condemned to the twin horrors of exposure and oblivion in the wilderness. According to the text, the only Israelites among the people granted an actual burial die as a result of God's plague at the end of chapter 11. The site of their burial is specifically mentioned: "That place was named Kibroth-hattaavah, because the people who had the craving were buried there" (Num. 11:34).

The fact that chapter 11 ends with a reference to a collective Israelite burial, that a grave is mentioned in Numbers 19:17, and that chapter 20 reports Miriam's burial suggests that the act of burial, even in the wilderness, is a detail considered pertinent enough to be included in a narrative of that period. In Numbers, however, the only mention of Israelite burial is that of chapter 11, which occurs *before* God's condemnation of the generation in Numbers 14. From chapter 14 until the last deaths of the generation in chapter 25 at Baal-Peor, the manner of death is repeatedly reported without reference to burial.

Could the lack of burial in all other references to the people be considered more than an indifference to their fate or even a simple reflection of the well-known laconic quality of the biblical narrative?[30] Could the lack of burial be a crucial ingredient in their punishment? Even if the biblical writer did not *purposefully* omit mention of burial (one would not be able to substantiate the writer's intent one way or another), the fact remains that after Numbers 11 the narrative does not refer to any additional burials of the members of the wilderness generation. Even without ascertaining the intent of the writers or the editors of Numbers, one could still consider what such an omission would mean to an Israelite audience hearing the account of the wilderness journey. What would abandonment outside the land as well as the concomitant absence of tomb or marker mean to that audience? Or, as put by Brian B. Schmidt in a recent article, "What constituted ... an 'acceptable' death in ancient Mediterranean West Asia and in Iron Age Israel?"[31] Of course, which Israelite audience is meant – preexilic (considered the late Iron Age) or postexilic (after the return from Babylon) – is subject to one's dating of the final version of Numbers, a matter still open to debate. For our purposes I rely on a consensus in the literature that during both periods there is evidence for the enormous importance of the proper burial and care of the dead.[32] After all, as Robert Pogue Harrison notes, "everywhere one looks across the spectrum of human culture one finds what we might call an obligation to the corpse, or the remains thereof ... a human imperative to dispose of the dead deliberately and ceremonially."[33]

An acceptable death

While actual practices differed from culture to culture, Israel shared its overall concern for the proper treatment of the dead with its neighbors in the ancient world. Therefore the following remarks weave together evidence from biblical as well as external sources. In general an acceptable death in the ancient world would comprise some sort of funeral that included lamentation, the proper burial of the dead, mourning, and some kind of care over time. The extent of that care (burial with implements, oil lamps or even more elaborate objects, and/or the recurring offering of food and drink) and the motives for that care (fear of the wrath of ancestors or a simple wish to honor one's dead) remain subject to debate and also differ between cultures as well as from period to period.[34] For the present argument one might agree in a general way with the conclusion of Brian Schmidt, that

> ancient Israelite society was characterized by a strong bond between kinship, family and religion. Whether one has in mind the Israelite societies in which the authors themselves lived, the ideal society depicted in their texts, or a more ancient society constituting a historical past ... all indications are that kinship, family and religion were closely intertwined. The care, feeding and commemoration of the dead attested to in the sources verifies the centrality of kinship and family in religious and social life ... the properly buried and regularly attended Israelite dead were pitied and their memory immortalized.[35]

The importance of proper burial, ongoing care of the site, and preservation of the memory of the dead long pre-dates the Israelites. For instance, Schmidt cites the reflection of Aqhat, a figure of renown in an Ugaritic epic, that "the best a mortal could hope for was a decent burial and the perpetuation of one's memory, so 'pick up your bow and make a name for yourself that will not be forgotten while you still can.'"[36] One might add to Aqhat's conclusion that based on the evidence, the best burial one could hope for would be in a tomb of one's ancestors "in the possession of the family."[37] The quality of such a tomb was also of concern. For instance, after examining the tale of the Egyptian character Sinuhe, Cyrus Gordon argued that "far more precious to an Egyptian than 'life, liberty and the pursuit of happiness' in this vale of tears is a stone pyramid, well located, well constructed and well carved."[38]

Within biblical texts, Jeremiah 16 provides a particularly comprehensive example of the proper treatment of the dead in a catalog of practices whose performance by Jeremiah is paradoxically forbidden by God.[39] Such proper practice includes lamentation, burial, and a condolence visit to a house of mourning. Forbidding all of that, God announces, instead:

> They shall die gruesome deaths. They shall not be lamented or buried; they shall be like dung on the surface of the ground . . . their corpses shall be food for the birds of the sky and the beasts of the earth. For thus said YHWH: Do not enter a house of mourning, Do not go to lament and to condole with them. (Jer. 16:4–5a, JPS trans.)

Thus the act of burial or its omission receives careful attention. The exposure of the corpses in Jeremiah is meant to shock.

If we turn to the archeological record, contra to the missing burials in the wilderness of Numbers, we can observe significant evidence of burial within the borders of the promised land. Elizabeth Bloch-Smith describes numerous examples of the different types of burial practice found in the area of ancient Israel and Judah from the late tenth through the sixth century B.C.E. These include burial in caves, simple graves, cist graves, jar burials, anthropoid coffins, bathtub coffins, and bench tombs. The most popular were simple graves or bench tombs. Bloch-Smith writes: "After a decrease in the number of sites where dead were interred during the ninth century BCE, the first half of the eighth century BCE witnessed an upsurge along the north coast, in the Shephelah and in the Judahite foothills and highlands. . . . During the seventh century BCE the majority of new burials were initiated in Judah."[40] The evidence suggests that the type of burial varied but that attention to the provision of either a grave or tomb was widespread among wealthy and poor alike.

Tombs, especially those of kings, would often be inscribed with curses and warnings. Such curses reflect an anxiety that tombs remain untouched and unharmed. A particularly clear expression of such anxiety on behalf of the dead can be found in Phoenician funeral inscriptions. Yitzhak Avishur has shown just how close these Phoenician inscriptions are to their Hebrew equivalent.[41] Several examples of Phoenician coffins have been excavated, each displaying a prominent warning and curse against any who would contemplate disturbing the sarcophagus. The Tabnit inscription is a case in point:

> don't, don't open my sarcophagus and don't disturb me for such a thing would be an abomination to Astarte. But if you do open up my sarcophagus

and if you disturb me may you have no seed among the living under the sun and a resting place with the spirits.[42]

Another example, found on the coffin of Eshmunazar, illustrates the depth of the concern:

the ruler or the man who shall open the box of this resting place or who lift up his casket, and the seed of that king or those men. May they have no root down below and no fruit up on top and foliage among the living under the sun.[43]

These curses exemplify the purpose of royal inscriptions as described by Peckham in his discussion of a royal Sidonian example. They are "concerned primarily with preserving the undisturbed tranquility of the dead. Potential violators of the royal tombs are exhorted, cajoled and finally threatened not to open their coffins or disturb their rest."[44] No doubt such warnings are motivated by the threat of looting, as the tombs of a royal family would be filled with riches meant to accompany the corpse. Yet in addition to such a worldly concern, the urgent warnings to protect the corpse from violation suggest an anxiety that the remains of the dead be protected from exposure. The graves or tombs that house them do precisely that. Therefore the tomb would require looking after, even with vigilance. If one keeps in mind that tombs were discovered not only in the royal capitals but throughout the land, one could extend that fear of exposure with its demand for vigilance to the general population, including not only Phoenician but Israelite kings as well as the general population.

In concrete terms, the desire to protect the remains vigilantly translated into continual and careful maintenance of the grave site. Maintenance over time created the likelihood not only that the immediate family of the deceased would keep track of the location of the tomb or grave site, but also that his or her descendants would do so. This likelihood was increased by the fairly common practice of burying members of the same family in one site. As a result of group burial practices, the tomb or grave site continued to function as a site of great importance for at least several generations and inevitably and naturally became the primary focus of rituals of commemoration. Note that this holds true for both the elite and the general population. Annual public recitations of the names of the deceased were a crucial component of such commemoration.[45] Public recitations prevented the fading of memory. They did battle with the anonymity of death as the names of the deceased remained in the minds of the living.

Gerdien Jonker describes the practice of invoking the names of the dead in both official and personal settings in Mesopotamia. In so doing, Jonker also distinguishes between written versus oral forms of memory:

> The King and the head of the family kept memory alive on behalf of the groups associated with them.... The sovereign had a system of writers and scholars at his command to assist him, who moulded the desired memory into a permanent written form.... The names which the head of a family "invoked" formed the basis of that family's prestige and self-image. Within the context of the family, securing something in written form played hardly any role; memory was transferred orally.[46]

Yet such recitals provide more than a pious tending to the memory of one's loved ones. They have an economic consequence as well. "The surest way to take possession of a place and secure it as one's own is to bury one's dead on it."[47] Repeated recitations of names establish public records of genealogical ties. A family could rely on such public records in matters of property dispute. Hence an ancestral tomb serves as a "physical marker of the family claim to the land; ... sometimes burials functioned as territorial boundary markers."[48] Obviously, the imagined death and abandonment of ancestors in the distant wilderness would preclude the possibility of such rituals and/or spiritual, psychological, or economic benefits.

Thus we have a general picture of what is considered "an acceptable death." In particular the importance of burial is widely attested. Herbert Brichto summarizes the evidence within ancient Israel:

> The frequent references to burial in the Bible, the thousands of tombs excavated by biblical archaeologists, *the horror of exposure of the corpse*...all testify to the importance of the practice and suggest not mere sentimental respect for the physical remains as the motivation for the practice, but rather an assumed connection between proper sepulture and the condition of the happiness of the deceased...[as well as to] the all-important tie between sepulture and ownership of land.[49] (emphasis added)

One might add to this description the idea that proper burial confirms the positive reputation of the deceased. "Peaceful burial with one's ancestors is itself seen as a reward for a good life."[50]

In contrast, sinners in the bible are repeatedly cursed with denial of burial.[51] Explicit expressions of the dread and horror of being left unburied, coupled with an understanding of such a death as severe punishment, appear in many different texts. Deuteronomy 28:26 lists this concern in the midst of a long list of curses: "Your carcasses shall become food for all the birds of the sky and all the beasts of the earth, with none to frighten them off." In a near echo of that sentiment, Jeremiah 7:33 announces: "The carcasses of this people shall be food for the birds of the sky and the beasts of the earth, with none to frighten them off." Royalty does not avoid such a fate. In I Kings 14:11, whether they dwell in the town or in the countryside, the descendants of King Jeroboam are doomed to a horrible end. Those of Jeroboam "who die in the town shall be devoured by dogs; and anyone who dies in the open country shall be eaten by the birds of the air." Isaiah 14:18–20 is another good example of such a punishment, this time meted out against the King of Babylon:

> All the kings of the nations, all of them, lie in honor, every one in his own house. But you are cast out from your grave like an abhorred offshoot, dressed in the garment of the slain, thrust through with a sword; like those who descend to the stones of the pit as a trampled corpse. You shall not be joined with them in burial, because you destroyed your land. . . .

In the case of Numbers, while not explicitly announcing that the corpses of an entire generation shall lie exposed in the wilderness, God does offer up a graphic image of "carcasses" falling in the desert at least three times in the midst of divine condemnation in Numbers 14. And as those carcasses begin to fall, the narrative provides no record of funerary rites or burial. Interestingly enough, there are only two other references to "carcasses" in the Five Books of Moses. In each instance, the carcasses appear exposed to the elements. The first occurs in Genesis 15:11. After Abraham cuts in two the carcasses of the animals and birds he is to offer God, he lays them out on the ground. He must then immediately chase away a bird of prey who swoops down to devour the exposed carcass. In Leviticus 26:30 God threatens the Israelites with a horrifying curse: "I will heap your carcasses upon your lifeless fetishes. I will spurn you." Here too the carcasses appear exposed to the elements.

A rabbinic commentator picks up on the image of fallen carcasses in Numbers and in fact assumes that they were left unburied. The omission of burial becomes a puzzle that demands a solution. In addition, the midrash illustrates that the concern for the proper treatment of the dead as well as a horror of the idea of the exposure of a corpse continues centuries later. Rabbi Nathan concludes that the absence of burial must be purposeful, providing sufficient punishment so that in the world to come, God would surely forgive the sinners:

> "It is a good sign for an individual when his sin is requited after his death. If he is not eulogized, not buried, devoured by a beast, or if rain falls upon him – these are good signs that his sin is requited after his death."[52]

Note that his associations lead from the lack of funeral ("no eulogy") to the lack of burial to the consequences of exposure: being devoured by a beast or rained upon. Rabbi Nathan could have added to this anxious catalog of omissions a worry that one might forget the name of the deceased. In ancient Israel, one established one's immortality "by the preservation of one's deeds, position or personhood in the mind of those one left behind long after one's departure from this world."[53] This preservation was concretized through the annual care and commemoration described above.

Yet Numbers denies such a possibility to an entire generation. No provisions are made for the ongoing care of the dead nor would such acts be feasible, because the dead are left behind in the wilderness. If one keeps in mind what we have observed of ancient attitudes and practices toward the dead, the depiction of the treatment of the Israelites who die in Numbers – the anonymity of their deaths, the indifference exhibited toward proper burial, and especially their unceremonious abandonment in the wilderness – would presumably create a significant, even horrifying, deterrent. Precisely such an "unacceptable death" is imposed on an entire generation, cut off from its children and deprived of human memory, left in the wilderness unnamed, unburied, and unmarked.

In this wilderness

In a fascinating study of memory in Mesopotamia, Gerdien Jonker refers to an insight of Maurice Halbwachs, a figure who was among the first to analyze collective memory systematically. Halbwachs points to the importance of physical space – whether the topography of a locale or a succession of physical loci (such as the Via Dolorosa in Jersualem) – as an aid to the construction of collective memory. Memories become anchored, and are developed, through their association with specific places or types of space.[54] Halbwachs's claim shaped Jonker's study of physical sites of memory in ancient Mesopotamia.[55] Jonker focuses on buildings and monuments, delineating the ways in which Mesopotamians trusted in the durability of their physical structures. "Repairs, reconstructions, and respect for earlier builders were the catchwords with which one generation summoned the next to administer their inheritance."[56] Jonker is on solid ground in focusing on buildings. Due to the antiquity of civilization in that area of the world, a Mesopotamian, even in 600 B.C.E, would have access to temples that would have long predated the observer. These buildings, especially due to their longevity and centrality in areas of population concentration, provided a mental geography for memories of the glories of the Mesopotamian past.[57] This idea of a mental geography in present time that contributes to, and becomes part of, collective notions of the past seems to be an especially apt contribution to the variety of forms taken by memory in the book of Numbers.

Yet as I considered the very durability of such ancient temples and monuments, I realized how different that Mesopotamian solidity was from the wilderness setting that provided the mental geography for the collective memories found in Numbers. Mortar and brick are replaced by a vast and parched emptiness. In fact the wilderness defies the very notion of durability and concreteness found in the Mesopotamian examples. Even when Numbers creates a mental geography on behalf of the collective memory similar to that proposed by Halbwachs with his succession of physical loci, such a mental geography reinforces the transient nature of the whole enterprise. I refer to the itinerary of chapter 33. The sites listed in such detail are mere stops along the way, defining the wilderness as a place one gets through in order to reach the other side. The task of getting to the other side becomes ever more urgent for the new generation as the wilderness increasingly becomes a repository of the Israelite dead. Thus the collective memory being constructed in Numbers resides in a mental geography of great desolation.

How is the wilderness transformed from a forbidding territory into something much worse – a realm of death? And to what end? For one thing, the omission of particular, discrete sites of burial has the effect of turning the wilderness *in its entirety* into a vast and terrible burying ground. Numbers

19:16 captures that image in its depiction of a landscape littered with corpses: "in the open field, anyone who touches a person who was killed or who died naturally, or a human bone, or a grave, shall be unclean seven days."[58] Wilderness has become wasteland.

In his work on sacred space in the bible, Robert L. Cohn reinforces the sense of wilderness as the realm of the dead when he observes that the narrative of the wilderness period does not contain the record of a single birth.[59] Only after the crossing of the Jordan do we realize that births must have occurred, because the Book of Joshua orders the circumcisions of those born in the wilderness (Joshua 5:5–8). Written records of birth and life belong to the realm of the promised land, not to that of the wilderness, the preeminent place of death. The wilderness barely sustains life. It is "a place of utter desolation: a vast void of parched earth, of utter cruelty."[60] If they want to live, the next generation must leave such a wasteland, as well as their parents, behind.

Thus does death transform the wilderness. In fact J. Pederson identifies the wilderness as one of three realms of death (or "non-worlds") within the bible. The other two are the sea and Sheol.[61] Psalm 107 is instructive in this regard, depicting both the wilderness and the sea as sites of danger and destruction from which God might rescue the repentant sufferer. While Sheol is not mentioned by name, the Psalmist refers to two other sites in terms often reserved for Sheol. These include a "place of darkness in the shadow of death" (verses 10 and 14) and the "gates of death" (verse 18). The pervasive topography found in Psalm 107 with its intimations of death powerfully captures the dismal atmosphere in which the condemned generation lives out its remaining days in the wilderness. And in fact both the sea and Sheol appear in Numbers, reinforcing the extent to which the wilderness is being prepared to become a realm of death. The sea is implicated in the tragedy as the source for the quails in Numbers 11:31 that lead to Israelite deaths. It is also the destination to which the Israelites must return in Numbers 14:25 once they are barred from the promised land. Sheol is none other than the destination of Dathan and Abiram (16:33).

If we examine the concept of Sheol in the bible, we can better observe its parallels to the wilderness as depicted in Numbers. The concept of Sheol evolved over time in ancient Israel but is generally considered to refer to a shadowy underworld, sometimes called "the pit." Theodore Lewis traces the word's connotations as a desolate or devastated place, best translated by "no land," a world remote from God.[62] This notion is close to that of Pederson's "non-world." The bible understands such a non-world as a place in which Israel cannot praise God: "For it is not She'ol that praises you, not [the land of] death that extols you; nor do they who descend into the Pit hope for your grace" (Isaiah 38:18) Psalm 6:6 echoes this description of Sheol. One cannot praise God from there because one is cut off. Psalm 88:6b makes this point explicit. For those in the pit "are cut off from thy hand." By the end of Numbers the similarity between Sheol and the transformed wilderness is striking. The generation is left in the wilderness to die because God has cut it off. The wilderness has in this sense become the equivalent of Sheol.

The wilderness that dominates the spatial geography of the journey is terrifying, but Numbers reminds us that it is made so by the Israelites who wander in it. The text brutally depicts the transformation of a space meant to serve as a temporary staging ground for new life in the land into the people's final destination. The people unwittingly express the desire to make the wilderness into such a space at the moment they cry out: "If only we had died in the land of Egypt ... or if only we would die in this wilderness" (Num. 14:2). God grants their wish, consigning them to oblivion in the wilderness. Their cry sets in motion the creation of a territory fit only for those cast out by society, a "refuge of the outlaw."[63] From that point on, the wilderness exists as a menacing and punishing site, outside the reach of memory, a place to which the new generation, if it transgresses and forgets, could forcibly be returned.[64]

Such a mental geography creates an unmistakable physical dichotomy between the wilderness as the realm of the dead versus the promised land as the site of the living. Through such a dichotomy the editors of Numbers clarify the choice before the people Israel in the most dramatic of terms. A brief perusal of the subject matter of Numbers in the concluding section of the book, 27–36, after the final deaths of the generation in the wilderness, illuminates the choice held out to Israel. The topics – each only relevant once in the land – include inheritance; a calendar of public sacrifice; the observance of the sabbath, the new moons, and the festivals; and the boundaries of the land. Concern with inheritance is particularly pointed. As noted in my chapter 2, a form of inheritance, נחלה, surfaces in these latter chapters in numerous examples: Numbers 26:53–56; 27:7–11; and 34:2 (not an exhaustive list). The repetition of נחלה in the narrative of the second generation reinforces the shift in focus from death in the wilderness to life in the land.

Together, these topics shape a future in which the new generation, after restoring its relationship with God, has resumed its collective life in a new space, the promised land. Note that collective life will be guided and led by the priestly class. This concluding vision of a successful and blessed future in a land not yet conquered remains the ultimate aim and message conveyed by Numbers. Tragically, if they choose correctly the children of Israel must abandon their parents in a wilderness that effectively becomes "a world set apart."[65]

Indeed, the territory inhabited by the dead will forever be cut off from the land of the living. The priestly editors insist that Israel, in each generation, understand that one cannot live in such a wilderness – a site in which appetites and urges dominate, over which priestly law and God's protection have little influence. The people must see they have no choice but to choose life in the land under the political and religious authority of the priests. Only the priests can ensure God's blessing and Israel's future by obtaining the divine presence in the priestly sanctuary.

To ensure the hopeful conclusion of Numbers, the editors do not rely on the power of a priestly vision alone. Seeking to create a deterrent powerful enough to sway each subsequent generation, they find it in the tale of the wilderness generation's fate. Terrifying images of that fate haunt the narrative. The thousands so carefully accounted for in the book's grand opening view of them end their days consigned to a fate of their own making, abandoned in anonymity and obscurity, at a site "no one on earth knows ... [enclosed by] heaps of hills piled up by the storm."[66]

SEVEN

Inheriting the Land

...the viability of a culture inheres in its capacity for resolving conflicts, for explicating differences and renegotiating communal meanings.[1]

The way a story is told is a clue to its meaning.[2]

We project ourselves...past the End, so as to see the structure whole, a thing we cannot do from our spot of time in the middle.[3]

Finally we come, at the end, back to the beginning. In the beginning there were multiple traditions: fragments of legends, tabernacle lists and tribal ones, marvelous poetry, tales of wilderness thirst and hunger, rebellious confrontations, and memories of dangers and desires. And someone (or, more likely, several anonymous figures over time) deftly ordered those diverse texts and impressions into a whole. In so doing the editor(s) produced a memorable narrative of a wilderness journey that lasted forty arduous years.

At journey's end our last glimpse of the new generation of Israelites is a positive one. At the edge of the promised land, they are busying themselves with tribal boundaries and allotments of territory as well as issues of inheritance. Most important, they have a plan for what to do once in the land. They possess a calendar of yearly sacrifices and festival celebrations, events that require the supervision of the priests, sons of Aaron. In other words, even before the new generation enters the land, it finds itself dependent on priestly arrangements, obligated to perform sacrifices in the years ahead under the direction of a clearly demarcated and hierarchical priestly class. The priestly editors crafted this particular concluding portrait of the children of Israel in Numbers by masterfully weaving the diverse collection of materials that came into their possession into a story about the distant past that led inexorably to a future of their devising.

In prior chapters of the present work we observed both the editorial methods and priestly strategies that led to this result. Editorial methods included the skillful weaving together of discrete materials, the juxtaposition of different ideas and events to great advantage, and the purposeful placement of certain independent texts, such as the censuses and the itinerary, at particular points within the broader narrative. Through such an analysis we discovered the extent to which Numbers was a multivocal text yet surprisingly coherent in its final form. Priestly strategies relied on these editorial methods. For instance, the editors shaped Israel's collective memory of the wilderness journey through creative juxtapositions of different types of memory, one leading to communal harmony, the other to chaos. Other strategies included placing the episodes of rebellion together for maximum effect and using the commemorative objects thus produced to counsel Israel to remember wisely so that it would choose wisely, to choose the side of God, Moses, and the priests. Finally, the priestly editors used the reports of Israelite deaths to amplify the terrifying fate of an entire generation liberated from Egypt only to die in the wilderness, reports designed to deter the new generation against repeating the mistakes of its elders. We were able to observe the extent to which each of these strategies assumed the malleability of tradition and the necessity of collective memory.

Both the weaving together of diverse materials and the implementation of the priestly strategies relied on narrative's proclivity to unfold over time. For instance, the editors had at hand a series of events riddled with anger and conflict – the complaints of the people, of Miriam and Aaron, of the scouts, and of Korah – and could use those events to heighten an atmosphere of tension within the camp that became so unbearable that the people Israel could avoid permanent disaster only through the destruction of an entire generation. In other words, the editors relied on the fundamental elements of narrative (plot, sequence, order) to generate a dramatic and highly polemical depiction of the journey as a whole, even if that journey was represented through a range of textual materials. In this final chapter I briefly review and highlight those particular dimensions of narrative relied on by the priestly editors to achieve their coherent version of communal life and authority in the wilderness. At its best, narrative can persuade its reader to accept a certain construction of reality. The priestly editors used the steady unfolding of the biblical narrative, piece by piece and text by discrete text, in order to convince the Israelite audience to accept their construction of reality.

Of course, all narratives have to arrive at an end. An ending is often indispensable to the larger narrative task of constructing and communicating meaning. An ending pulls together the entire narrative, by confirming what came before, recapitulating or summing up the main events, or asserting the "moral" of the tale or its message. This holds true for Numbers, even in, or perhaps because of, its rather curious and anti-climactic final chapter. I intend to account for that final chapter and, in so doing, arrive at the end of the present work.

∾ The narrative process and the making of meaning

In earlier chapters we observed the extent to which the biblical editors made their presence felt through the sequencing of events and the framing of those sequences, the basic building blocks of narrative. It is through just such sequencing and framing of specific texts that the broader message or argument of the narrative is communicated to the reader. After all, narrative will fail to make much sense unless the wide variety of events and actions out of which it is comprised are placed in some kind of chronology. Nowhere is this need for sequence and order more apparent than in a composition such as Numbers, the one biblical work of the Five Books of Moses closest to the model of an anthology. The variety of texts in Numbers must somehow be arranged and ordered. For instance, because it did not begin the book of Numbers but comes in its middle, the Israelite lusting after meat must necessarily follow something else. So the editors place the pivotal tale immediately after the celebratory blowing of trumpets. Or in another example of the sequencing of materials, the announcement of rules in the land for the new generation immediately follows the story in which God condemns their parents. As I have argued in prior chapters, this ordering of events is far more than a tidy putting together of disparate texts. It is not a random decision or coincidence. The meaning of both the specific tale and the larger narrative in which it is embedded lies in the ordering and sequencing of actions and events. As suggested by Labov, the "meaning of 'what happened' is strictly determined by the order and form of its sequence."[4] One can discern the poignancy and perhaps the value of the celebratory blowing of trumpets only by experiencing the loss of those joyous notes in the ominous complaints that follow, complaints that threaten to undo the very possibility of that imagined future in the land. Or one recognizes the source for the new generation's enormous relief as it receives regulations for sacrifices in the land by remembering that just prior to those seemingly dry regulations, the older generation learned that it was denied the chance to enter that land to fulfill them, having itself become a different sort of sacrifice. Meaning emerges out of sequence.

Meaning is also found in the framing of sequential events. As I pointed out in chapter 2, in the case of Numbers we can detect the priestly editing precisely in the way in which the editors framed the consecration of tabernacle and Levite, the rebellions and deaths, with the opening numbering and naming of Israelites, tribe by tribe, in the wilderness camp, a numbering and naming to which they return toward Numbers' end. "Framing provides a means of 'constructing' a world, of characterizing its flow, of segmenting events within that world."[5] In fact, the vivid, at times terrifying world of the wilderness is introduced and contained by a frame that reassures us, focusing us at the beginning and again at the end on the Israelites numbered, ordered, and encamped in the wilderness, first at Sinai and then later on the steppes of Moab. Hope and possibility exist in the frame of the narrative, both at the start of the journey and at its end, but not at its core.

Through such acts as the sequencing and framing of events, narrative conveys its meaning to the reader or listener. And because biblical narrative is collective property, its meaning has been intentionally rendered accessible and public. It provides an arena in which conflicts or simple alternative possibilities, allegedly from the past but with equal claims on the reader's present, can be examined openly. At its most successful, narrative offers us a conception of reality in which such conflicts get resolved and harmony restored. We saw this aspect of narrative at work in the series of increasingly tense, even violent challenges of the scouts, the rebels, and the people to the authority of Moses, Aaron, and God. Bruner reminds us that "the viability of a culture inheres in its capacity for resolving conflicts, for explicating differences and renegotiating communal meanings."[6] Biblical texts such as the social dramas of Numbers 15–17 play a significant role in ensuring the viability of a culture by renegotiating communal meanings and either resolving or, at times, reinforcing communal arrangements. A specific reality becomes so compelling, for whatever reason, that we accept its definition – at times wholeheartedly, at times reluctantly. We have been persuaded.

Of course in the case of Numbers it is most likely the persuasive powers of a series of editors who, over time, have created a narrative of the journey through the wilderness. We have seen the editors shape the biblical narrative through subtle accretions, tinkering with a word here, adding a verse or phrase there. They have also expanded whole sections by supplying more details or placing a self-contained tradition in the midst of a crisis in the wilderness camp in order to elaborate on a point or provide an urgently needed remedy (such as the creation of a special decontaminant in Numbers 19 if one touches a corpse, a growing possibility considering the upsurge in Israelite deaths and the deaths of the spies). We have especially seen the results of the editorial juxtaposition of seemingly contradictory understandings of such key concepts as memory. They rely on narrative sequence and chronology to do their work. This process is described succinctly in the following: "[The priestly editors] adapted from generation to generation the traditions about the past, and shaped them in view of their importance for their own time. In their emerging narrative, traditional memory and new interpretation were interwoven."[7]

∽ Editing the past

What then were the goals of priestly editors in shaping a narrative of the past for their own time? What drove them to deploy the various strategies I have identified in my argument? We attempted to answer those questions in prior chapters by observing the evidence for the creation of a particular set of communal arrangements under priestly rule that aimed to construct a particular reality relevant for the time of the priestly editors. We observed the attempt of the priestly editors to legitimize that particular priestly vision and power structure by placing it in the wilderness past. Thus the line of Aaron dominated the camp (and the Temple complex), while the other Levites remained subjugated to that of Aaron's sons, not just in the wilderness but in perpetuity.

In fact, the influence of the Aaronites was felt throughout the various episodes, and in the final form, of Numbers. Such influence expands through additional ordinances [those found in Num. 1–10 as highlighted in chapter 3] what had already been established earlier in the Sinai revelation: the program for the life of the holy community in purity in the promised land. It envisions a hierocratically constituted community under that priesthood whose authority was established before the time in the land, before the monarchy and its authorizations. Indeed, the priesthood's authority was derived from Yahweh's own revealed instructions to Moses.... for these writers, the meaning also of their campaign story had – and has – to be transparent for their own time. Their story serves as the reminder of the past generations that perished in the wilderness, of their existence outside the promised land, of the abiding promise for their own and their future generations, and of the expectation of compliance with the prescribed ordinances.[8]

In other words, the biblical account serves specific priestly interests. Bruner points out what happens when narrative accounts are no longer neutral. "They have rhetorical aims or illocutionary intentions that are not merely expository but rather partisan, designed to put the case if not adversarially, then at least convincingly in behalf of a particular interpretation."[9] This claim is certainly illustrated in the final form of Numbers. The priestly editors are motivated by their partisan interests to put forward a series of arguments that would lead Israel to feel that they have no choice but to choose the priestly platform. Over and over, we have witnessed the priestly placement of a choice in front of Israel – remember Sinai, not Egypt, so that you may live. Remember the rebels this way, not that, in order that you may live. Choose the side of Moses and Aaron, not that of Korah, so that you are not swallowed by the earth. Choose God's side, not that of your parents, so that you avoid the horror of abandonment in the wilderness. And they have the texts in hand that could create that choice. Through juxtapositions of memory, through social dramas and the objects thus produced, and through the terrible threat at the core of Numbers – the very erasure of memory – the priestly editors indeed show themselves to be highly and intently partisan.

And they are also highly skilled. They have edited together a series of deterrents that would shock any reader out of complacency and gain his or her attention. After all, Numbers is about the destruction of an entire generation, of deaths that number in the thousands. Numbers is about the horror of bodies abandoned to their fate in the obscurity of wilderness, of God's unforgiving fury at that one generation. Yet in the tragedy of the generation the priestly editors find their most imaginative images and arguments, their most fruitful transactions with prior texts and images. They daringly use the fate of the wilderness generation to construct their version of a meaningful future. In fact, they bring about renewed promise not only for the children of those killed off in the wilderness but for their own generation. The editors do not just recount the facts of the journey but somehow find a way to justify the terrible price paid by the wilderness generation.[10] That justification resides in the future possibilities offered to the next generation and those that follow. In other words, the way in which Numbers ends – with the provision of a vividly imagined future life in the land – is as necessary to the priestly editors as the journey itself.

∼ At journey's end

Images of death and abandonment, found in the central chapters of Numbers, are followed in the concluding chapters with an abundance of a very different series of images and a very different sort of detail (as I briefly noted in chapter 6). These images and details convey a people in the midst of vibrant activity in a flourishing community. The Israelites are told how much oil and how much flour will be needed for future sacrifices in the land, and are reminded that a libation needs a hin of wine and a sin offering a single goat. Celebrations of yearly festivals are eagerly anticipated. New leaders will be appointed. Cities of refuge will be established, land divided tribe by tribe, inheritances decreed, even among daughters if no son exists to inherit. Laws will certainly get enacted. Pledges and vows are taken up. A man must not break his pledge. But what of a woman? Shall her vow stand?

It is noteworthy that the variety of topics discussed in the final chapters of Numbers include several legal issues pertaining to women. These issues include the status of vows, concerning not only those taken by daughters and wives but those of a divorced or widowed woman (Num. 30:10). The vows of daughters and wives depend on the confirmation of their fathers or husbands. On the other hand, in the case of divorced or widowed women, the vows they themselves make are binding. The legal system envisioned by the writers of Numbers both constrains and expands the obligations of the female Israelite at the very moment that she is to enter the land. Chapter 30 does make a woman's subordination to the authority of her father or husband quite clear, just as the rest of the narrative in Numbers makes the subordination of the children of Israel to the priestly authority quite clear.

Yet the variety of ordinances found in the last third of Numbers and the discussion of legal fine points also make another point crystal clear. Israel will enter the land with a legal system already subject to revision even while the people are still encamped in the wilderness. In fact, the book of Numbers ends in chapter 36 with just such a revision, that of female inheritance, first described in Numbers 27. My final task will be to account for the ending of Numbers and, in so doing, to find further evidence of the priestly agenda described above, an agenda that shapes and edits the narrative of the journey up until, and including, its end. As Frank Kermode reminds us, "We cannot, of course, be denied an end; it is one of the great charms of books that they have to end."[11]

At first glance it is not surprising that we might miss the charm of Numbers' ending. It is true that the reader has been prepared for a dry, even dull ending because the conflict and violence of the middle chapters of Numbers has long since been replaced with an abundance of rather technical details for the future life in the land. Even so, the matter-of-fact account that forms the ending of Numbers is strikingly anti-climactic even within the context of the last chapters of Numbers. It is also strikingly brief, a mere thirteen verses. The last chapter of Numbers records the complaint of the heads of the clan of the descendants of Gilead who object to a recent ruling concerning the daughters of Zelophehad. Moses acknowledges their complaint and adjusts the regulation accordingly. He then lapses into silence, thus concluding the encounter. In the penultimate verse of Numbers 36 we learn that the daughters marry wisely and thus keep the shares of their father's property within their father's clan. The final verse of Numbers concludes: "These are the commandments and regulations that YHWH commanded by the hand of Moses to the children of Israel on the steppes of Moab, at the Jordan near Jericho." That is it. Indeed, it is rather perplexing and, as such, invites explanation.

I begin with Frank Kermode's proposed function of an ending. He claims that the reader makes a "considerable imaginative investment in coherent patterns which, by the provision of an end, makes possible a satisfying consonance with the origins and with the middle."[12] In the biblical case it is more pertinent to consider how the particular end just described might provide the sought-out coherence not only for the reader but also for the priestly editors. How does the ending provide a "satisfying consonance" with the beginning and middle of the narrative as edited in Numbers? How does the ending serve priestly purposes? Does the revision of a rule of inheritance somehow strengthen the priestly construction of Israel's future reality? In other words, we need to consider why Numbers ends in the fashion that it does.

While we are talking of endings, let me repeat the final verse of Numbers cited above. "These are the commandments and regulations that YHWH commanded by the hand of Moses to the children of Israel on the steppes of Moab, at the Jordan near Jericho." What one immediately notices in this last verse of the book is an echo of the very first verse that opens Numbers: "And YHWH spoke to Moses in the wilderness of Sinai in the tent of meeting on the first day of the second month, in the second year following the exodus from the land of Egypt." In the beginning and in the end God speaks to Moses in a specific setting. Of course, geographical progress has been made on the journey. The wilderness of Sinai has been replaced at journey's end by the steppes of Moab. More significant, God is no longer speaking only to Moses but through Moses to the Israelites, a fitting enough change considering Moses' imminent death outside the land.

But in the end, as in the beginning, the people Israel are not yet in the land. In the end, the very promise of movement is supplanted by details of law and regulation for the eventualities of a still theoretical future. The narrative perspective has changed to reflect that slowing down. Instead of the opening chapters' vista of an entire camp spread out around the tabernacle, the movements of thousands of males over twenty preparing for the census, our vision narrows to a small group comprised of the heads of a single clan presenting a legal matter to Moses, worrying over a ruling that establishes a precedent that they find objectionable. Before entering the land and fulfilling the promise of the opening chapters, apparently the objection of this one clan must be met. In Moses' quick response to their worry and objection, we have a significant clue to the explanation for why Numbers ends in the way that it does. *A legal ruling can and will be revised.* One must assume that this example of legal adaptation is crucial to the broader message of the priestly editors, so crucial that Israel cannot enter the land without establishing a precedent and settling the matter. To make a full accounting of a legal revision as ending, we must begin with the ruling as first developed in Numbers 27.

Numbers 27 opens, as many chapters in the bible, without an obvious association to the preceding chapter. "And the daughters of Zelophehad, son of Hepher son of Gilead son of Machir son of Manasseh, of Manassite family, son of Joseph – came forward and these are the names of the daughters:

Mahlah, Noah, Hoglah, Milcah, and Tirzah." So many names. If we were paying attention, we would remember hearing about these daughters of Zelophehad before. They are listed, somewhat conspicuously because they are part of a much longer list dominated by male names, in the prior chapter, in Numbers 26:33. Not only that, but the prior chapter makes clear that the entire generation of which Zelophehad was a member exists no more, having been condemned by God to die in the wilderness. Thus Numbers 27 fittingly enough opens with a story that concerns the new generation. Rather unusually, it is the story of a new generation of daughters.

Even though the daughters come forward in Numbers 27:1 we are not immediately informed of their reason for doing so. No obvious object of the verb is mentioned in verse 1. We are left hanging. The lack of an object of the verb reminds one of the "taking" of Korah in Numbers 16:1, as that verse also fails to mention a direct object. Of course, the difference in the two situations could not be more striking. In the case of Korah, the disagreement is resolved only through the rather dramatic killing off of the dissenters. Here, as we shall see momentarily, the disagreement will be resolved peacefully. This peaceful resolution of disagreement in the new generation signals a return to the smooth functioning that marked the opening chapters of Numbers.

As the daughters speak, they make the connection obvious between the demise of the previous generation in Numbers 26 and their present concern. They are worried about the preservation of their father's name:

> Our father died in the wilderness but he was not among the assembled faction against YHWH, in the assembly of Korah but rather in his own sin he died; and he had no sons. Why let our father's name be lost from his family because he has no son? Give us a holding in the midst of our father's kinsmen! (Num. 27:3–4)

The daughters articulate a shrewd, worldly concern. They are anxious about property and the proper channels of inheritance. The agreed-upon rules apparently fail to consider just such an eventuality – living in a family without a brother who would typically inherit the father's property. The daughters of Zelophehad are right to be concerned. Their future financial security depends on the clarification of such uncertainty and the closing of such a gap in the laws of inheritance. Their worry takes the form of an anxiety over the loss of their father's name. As we have seen, the linking of a family name and property is important precisely because it establishes a claim on behalf of the next generation. But in the present context, such an anxiety is not only pragmatic but poignant. After all, an entire generation has just been wiped out in a rather anonymous and abrupt fashion. We can well imagine that the preservation or loss of countless names would be a pressing matter among the new generation. Perhaps for that very reason, the names of the five daughters are listed not just once but three times, in Numbers 26:33, 27:1, and 36:11, as if to reassure the new generation that it will not share the fate of its elders.

In fact, the new generation is immediately assured of the continuation of a particular family line and, in contrast to the dead in the desert, especially assured of that line's interdependence with property in the land. Reassurance comes about through Moses' handling of a question of inheritance. It cannot be a coincidence that the first issue for Moses to resolve on behalf of the next generation has to do with this question of posterity, of names lost or preserved, and of land in which such preservation and commemoration might be guaranteed in the future. In other words, the confirmation of the prior generation's demise in the wilderness in Numbers 26:64–65 directly raises the issue of continuity and transmission, of the transfer of land from fathers to their sons – or in our present case, to their daughters – and of the inexorable passage of time. Notably, the present example provides yet another example of the concern with memory and the forms that it takes that is a hallmark of the priestly editing of Numbers. This time the relationship between the generations and the memory of the past is mediated through issues of inheritance and holdings of land.

After the daughters come forward, Moses matches their action by his own parallel act of coming forward. He seeks a judgment from God.[13] God labels the daughters' objection to current arrangements of inheritance correct (כן in the Hebrew) and instructs Moses to give them a "hereditary holding" (JPS trans.) among their father's kinsmen in language that is identical to their original request in verse 4.[14] The verse is almost poetic:

> You shall surely give them a hereditary holding in the midst of their father's kinsmen And you shall transfer their father's inheritance to them. (Num. 27:7)

"Surely give" and "transfer" are in parallel to one another. So too are "hereditary holding" and "father's inheritance." The "father's kinsmen" is parallel to "them" (in the Hebrew plural feminine). The last parallelism in particular makes the point. Female daughters will legally replace more distantly related male kinsmen when it comes to inheriting the holdings of their fathers.

Yet God has not finished speaking. Instead of defining the matter as a specific case concerning the daughters of Zelophehad and leaving it there, God elaborates on the divine judgment by stating a general principle. Whenever a man dies without leaving behind a son, his property shall be transferred to his daughter. If he has no daughter, then his property can be transferred to his brothers. Failing that, the property can be transferred to the man's father's brothers or, as a last resort, to the nearest relatives within the clan. The whole incident concludes with a statement defining the regulation as a law of procedure (חקת משפט) for the children of Israel as God commanded Moses. We have a rather straightforward account of a legal issue peacefully and quickly resolved and a wonderful example of female agency.[15]

That the legal issue concerns the preservation of a name as well as issues of inheritance suggests an awareness on the part of the priestly editors that a new chapter in the life of Israel has begun. An entire generation has just been irrevocably lost, as Numbers 26 makes brutally clear. Now, in the very next chapter, the children of Israel learn that they can avoid the terrors of anonymous death by preserving a father's name in the concrete rules of inheritance and land holding among members of a clan. The rest of Numbers 27 continues to develop this theme of a new chapter in the life of Israel. The shift between generations is highlighted when we are reminded of the imminent death of Moses. He will be replaced by Joshua. The establishment of a law of procedure at the opening of Numbers 27 functions to preserve a memory of Moses as a legal adjudicator while at the same time presenting a legal principle that will outlast Moses.

But does it? In chapter 36, Moses revises the ruling of chapter 27. The chapter opens abruptly, appearing at first glance to have nothing in common with prior chapters after chapter 27, especially the chapter that it immediately follows. On closer observation, Numbers 35:1 and the final verse of Numbers 36 form an *inclusio*. In both verses, but nowhere else in either chapter, God speaks to or through Moses at the steppes of Moab. A more significant connection between the two chapters exists, having to do with *additional refinements of the rules of land holdings*. Chapter 35 develops rules for the Levites to inhabit particular cities once in the land that will also function as cities of refuge. To do so, chapter 35 tinkers with the recently established laws of inheritance. "In assigning towns from the holdings of the Israelites, take more from the larger groups and less from the smaller, so that each assigns towns to the Levites in proportion to the share it receives"(Num. 35:8, JPS trans.). In addition, one who claims sanctuary in the cities of refuge inhabited by the Levites may return to his own property holding after the death of the high priest (35:28). As we have seen, Moses returns to the topic of land holdings in chapter 36. Perhaps there is even a connection between chapters 35 and 36, though admittedly more tenuous, in the last words of chapter 35. God directly speaks to the people, reminding them that God will dwell in their midst in the land. Yet as chapter 36 makes apparent, before the people can secure that outcome and obtain God's presence in their midst by entering the land, the question of inheritance must once more be addressed, this time leading to a revision of God's ruling in Numbers 27. Returning to that topic suggests something crucial, even urgent, must be at stake. Israel will not enter the land before the resolution of the objections of the clan of Gilead.

Chapters 27 and 36 obviously have a great deal in common. In fact, they form a mini frame for the final section of Numbers, a section devoted to the future in the land as described above. "The accounts of the daughters of Zelophehad in Numbers 27 and 36 ... form an *inclusio* of the events and organization of the new generation whose emergence is marked by the second census list in chapter 26."[16] But chapter 36 does more than reiterate the events of chapter 27 as a neat conclusion to this leg of the journey. Chapter 36 *alters* God's earlier ruling on behalf of the daughters of Zelophehad, curtailing their freedom of choice when it comes to whom they may marry in order to keep the land holding of their father within the same clan.

In place of the daughters, in chapter 36 it is the heads of the clan of the descendants of Gilead that come forward to speak. Noting first that God had instructed Moses to assign the land in Israel by lot, they reiterate God's command to Moses that the inheritance of Zelophehad goes to his daughters. It is striking that in their recapitulation of the earlier ruling they leave out the expressed concern by the daughters over the loss of their father's name. This is not a concern shared by the rest of the members of the clan of Gilead. They then launch into their complaint:

> Now if they marry members of (another) tribe of the Children of Israel their inheritance will be lost from the inheritance of our fathers and be added to the inheritance of the tribe into which they marry; from our allotted inheritance it will be lost. (Num. 36:3)[17]

In the subtle fashion of the biblical text, the verb in 36:3 used to describe their fear that the portion will be "lost," נגרע, is precisely the same root used by the daughter themselves when announcing the loss, יגרע, of their father's name in 27:4. The incident highlights the struggle between competing claims – immediate family memory as represented by the name of Zelophehad in addition to female inheritance of his property juxtaposed to broader rights of property as represented by the heads of the clan. Thus we can understand why the heads of the clan begin by mentioning the lot. It was intended, at least in part, to ensure the distribution of the land of Israel among the tribes and clans in an orderly fashion. If the daughters can marry away from their clan, taking their land with them, that careful distribution will be upset to the detriment of the clan. Thus an unintended consequence, or a loophole, has been pointed out, an exception that works to the detriment of the other members of the clan.

The legal problem presented by Numbers 27 has to be dealt with before Numbers can end. Moses quickly responds in Numbers 36 by revising God's original pronouncement. Notably, the narration at this point omits any description of Moses approaching God. Moses now only reports having done so (Num. 36:5). Thus while in Numbers 27 God acknowledges the daughters' claim directly, now that claim is revised indirectly through Moses. Even so, it stands. The new pronouncement instructs the daughters of Zelophehad to marry into a clan within their father's tribe. Again the ruling moves from the particular case to include a more general principle, but again only through Moses' recounting of it. Moses announces the final ruling in strikingly repetitive language:

> No inheritance of the Israelites may pass over from one tribe to another, but the Israelites must remain bound each to the ancestral portion of his tribe. Every daughter among the Israelite tribes who inherits a share must marry someone from a clan of her father's tribe, in order that every Israelite may keep his ancestral share. Thus no inheritance shall pass over from one tribe to another, but the Israelite tribes shall remain bound each to its portion. (Num. 36:7–9, JPS trans.)

Note that the third verse basically repeats the first verse, thereby drawing attention to the all-important middle verse, which states the revised rule. In this fashion chapter 36 limits "the circumstances under which the original judgment can be applied. And the purpose for the limitation is to hold heritable property within the clan of the dead father."[18]

The incident ends without protest. The daughters of Zelophehad, whose names are again listed for the reader, dutifully acquiesce in Moses' judgment and marry within their clan. Finally, as mentioned above, the very last verse of Numbers shifts our attention away from the particulars of this case to inform us of the entirety of God's commandments and regulations, at least those given on the steppes of Moab.

In the present rereading of Numbers I have repeatedly sought to account for seemingly random or contradictory insertions and/or juxtapositions of texts. In so doing I have often been able to propose the editorial logic of such juxtapositions, usually through considering how two obviously diverse texts interact, what language they might share, which viewpoint they might challenge by being placed next to one another, or which point of view might be reinforced by such placement. More often than not, the sequencing of texts is driven by the strategies, rhetoric, and persuasive power of the priestly editors. The placement of chapter 36 at the end of Numbers provides a final example of the work of the priestly editors. This is so even if, as some commentators have argued, chapter 36 was placed at the end of Numbers as an afterthought. Even as an afterthought, it concludes the book and remains the final impression offered the reader of the journey and its end.[19]

Why then should Numbers end in such a legalistic and dry fashion? Why should we return to an established legal ruling only to revise it? Most intriguingly, why do we again hear the names of the five daughters of Zelophehad? The very last event, an event that leaves an indelible impression in the mind of the reader because it is last, informs us that Israel is entering the land with the most important possession of all, the knowledge that the community will be governed by law and legal stipulations, but that such rulings are subject to legal review and revision (unfortunately in our present case through restricting who the daughters of Israel might marry). In other words, the legal culture that Israel is to inherit from Moses and to take into the land under priestly supervision is a living and growing one. As they enter their future lives, the children of Israel receive a reassuring clarification of the contours of that life. Their community will be shaped and guided by a flexible legal culture that is their legacy, originating, so the priestly editors endeavor to show us, in the wilderness.

That those legal stipulations are concerned with the relationship between a father and his daughters beautifully reinforces the underlying, even haunting force of this narrative of two generations. As such, chapter 36 provides a satisfying conclusion to the book of Numbers. Not only is the name of Zelophehad preserved, but so are those of his daughters. In so doing, the narrator personifies the core concern of Numbers – the preservation and transmission of tradition and collective memory – and the ultimate resolution of that concern in the new generation through the way in which the narrative ends. Thanks to the thrice-stated recitation of their names, the memory of Mahlah, Tirzah, Hoglah, Milcah, and Noah, even their agency, is preserved. It is fitting that at journey's end, and the very ending of the book, we are left with the names not of those bound by the desert but those who will at any moment leave it behind.

The Priestly Sphere of Activity
in the Book of Numbers

	Chapter
Aaron the high priest	
Aaron joins Moses in numbering the people	1:3
Aaron and his sons bless the children of Israel	6
Aaron mounts the lamps of the menorah	8:3
Aaron officiates in turning the Levites into elevated offerings	8
Aaron and sons supervise the service of the Levites in the tent of meeting	8:22
Aaron aids Moses in ruling on who can celebrate Pesach	9:6
Shabbat violator brought before Moses and Aaron	15:33
Aaron confronts competing claims of holiness by Korah the Levite	16
Aaron saves the people by standing between the living and the dead	17:11–15
Aaron's flowering rod	17:23
Formalization of the functions of Aaron and his descendants	18
Aaron deals with shrine and altar	18:5
Again the Levites are subordinate to Aaron and his sons	18:6
Payments to the Aaronites (the various sacrifices and shekalim)	18:8–20
An everlasting covenant of salt for Aaron and his descendants	18:19
Aaron implicated at the Rock; priestly succession to Eleazar	20
The sons of Aaron (and his grandson)	
Eleazar and Ithamar serve as priests for Aaron	3:4
Eleazar supervises the Levites	3:32
Aaron and his sons bless the children of Israel	6:23
Ithamar supervises the Merarites	7:8

The sons of Aaron blow the trumpets	10:8
Eleazar collects the ashes and the fire pans	17:1–5
Eleazar deals with the purifying substance formed from the red heifer	19
Eleazar receives his father's vestments	20
Phinehas (son of Eleazar, son of Aaron) slays Cozbi and Zimri	25:7–8
Phinehas and his seed receive the eternal priestly covenant	25:12–13
Eleazar helps Moses take a new census	26
Eleazar listens to the judicial case with Moses	27
Eleazar will give Joshua advice from the Urim	27:21
Phinehas accompanies Israel into battle with the trumpets	31:6
Eleazar instructs the people on rules for purifying booty	31:21
He is also involved in all inquiries	31
Eleazar and Moses listen to the Reubenites and Gadites	32:2
Eleazar and Joshua split the land along with the elders	34:16–17

Generic "Cohen"

Supervises a variety of regulations	5–6
Makes expiation on behalf of the community and the individual for inadvertent error	15
Supervises the proceedings involving the red heifer	19:6

The Levites

They take care of the tabernacle	1:48–59
Details for taking apart and transporting the tabernacle	3–4
Receive the gifts of the tribes from Moses	7:5–9
Attend to Aaron and his sons	8:13
Serve Aaron and his sons and receive tithes from the people	18
Cities of Levites – cities of refuge	35

The Use and Variation of God's Address
to Moses and to Aaron

The details of the address

1. The formula וידבר יהוה אל משה occurs at least forty-two times.

2. It also occurs a few times with the addition of Aaron.

3. A different version ויאמר יהוה אל משה appears in Numbers 11:16 and 23, a distinct unit (likely to be nonpriestly) concerning the gathering of seventy elders and of quail that the redactor might have left untouched from an earlier version. In addition, the same formula reappears in chapter 12, also a distinct, nonpriestly unit containing the challenge of the siblings against Moses.

4. God also speaks only to Aaron: ויאמר יהוה אל אהרן

Interpreting the distinctions in address

The more common formula of וידבר יהוה אל משה לאמר is found in almost every chapter of Numbers. It usually introduces a new piece of legislation or a commandment that requires the weight and authority of God. The formula creates a situation in which Israel becomes "the special creation by word (commandments and the like) of God...."[1] Certain traditions – the precise treatment of skin eruptions, confessions of wrongdoing, the steps in becoming a nazir – are being legitimated by the authority of divine command.

Aaron is included in the formula when the topic to be introduced directly concerns him, especially in Numbers 4 when the dominance of Aaron and his sons over the Levites is clearly established. There are also times when God addresses only Aaron, such as in 18:1, 18:8, and 18:20.[2] Chapter 18 contains matters of great priestly concern. Therefore it makes sense that the formula would exclusively single out Aaron and exclude Moses. Through such attention to formulaic phrases on the micro-level one detects the hand of a later presence organizing and linking the various rituals, laws, and commandments while at the same time legitimating them through their attribution to God's word spoken to Moses or, on rare but significant occasion, to Aaron alone.

Death Reports

In what follows, I summarize the ways in which three groups die in the wilderness as narrated in Numbers 11–25. These include the wilderness generation, the dissenters and idolaters, and the leaders Miriam and Aaron. In identifying the length of reports, I omit much of the narrative leading up to the death but rather focus exclusively on the immediate action and moment of death. I also note whether burial is mentioned.

Chapter, verse, and subject	Question of burial	Length
11:1 A portion of the people are threatened in a consuming fire of the Lord.	No mention of burial	One verse
11:33–34 The meat eaters die by plague/מכה.	This report includes the only mention of the people receiving a burial. The site is named after the incident: *Kibroth-hattaavah,* literally, burial places of the craving.	Two verses
14:36–38 The spies die by plague, מגפה.	No mention of burial	Three verses
14:45 The attempted conquerors die from the shattering blows of their enemies.	No mention of burial	One verse
15:35–36 The wood gatherer is stoned by the community.	No mention of burial	Two verses

Chapter, verse and subject	Question of burial	Length
16:27–33 The families of Dathan and Abiram are swallowed by the earth.	Buried alive	Seven verses
16:35 The 250 supporters of Korah die in a consuming fire of the Lord.	Refers to charred remains, (Num. 17:1) but no mention of burial	One verse
17:11–15 The protesters of the deaths of "the Lord's people" are killed in a plague, נגף / מגפה.	No mention of burial	Five verses (Israelite deaths occur in 17:14)*
20:1 Miriam's death.	She is buried	One verse
20: 23–29 Aaron's death.	No burial is mentioned, only the location	Seven verses
21:6 Many Israelites die.	No mention of burial	One verse
25:6–15 Phinehas slays the Israelite and the Moabite woman. The remainder of the generation die at Baal-Peor in a plague, מגפה.	No mention of burial	Ten verses (Israelite deaths occur in 25:9)*

* Note that in chapters 17 and 25, the priest stops the plague. Thus in both, the death reports of the generation are longer and more complicated in order to highlight the role of the priest.

Proper and Improper Treatment of the Dead

A partial list of biblical references to the proper and improper treatment of the dead outside the book of Numbers.

I. Within Torah

Genesis 23:4 Abraham negotiates for a family tomb on behalf of his deceased wife Sarah. The episode illustrates the importance of having property in order to have a tomb to bury one's loved ones.

Exodus 14:11 "Were there no graves in Egypt that you brought us out to die in this wilderness?" A matter-of-fact statement that Israelites expected to be buried in graves at the time of death.

Deuteronomy 28:26 In the midst of the curses against Israel: "Your carcasses shall become food for all the birds of the sky and all the beasts of the earth, with none to frighten them off." Note that this is nearly identical to Jeremiah 7:33.

II. Within Prophets

I Samuel 31 This chapter describes the humiliating way in which the Philistines treated Saul. The disrespect to his corpse triggered shock and humiliation among the children of Israel. After his death he lay exposed on the hill for a day, had his head cut off and armor spread among the Philistines, and then was impaled on a wall at Beth Shean. The next day the inhabitants of Jabesh-gilead heard about it and removed him, burned him, and buried his bones under a tree.

I Kings 13 This chapter narrates the story of a prophet from Judah who prophesized against Jeroboam but ended up disobeying God by eating and drinking with the local elderly prophet. His punishment is announced in verse 22: "your corpse shall not come to the grave of your fathers." After being struck down by a lion, his corpse remains lying alongside the road, exposed until the elderly prophet comes and buries him. He will be buried by the old prophet in the prophet's own grave, but will not be able to be gathered to his own fathers in Judah.

This tale conveys both the importance of burial, the horror of exposure, usually associated with divine wrath, and the practice of being buried in a family tomb.

I Kings 14:11 God's punishment against the house of Jeroboam: "Anyone belonging to Jeroboam who dies in the town shall be devoured by dogs; and anyone who dies in the open country shall be eaten by the birds of the air; for YHWH has spoken."

Isaiah 14

This chapter offers excellent insight into ideas of what happens after death as well as a reference to the strong political dimensions of dying, including the question of one's location after death. The target of wrath is the king of Babylon. The shades of all earth's chieftains were roused in Sheol in order to greet the king of Babylon. In 14:10b–11a they announce:

> So you have become stricken as we were,
> You have become like us!
> Your pomp is brought down to Sheol.

He will find a bed of worms and a blanket of maggots in Sheol.

This is clearly envisioned as the opposite of where as a king he might have expected to spend his death, in the heavens.

Now the real punishment of this king is spelled out in verse 18. Other kings were properly laid in their tombs in honor. But not this reviled king. Verses 19–20 describe his fate:

> While you were left lying unburied
> Like loathsome carrion
> Like a trampled corpse . . .
> You shall not have a burial like them.

Isaiah 38:18

Mention of "Death" as a physical location equivalent to Sheol. One descends into Sheol, also referred to as the pit.

Jeremiah 7

In this chapter Jeremiah condemns the people of Judah; how shall they be punished? They will run out of room for burial – even in a place like Tophet.

7:33: "The carcasses of this people shall be food for the birds of the sky and the beasts of the earth, with none to frighten them off."

The result:

7:34: "For the land shall be desolate" (in effect, returning to a state of wilderness as depicted in Numbers).

Jeremiah 16

Describes the proper practices when you visit a house of mourning: lamentation and condolence. But in the time of Jeremiah God prohibits those practices.

> 16:6 Great and small shall die in this land
> They shall not be buried; men shall not lament them
> Nor gash and tonsure themselves for them
> 16:7 Nor break bread for a mourner
> To comfort him for bereavement,
> Nor offer a cup of consolation.

Translations, Jewish Publication Society.

Notes

CHAPTER 1 DESERT BOUND

1. Hayyim Nahman Bialik, "Metei Midbar," in *Selected Poems*, trans. Ruth Nevo (Israel: Dvir, 1981).

2. Stephen Owen, *Remembrances* (Cambridge: Harvard University Press, 1986), 102.

3. Referring to Numbers as a "book" is of course inaccurate. I do so for convenience. The five "books" of the Torah were originally written on scrolls and only later printed in book form. For a history of writing the Torah, see the work and bibliography of William Schniedewind, *How the Bible Became a Book* (Cambridge: Cambridge University Press, 2004); Isaac Rabinowitz, Ross Brann, and David I. Owen, *A Witness Forever* (Bethesda: CDL Press, 1993); and D. J. Wiseman, "Books in the Ancient World," in *The Cambridge History of the Bible* vol. 1, ed. Peter Ackroyd and Christopher Evans (Cambridge: Cambridge University Press, 1970).

4. The stock of traditions of the wilderness period include Hosea 2, 9; Deuteronomy 8, 29, 32; Jeremiah 2, 31 ; Ezekiel 20, and Psalm 106. See also Shemaryahu Talmon, "The Desert Motif in the Bible and in Qumran Literature," in *Biblical Motifs, Origins and Transformations*, ed. Alexander Altmann (Cambridge: Harvard University Press, 1966).

5. In chapter 3 I examine the interests that shaped the priestly editing of Numbers and survey the possible historical contexts in which they wrote.

6. Daniele Hervieu-Leger, *Religion as a Chain of Memory*, trans. Simon Lee (New Brunswick, N. J.: Rutgers University Press, 2000), 126.

7. Bialik, "Metei Midbar."

8. Robert Pogue Harrison's stunning description comes in the midst of a study of Conrad's use of the sea in *The Dominion of the Dead* (Chicago: University of Chicago Press, 2003), 12.

9. For a useful discussion of the relation between narrative and the development of communal identity, see *We Are a People*, ed. Paul R. Spickard and W. Jeffrey

Burroughs (Philadelphia: Temple University Press, 2000), esp. Stephen Cornell, "That's the Story of Our Life" (41–53).

10. In a discussion of Jerome Bruner's work by Cornell, "That's the Story of Our Life," 45 and n. 10.

11. The notion that narrative may embody evidence of both intra- and intergroup struggle is developed at length in the work of Stephen Cornell. He writes: "Different insiders may tell radically different versions of their own story, and one subgroup may have sufficient resources to dominate the storytelling and control the more public narrative. Much of the dynamic of both inter- and intra-group relations is a contest for whose version of a particular identity narrative will prevail." Cornell, "That's the Story of Our Life," 47. Raymond Williams describes the ways in which different versions of tradition compete in even more forceful tones, writing: "It is at the vital points of connection, where a version of the past is used to ratify the present and to indicate directions for the future, that a selective tradition is at once powerful and vulnerable. Powerful because it is so skilled in making active selective connections, dismissing those it does not want. . . . attacking those it cannot incorporate as 'unprecedented' or alien. Vulnerable because the real record is effectively recoverable, and many of the alternative or opposing practical continuities are still available." Raymond Williams, *Notes on Marxism and Literature* (Oxford: Oxford University Press, 1977), 116. I am using the biblical narratives in Numbers as data to substantiate the observations made by Cornell and Williams.

12. As quoted in Hervieu-Leger, *Chain of Memory*, 126.

13. Deuteronomy has long been considered a separate book, containing fewer priestly materials and less focus on a priestly leadership than Exodus, Leviticus, or Numbers. However, it was probably placed in its present position as the conclusion to the Torah by the priestly redactors of those works.

14. In Deuteronomy Moses looks back on the events of forty years, having resigned himself to the fate of the generation and having lived through it. The sense of immediate crisis so palpable in Numbers is gone, though it is replaced by a brooding over an ominous future in which Israel will again fail God.

15. Harrison, *Dominion of the Dead*, 22.

16. For further details on these finds, see Baruch A. Levine, *Numbers* (New York: Doubleday, 1993), 73 and 77. For a recent discussion of the issues as well as a bibliography on memory and historicity in relation to the Exodus from Egypt, see Ronald Hendel, "The Exodus in Biblical Memory," in *Remembering Abraham* (Oxford: Oxford University Press, 2005).

17. Edward Shils, *Tradition* (Chicago: University of Chicago Press, 1981), 12.

18. Eric Hobsbawm and Terence Ranger, *The Invention of Tradition* (Cambridge: Cambridge University Press, 1983), 9.

19. Joseph Blenkinsopp, *Sage Priest Prophet* (Kentucky: Westminster John Knox Press, 1995), 7.

20. Marc Zvi Brettler, *How to Read the Bible* (Philadelphia: Jewish Publication Society, 2005), 35–36.
21. Shils, *Tradition*, 24.
22. The phrase appears three times in Numbers: 10:8, 15:15, and 18: 23. For the broader discussion of the phrase, see Israel Knohl, *The Sanctuary of Silence* (Minneapolis: Fortress Press, 1995), 46–55. Let me cite Baruch Levine's explanation for the spelling of YHWH. It is "a consonantal transcription of the Tetragrammaton that avoids the form 'Yahweh' which I regard as uncertain" (*Numbers*, 88). I have used YHWH as a translation of the tetragrammaton in order to avoid using "Lord." Because the biblical God is envisioned in male terms, the use of the male pronoun is unavoidable as I translate the relevant texts. The use of such pronouns, however, by no means assumes that God is male but rather that God is portrayed thus in the bible. Please note that there is evidence within the biblical text of female imagery for God, most particularly in Isaiah.
23. Avishai Margalit, *The Ethics of Memory* (Cambridge: Harvard University Press, 2002), 61.
24. For instance, though memory is inextricably linked to tradition, its very selectivity makes the transmission of tradition necessarily partial and incomplete. George Allan captures the dynamic: "I don't create my heritage out of whole cloth. I remember it, and in cooperation with others give it new saliencies depending on what we might think important enough to preserve." Allan, *The Importance of the Past* (Albany: State University of New York Press, 1986), 77.

    Another interesting study of the interaction between tradition and memory to which I am indebted is that of Angelika Rauch, *The Hieroglyph of Tradition* (Teaneck, N.J.: Fairleigh Dickinson University Press, 2000). The work of Ilana Pardes, *Countertraditions in the Bible* (Cambridge: Harvard University Press, 1992), has influenced my readings of the "counternarratives" of Numbers as I attend to multiple voices and views present in the text, particularly a text with such a long and varied history of composition. Two additional works of Pardes that are relevant include an essay titled: "The Biography of Ancient Israel: Imagining the Birth of a Nation," *Comparative Literature* 49, no. 1 (Winter 1997): 24–41, and *The Biography of Ancient Israel* (Berkeley: University of California Press, 2000).

    Finally, two recent works already mentioned nicely corroborate much of my method of reading the Hebrew bible while paying attention to how memory operates within its texts. These works include Mark Smith, *The Memoirs of God* (Minneapolis: Augsburg Fortress Press, 2004), and Ronald Hendel, *Remembering Abraham*.
25. In spite of the absence of individual memory, the term often used for the people in Hebrew – עַם – does capture the movement between individual and collective remembering. It is a flexible noun, accompanied either by a singular

or a plural verb, as in the following examples: "And the people cried out (ויצעק העם, singular) to Moses" (Num. 11:2). Three chapters later, the verb is in the plural: "and the people wept that night" (ויבכו העם בלילה ההוא) (Num. 14:1).

26. Noa Gedi and Yigal Elam, "Collective Memory – What Is It?" *History and Memory* 8, no. 1 (Spring/Summer 1996): 30–50, 34.

27. Ibid., 43.

28. Gerdien Jonker, *The Topography of Remembrance* (New York: E. J. Brill Leiden, 1995), 28. See also Jonker's useful discussion of the theory of Maurice Halbwachs, 18–29.

29. Margalit, *Ethics of Memory*, 147.

30. Natalie Zemon Davis and Randolph Starn, "Introduction," *Representations* 26 (Spring 1989): 1–6, 2.

31. Pierre Nora, "Between Memory and History: Les Lieux de Memoire" *Representations* 26 (Spring 1989): 7–24, 9.

32. For an example of such an approach, see Amos Funkenstein, *Perceptions of Jewish History* (Berkeley: University of California Press, 1993).

33. Owen, *Remembrances*, 114. On the anniversary of the bombings of the World Trade Center, Leon Wieseltier reflected on the character of collective memory: "Most of us will be remembering an event that we never saw . . . we were not strictly speaking, witnesses of what happened; and yet we gained a kind of knowledge by acquaintance." Leon Wieseltier, "Washington Diarist: A Year Later," *The New Republic*, September 2, 2002.

34. Richard Terdiman, *Present Past* (Ithaca: Cornell University Press, 1993), 225.

35. For details, see David Lowenthal, *The Past Is a Foreign Country* (Cambridge: Cambridge University Press, 1985).

36. Ibid., 206.

37. For specific citations of the uses of זכר as a noun and as a verb in the Torah, see Gerhard Lisowsky, *Konkordanz Zum Hebraischen Alten Testament* (Stuttgart: Wurttembergische Bibelanstalt, 1958), 444–447.

38. In addition to זכר, two other Herbrew terms connected to keeping the past in mind also occur in Exodus 12–13 – שמר, "observe," and פקד, "surely take notice." These three terms – remember, observe, and take notice – are the key verbs in the Torah for dealing with the past. It is not a surprise that all three are in use during the foundational narrative of Israelite history – the liberation from Egypt and all that event entails for the future relationship of God and Israel.

39. God's liberation of Israel from Egypt does not provide the only motive for Israel's behavior in the ritual and ethical realm. God's creation motivates the memory and observance of the Shabbat in Exodus 20:8. Additionally, the collective memory of slavery compels the people to treat their own dependents justly as commanded in Deuteronomy 5:15, 16:12, and 24:18, 22.

40. In this regard, note the difference between Exodus and Deuteronomy concerning the command to place a sign between the eyes. In Exodus 13:9 you shall place a sign (אות) on your hands and a reminder (זכרון) between your eyes. In

Deuteronomy the sign on your hands remains but the reminder between your eyes is now a frontlet (טוטפת).

41. Rabinowitz et. al., *A Witness Forever*, 40.

42. In contrast to Deuteronomy, Numbers cites very few examples of writing. It is used twice in ritual contexts – the ordeal of the *sotah* in chapter 5 and in writing Aaron's name upon a rod that subsequently flowers in Numbers 17. As part of the ordeal in Numbers 5, the priest writes a curse on parchment. He then rubs the ink off in water, creating a mixture called the "waters of bitterness." The curses written in ink are meant to dissolve into the water and induce a spell. The defendant must then drink the mixture to determine guilt or innocence. Writing in this context should be considered not a strategy of preservation, but rather a key diagnostic ingredient in a punishing ordeal. In Numbers 17 the writing of Aaron's name is also utilitarian – confirming and certifying his role as leader of the tribe of Levi. There is one example of writing in Numbers that is noteworthy for our purposes. Moses writes down an itinerary of the journey in Numbers 33:2, thus creating a record of the past. But nowhere else in Numbers is writing used to preserve the past.

43. H. Eising's discussion and citation of Schottroff's point of view can be found in G. Johannes Botterweck and Helmer Ringgren, *Theological Dictionary of the Old Testament*, vol. 4, (Grand Rapids: William B. Eerdmans, 1980), 81.

44. Brevard S. Childs, *Memory and Tradition in Israel* (Naperville, Ill.: A. R. Allenson, 1962), 89.

45. Yosef Hayim Yerushalmi, *Zakhor* (Seattle: University of Washington Press, 1982), 5.

46. Ibid., 5.

47. Ibid., 10.

48. Ibid., 11.

49. Ibid., 10.

50. See, e.g., Yerushalmi's comments on the use of memory in *Zakhor*: "they reach a crescendo in the Deuteronomic history and in the prophets," ibid., 9.

51. Even the two most recent and highly insightful studies of memory cited in note 24 above, that of Mark Smith and Ronald Hendel, overlook the remarkable problem that memory poses for Moses and the priestly editors in Numbers.

52. Owen, *Remembrances*, 102.

53. Mary Douglas assumes the purposefulness of the editors of Numbers: "the book has been carefully constructed.... the many repetitions and jumps of context are not accidental." See Douglas, *In the Wilderness* (Sheffield: JSOT Press, 1993), 83.

CHAPTER 2 WEAVING BY DESIGN

1. John Barton's collapse of method and theory is worth mentioning at the outset: "Biblical 'methods' are theories rather than methods: theories which result

from the formalizing of intelligent intuitions about the meaning of biblical texts." John Barton, *Reading the Old Testament* (Philadelphia: Westminster Press, 1984), 205, as quoted in Edward L. Greenstein, *Essays on Biblical Method and Translation* (Atlanta: Scholars Press, 1989), 21.

2. For an early attempt at identifying the sources in Numbers, see George Gray, *A Critical and Exegetical Commentary on Numbers* (Edinburgh: T. T. Clark, 1903). For more recent attempts, see the work of Jacob Milgrom and Baruch Levine, both of whom have written commentaries on the book of Numbers in which they identify texts as belonging to different sources or in some instances, outside the sources of the documentary hypothesis. See Jacob Milgrom, *Numbers, JPS Torah Commentary* (Philadelphia: Jewish Publication Society, 1990), and Levine, *Numbers.* For an attempt to discuss the composite sources of Numbers 11 as well as additional bibliographic references to those seeking to precisely identify sources in Numbers, see the article and notes of Benjamin Sommer, "Reflecting on Moses: The Redaction of Numbers 11," *Journal of Biblical Literature* 118, no. 4 (Winter 1999): 601–624.

3. Ernst Nicholson, *The Pentateuch in the Twentieth Century* (Oxford: Clarendon Press, 1998), 268.

4. Jeffrey Tigay, *The JPS Commentary, Deuteronomy* (Philadelphia: Jewish Publication Society, 1996), 429. Stephen Geller recently considered the implications of the Torah's multivocality for a reconstruction of ancient Israelite versus biblical religion in "The Religion of the Bible," in *The Jewish Study Bible* (Oxford: Oxford University Press, 1999), 2021–2040, esp. 2039–2040.

5. Richard Elliot Friedman, *The Creation of Sacred Literature* (Berkeley: University of California Press, 1981), 25, 34. Joel Rosenberg formulates the relationship of the redactor to his source material in similar fashion while identifying both the limitations and the possibilities present to the redactor (whom he pointedly calls the author): "the author of the story's finished structure was, after all, a traditional collector, limited by the obligation to preserve the character and uniqueness (if not the actual verbatim formulation) of each inherited element while simultaneously seeking an arrangement of elements that would make a statement of its own." Joel Rosenberg, "The Garden Story Forward and Backward," *Prooftexts* 1, no. 1 (Jan. 1981): 1–27, 4. Thomas W. Mann summarizes various proposals for the redaction of Numbers in an analysis of its middle chapters in "Holiness and Death in the Redaction of Numbers 16:1–20:13," in *Love and Death in the Ancient Near East*, ed. Marvin H. Pope, John H. Marks, and Robert McClive Good (Guilford, Conn.: Four Quarters Publishing, 1987), 181–190, 182.

6. Levine, *Numbers,* 280. For those interested in a treatment of Numbers as part of the larger wilderness narratives, see Aaron Schart, *Mose und Israel in Konflikt* (Gottingen: Vandenhoeck and Ruprecht, 1990).

7. An emphasis on results is suggested by Benjamin Sommer in analyzing a non-priestly text, Numbers 11: "The redactor who combined these disparate texts

was, I presume, neither suffering from aphasia nor blindly pasting together random scraps in a darkened room. I do not see any cause to resist the assertion that the redactor combined texts in a surprising way for some reasons, and that we can attempt to reconstruct these reasons by evaluating the results...produced." Sommer, "Reflecting on Moses: The Redaction of Numbers 11," 615. Jacob Milgrom describes redaction criticism in the following terms: "It refuses to dissect the whole into parts and then consider these parts as having meaning apart from the whole. Rather, it studies a literary piece as a whole by demonstrating the interaction of its parts." Milgrom, *Numbers*, xii. Perhaps it is merely a matter of emphasis. I assume that separate materials do in fact have meaning apart from that whole. Therefore they first demand a separate analysis, the approach I take in chapter 4.

8. Rabinowitz et al., *A Witness Forever*, 113.
9. As argued by Eric Voegelin and quoted in Marc Zvi Brettler, *The Creation of History in Ancient Israel* (London and New York: Routledge, 1995) 206.
10. Rolf Rendtorff, "Directions in Pentateuchal Studies," *Currents in Research: Biblical Studies* 5 (1997): 43–65, 50.
11. Ibid., 49.
12. For a recent discussion of the status of the documentary hypothesis in the last decade, see my "Reading the Seams," *Journal for the Study of the Old Testament* 29 (2005): 259–287. In that article I discuss both the supporters of the documentary hypothesis and those who have proposed alternative models. Chief among the former is Alexander Rofe, *Introduction to the Composition of the Pentateuch* (Sheffield: Sheffield Academic Press, 1999), and Nicholson, *The Pentateuch in the Twentieth Century*. In his work, while defending the documentary hypothesis, Nicholson provides a survey of those who have largely rejected it. These include Rolf Rendtorff, *The Problem of the Process of Transmission in the Pentateuch* (JSOT, Sup 89; Sheffield: Sheffield Academic Press, 1990), and "Directions in Pentateuchal Studies," *Currents in Research* 5 (1997): 43–65, and Erhard Blum, *Studien zur Komposition des Pentaeuch* (Berlin: Walter de Gruyter, 1990). For an excellent English treatment of Blum's proposals, see David Carr, "Controversy and Convergence in Recent Studies of the Formation of the Pentateuch," *Religious Studies Review* 23, no. 1 (January, 1997): 22–30. In addition, for a continued and vigorous defense of the documentary hypothesis as well as a concise introduction, see Richard Elliott Friedman, *The Bible with Sources Revealed* (San Francisco: Harper, 2003).
13. For a brief description of RJE, see Friedman, *The Bible with Sources Revealed*, 4.
14. Levine, *Numbers*, 76–77.
15. Rolf P. Knierim and George W. Coats, *Numbers* (Grand Rapids, Michigan: William B. Eerdmans, 2005) 22.
16. See Appendix A.
17. Though not necessarily his identification of that layer as H. For the details of his argument, including the importance of the prophet Isaiah, see Israel

Knohl, *The Sanctuary of Silence* (Minneapolis: Fortress Press, 1995), esp. 199–224.

18. Levine, *Numbers,* 71, and Knierim and Coats, *Numbers,* 7.

19. For a discussion of the nonpriestly materials of Numbers, see Levine, *Numbers,* esp. 48–49 and 63, as well as Sommer, "Reflecting or Moses."

20. As suggested by Levine's reconstruction, *Numbers,* 105–108.

21. Rosenberg, "The Garden Story Forward and Backward," 3. Throughout my re-reading of Numbers I try to rely on observations of the text itself rather than a specific theory of its composition as suggested by Nicholson, *The Pentateuch*: "We should always begin with the text, not with theories about it" (131). For a more detailed description of the editorial design of Numbers than that provided in the present work, see Milgrom, *Numbers,* especially his thorough introduction (xxii–xxxii).

22. The following discussion will not exhaust the possibilities for editorial interventions in the five books of Moses or even in the book of Numbers. A partial bibliography of works describing redactional activity in the bible includes Umberto Cassuto, *Biblical and Oriental Studies* (Jerusalem; Magnes Press, 1973), esp. "The Sequence and Arrangement of the Biblical Sections" (1–6); Isaac B. Gottlieb, "*Sof Davar*: Biblical Endings," *Prooftexts* 11 (1991): 213–224; Samuel Sandmel, "The Haggada within Scripture," *Journal of Biblical Literature* (hereafter *JBL*) 80 (1961): 105–22; Jeffrey H. Tigay, "Conflation as a Redactional Technique," in *Empirical Models for Biblical Criticism,* ed. Jeffrey H. Tigay (Philadelphia: University of Pennsylvania Press, 1985); and H. Van Dyke Parunak, "Transitional Techniques in the Bible," *JBL* 102, no. 4 (1983): 525–548.

23. Dennis Olson discusses the census in great detail in *The Death of the Old and the Birth of the New* (Chico: Scholars Press, 1985), esp. ch. 5.

24. Mary Douglas, *In the Wilderness* (Sheffield: JSOT Press, 1993), argues that the reference to Jacob and his twelve sons in the opening of Numbers introduces a series of interconnections between Genesis and Numbers. She writes that "the parallels between Numbers and Genesis, where the names of Moab and Edom are prominent, point to grave matters of foreign policy remembered by the Second Temple community" (101). Douglas notes that Genesis 19, the seduction of Lot by his daughters, produces Ammon and Moab. Numbers 25 echoes that seduction in the acts of the daughters of Moab. Such inner-biblical dialogue is worth noting as it enriches a reading of any given book.

25. See the charts of the camp devised by Douglas, ibid., 175, 178.

26. Martin Noth articulates such a perspective: "From the point of view of its contents, the book lacks unity and it is difficult to see any pattern in its construction. . . . [Numbers is] a collection of very varied material with little inner cohesion." Martin Noth, *Numbers* (Philadelphia: Westminster Press, 1968), 1–2.

27. Olson, *The Death of the Old,* 55. George Medenhall reminds the reader of the most obvious functions of the census lists: "to serve as the basis for levying and

collecting texts and to serve as a register of those men subject to military duty" (54). See George Medenhall, "The Census Lists of Numbers 1 and 26," *JBL* 77 (1958): 52–66. Such a description fails to take into account the literary use and placement of the censuses.

28. Olson, *The Death of the Old*, 198.

29. Ibid., 66, 79.

30. Midrash provides a fascinating biography for the mysterious female character Serach bat Asher. For specific citations, see Leila Leah Bronner, "Serah bat Asher: The Transformative Power of Aggadic Invention," in *From Eve to Esther* (Louisville, KY.: Westminster John Knox Press, 1994), 42–60.

31. See Milgrom, *Numbers*, 336–339, for a historical reconstruction and early date for the census.

32. As an example, in his commentary Rashi asks, "Why was the passage of the spies placed next to the passage of Miriam?" *The Torah with Rashi's Commentary* (New York: Mesorah Publication, 1997), 148. On numerous occasions Rashi raises the same question and often provides a plausible and illuminating solution to his query.

33. A relevant discussion of the itinerary, including its possible dating, can be found in Gray, who points out that the itinerary records only two dates: the journey's start and Aaron's death, in *A Critical and Exegetical Commentary on Numbers*, 442–443. Milgrom raises the problem of dates for the events listed in the itinerary versus their mention in the broader narrative in *Numbers*, esp. 67, 277, and 498.

34. See, e.g., the maps reprinted and adapted from G. J. Wenham in Milgrom, *Numbers*, lvii, lviii, lix.

35. As quoted by Jonathan Z. Smith, *To Take Place* (Chicago: University of Chicago Press, 1987), 28.

36. As pointed out by Milgrom, *Numbers*, 172. See James Ackerman on the use of foreshadowing in the deaths of Aaron and Moses in "Numbers," in *The Literary Guide to the Bible*, ed. Robert Alter and Frank Kermode (Cambridge, Mass.: Belknap Press, 1987), 86. For a discussion of the chronological notices, see Olson, *The Death of the Old*, 84, and my dissertation, "Monumental Tasks: The Problem of Memory in the Book of Numbers," University of California, Berkeley (2000), 40–41. For a different analysis of the itinerary, including its possible relationship to themes found in Deuteronomy, see Z. Kallai, "The Wandering Traditions from Kadesh-Barnesa to Canaan: A Study in Biblical Historiography," *Journal of Jewish Studies* (Spring-Autumn 1982): 175–184.

37. David Damrosch has described a priestly conception of time that confirms what I have observed in Numbers. Damrosch writes that for the priests, "the fulfillment of past history is to be anticipated in the coming restoration of full religious observance in Israel. Past and future merge in the iterative present of ritual." David Damrosch, *The Narrative Covenant* (San Francisco: Harper and Row, 1987), 281.

CHAPTER 3 PRIESTLY PURPOSES

1. It is striking that both Miriam and Aaron are implicated but only Miriam publicly humiliated. I take up the politics of gender as represented in God's differential treatment of the two siblings in chapter 6.

2. God's statement provides a poetic snippet in the midst of a prose narrative. The parallelism that suggests poetry is present in the different ways in which God makes the divine self known to his prophet. Such poetic form functions to elevate God's speech in this encounter, lending it a lofty, rhetorical flourish. For further arguments concerning the interweaving of poetry and prose in biblical texts, see Moshe Greenberg, *Biblical Prose Prayer* (Berkeley: University of California Press, 1983).

3. Of course the tension between priestly and prophetic power has a broader history in the biblical materials and in ancient Israel. Consider the famous attacks on priestly insularity and excessive attention to the details of sacrifice found in Isaiah and in Micah. Within the Torah itself (rather than the prophetic material) that tension is less about the role of prophet versus priest and more about the priestly cult versus other religious forms and expressions that are not exclusively tied to the priests. In his commentary on Deuteronomy, Jeffrey Tigay argues: "Deuteronomy's aim is to spiritualize religion by freeing it from excessive dependence on sacrifice and priesthood." Tigay, *Deuteronomy*, xvii.

4. The other biblical prophet who, like Moses, acts as a ruling authority would be the prophet Samuel. In contrast to these two, other biblical prophets have an antagonistic relationship with the governing authority. Of course Moses exhibits antagonism against the Pharaoh at the start of his career as a prophet, while Samuel is quite antagonistic near the end of his career against the new king Saul, who usurps prophetic authority.

5. An illuminating discussion of the biblical prophet can be found in Yochanan Muffs, *Love and Joy* (New York: Jewish Theological Seminary of America, 1992). In addition, I find the brief article "Prophecy and Prophets" by Shalom Paul in the collection found in *Etz Hayim* (Philadelphia: Jewish Publication Society, 2001), 1407–1412, to be an extremely useful analysis of the trends within biblical prophecy.

6. As examples of Moses' reliance on the priest to implement God's instructions, consider that in Numbers 5 and 6 God instructs Moses on how to make restitution for wrongdoing, how to deal with a jealous husband, and what happens if a Nazir comes in contact with a corpse. In each instance Moses requires the services of a priest to make expiation or otherwise officiate in some fashion. For the details of God's formulaic address to Moses, to Moses and Aaron, and to Aaron alone, see Appendix B.

7. Milgrom, *Numbers*, xl.

8. See ibid., 257 n. 6, for speculation on which vessels are meant. Rules for engagement in battle, including the provision of a priest, can be found in Deuteronomy

20. An example of the use of the ark in battle, with mixed and entertaining results, can be found in I Samuel 4–6.

9. See Appendix A for a list of the main priestly activities associated with Aaron or his descendants.

10. Levine, *Numbers*, 65.

11. What profession Balaam follows is not exactly clear. For an illuminating discussion of the possibilities, see Milgrom, *Numbers*, 471–473.

12. Levine, *Numbers*, 73–76, and Milgrom, *Numbers*, 473–476.

13. Douglas, *In the Wilderness*, 96–97. David Damrosch distinguishes between the composition of materials, ranging over several hundred years, and the assembly of those materials in response to the social crisis of exile. A crisis, "that began with the fall of the North and culminated in the Exile would have provided the impetus for the joining together of the different Yahwistic materials as the Hebrews struggled to hold on to their endangered traditions and use them to make sense of the disaster that had befallen them." Damrosch, *The Narrative Covenant* (San Francisco: Harper and Row, 1987), 165. This seems a plausible scenario not only for Yahwistic materials but for priestly ones as well. Edward Greenstein explicitly links the exile with the redaction of the Torah. He writes: "The Torah may incorporate ancient material; it may remember old concerns. But the form in which it was finally shaped addressed the particular situation of the exilic community, the one that first made it Torah." Greenstein, *Essays on Biblical Method and Translation* (Atlanta: Scholar's Press, 1989), 51.

14. For a history of the Levites and the basis of my subsequent comments, see Blenkinsopp, *Sage, Priest, Prophet*; Knohl, *The Sanctuary of Silence*, 73–85; Levine, *Numbers*, esp. 104–107, 280–289; and Milgrom, *Numbers*, esp. his introduction, xxxiv–xxxv. Cooper and Goldstein summarize the argument of Ellis Rivkin, who claims that Numbers 16, the rebellion of Korah, marks the end point of Torah redaction. That rebellion signifies the final ascendancy of the Aaronids. For details, see Alan Cooper and Bernard Goldstein, "At the Entrance to the Tent: More Cultic Resonances in Biblical Narrative," JBL 116, no. 2 (1997): 201–215, 201.

15. Levine, *Numbers*, 285. For a recent description of the roles and functions of the Levites, see Jeffrey C. Geoghegan, *The Time, Place and Purpose of the Deuteronomic History* (Providence, R.I.: Brown Judaic Studies, 2006).

16. Among the authors depicting the period of Hezekiah-Josiah as crucial to the development of the priestly class and as a time of great literary output, see Menaham Haran, "Behind the Scenes of History: Determining the Date of the Priestly Source," JBL 100, no. 3 (1981): 321–333, and Moshe Weinfeld, "The Scribal Role in the Crystallization of Deuteronomy," in *Deuteronomy and the Deuteronomic School* (Oxford: Clarendon Press, 1972), 158–178.

17. Milgrom, *Numbers*, xxxiii–xxxiv. Milgrom also dates the creation of the levitical cities to an early period, the time of Solomon or soon after, in excursus 75,

Numbers, 504–509. If he is correct, then these cities are from an earlier time than the period under discussion.

18. For the reading of Korah's rebellion, see ibid., 420. Whether the Korah rebellion leads one to posit an early or a late date for the redaction of Numbers, it is clear that the redactor of that story intended his audience to understand that Korah, and therefore the Levites, were upstarts who failed miserably. As Saul Olyan writes: "The elite writers of most surviving biblical texts have a vested interest in portraying these challenges as illegitimate failures and so they do." Saul M. Olyan, *Rites and Rank* (Princeton: Princeton University Press, 2000), 118. I discuss the rebellion of Korah at length in chapter 5. For additional comments on the redaction of Numbers 11–16, see Jacob Milgrom, "The Structure of Numbers: Chapters 11–12 and 13–14 and Their Redaction. Preliminary Gropings," in *Judaic Perspectives on Ancient Israel*, ed. Jacob Neusner, Baruch A. Levine, Ernest S. Frerichs, and Caroline McCracken–Flesher (Philadelphia: Fortress Press, 1987), 49–61.

19. Knohl, *Sanctuary of Silence*, 211; for discussion of dating, see pp. 208–211.

20. Ibid., 198. Jacob Milgrom extensively responds to Knohl's arguments in *Leviticus 1–16* (New York: Doubleday, 1991), 13–35. Knohl responds in *The Sanctuary of Silence*, excursus 5, 225–230. Benjamin D. Sommer favorably picks up on Knohl's divisions between PT and HS in "Conflicting Constructions of Divine Presence in the Priestly Tabernacle," *Biblical Interpretation* 9 (Leiden: 1 Koninklijke Brill NV, 2001), 41–63, 45 n. 14. For a further development of the distinction between P and H based on Knohl but disagreeing with him in particulars, see Alan Cooper and Bernard R. Goldstein, "The Development of the Priestly Calendars (I)," *Hebrew Union College Annual* 74 (2003): 1–20. They date the reworking of P by H "to be predominantly post-exilic" (5). Without referring to it as the "holiness school," Robert Alter cites such a priestly editorial presence: "some of it may have been written as early as the eighth century B.C.E. though the principal stratum is in all likelihood a product of the sixth century B.C.E., when these same Priestly writers were also drawing together editorially all the previous sources with their own work into a single text." Robert Alter, *The Five Books of Moses* (New York: W. W. Norton, 2004), xi.

21. For details of his argument, see Schniedewind, *How the Bible Became a Book*. Rabinowitz et al., treats the same period in compelling fashion in *A Witness Forever*.

22. William Schniedewind, personal communication.

23. Levine, *Numbers*, 71.

24. Ibid., 104. The relationship of the priestly school to Ezekiel is quite complex. For details, see ibid., esp. 289. See also Cooper and Goldstein, "The Development of the Priestly Calendars," who summarize their conclusion concerning the relationship of P and Ezekiel: "H edits or augments P legislation, while Ezekiel apparently preserves a prior state of P. This is not to say that Ezekiel presents

us with P in its original form; rather, Ezekiel represents what we would term a 'transitional text' situated between P and H" (10). Menahem Haran argues that the material in Ezekiel does postdate the priestly material: "the historical cross-section reflected in P is much earlier, and the source displays far more perfection and originality than Ezek. 40–48." Haran, "Behind the Scenes of History," 327.

25. Levine, *Numbers*, 103. For an excellent survey of approaches to the Persian period, see Tamara C. Eskenazi, "Current Perspectives on Ezra-Nehemiah and the Persian Period," *Currents in Research: Biblical Studies* 1 (1993): 59–86. For a recent study of the period, see Charles E. Carter, *The Emergence of Yehud in the Persian Period* (Sheffield: Sheffield Academic Press, 1999), esp. 249–324.

26. See Levine's discussion of terms such as *degel* and *issa*, which he identifies as late in *Numbers*, 107. See also the essays of Baruch Levine and Avi Hurvitz concerning the use of terminology in dating the priestly source: Baruch Levine, "Late Language in the Priestly Source: Some Literary and Historical Observations," and Avi Hurvitz, "The Language of the Priestly Source and Its Historical Setting – The Case for an Early Date," in *The Proceedings of the Eighth World Congress of Jewish Studies* (Jerusalem: World Union of Jewish Studies, 1983).

27. In Baruch A. Levine, *Leviticus* (Philadelphia: Jewish Publication Society, 1989), xxix.

28. Blenkinsopp, *Sage, Priest, Prophet*, 64.

29. Ibid., 68.

30. Ibid., 92.

31. Ibid., 93.

32. Ibid., 108. Mary Douglas identifies the same period as crucial but offers quite a different historical reconstruction. See Douglas, *In the Wilderness*, 173–182, 232–233.

33. Douglas, *In the Wilderness*, 83.

CHAPTER 4 VARIATIONS ON A THEME

1. This quote was attributed to H. Gross in the entry "zakhar," *Theological Dictionary of the Old Testament*, vol. 4, ed. Botterweck et al., 80.

2. The observed link between the request of the Reubenites in chapter 32 and the actions of their parents during Korah's revolt in chapter 16 originated in an advanced seminar on Numbers I taught in the spring of 2001 at the Hebrew Union College/Jewish Institute of Religion in Los Angeles. I am indebted to the students of that seminar for lively and stimulating discussions of Numbers. Relevant comments on chapter 32's connection to the earlier narrative can also be found in Olson, *The Death of the Old and the Birth of the New*, 93.

3. Hendel, *Remembering Abraham*, 32.

4. For the difficulties in translating לַהֲנִיחוֹ as "abandons them," see the discussion in Milgrom, *Numbers,* 329, n. 20.

5. Marc Brettler notes this use of memory in "Memory in Ancient Israel," in *Memory and History in Christianity and Judaism,* ed. Michael Alan Signer (Notre Dame: University of Notre Dame Press, 2001), 11.

6. Seth Schwartz reminds us that rabbinic documents are not simply "repositories of tradition, but careful selections of material, shaped by the interests, including the self-interest, of tradents and redactors." Seth Schwartz, *Imperialism and Jewish Society 200 BCE to 600 CE* (Princeton: Princeton University Press, 2001), 8. I assume that such a claim holds equally true for biblical texts and their redactors.

7. Mark Smith, *The Memoirs of God* (Minneapolis: Fortress Press, 2004), 18.

8. Eugene Ulrich, *The Dead Sea Scrolls and the Origins of the Bible* (Grand Rapids, Mich.: Eerdmans, 1999), 5.

9. Smith, *The Memoirs of God,* 161.

10. Paul Connerton, *How Societies Remember* (Cambridge: Cambridge University Press, 1989) 1.

11. Ibid., 137.

12. Jacques Le Goff argues that the possession of highly technical knowledge reinforces and strengthens the position of the rulers within a hierarchical system. Le Goff, *History and Memory* (New York: Columbia University Press, 1992), 58. Milgrom, *Numbers,* xxxii–xxxv, has identified the materials relevant to the present discussion as priestly. While presenting a dating scheme for the priestly materials very different from that of Jacob Milgrom, Baruch Levine also identifies the relevant chapters (1–10) as priestly in the most explicit of terms: "all of Num 1:1–10:28 is the work of P." Levine, *Numbers,* 64. For further details of Levine's claim that P edited Numbers, see his introduction in that volume. Most recently, see Friedman, *The Bible with Sources Revealed,* particularly his list of P's terminology found on pp. 8–9 and his identification of P, R, J, and E in Numbers. For a more specific listing of priestly activity in Numbers, see my Appendix A.

13. Joseph Blenkinsopp, "The Structure of P," in *The Catholic Biblical Quarterly* 38 (1976): 275–292, 275.

14. Gerhard Lisowsky, *Konkordanz Zum Hebraischen Alten Testament* (Stuttgart: Deutsche Bibelgesellschaft, 1981), 1179–1182. Gerdien Jonker discusses the findings of Jo Ann Scurlock in the Mesopotamian context concerning *zakaru* and *paqadu*: "it can clearly be seen that *suma zakaru* 'the invocation of the name' and *zakir sumi* 'the one who invokes the name' occupy special places in the care of the dead. . . . Here *zakaru* is accompanied by the regularly recurring verb *paqadu*, to provide the dead with food and drink." Gerdien Jonker, *The Topography of Remembrance: The Dead, Tradition and Collective Memory in Mesopotamia* (New York: E. J. Brill, 1995), 2. The linkage of the two terms is highly suggestive for the biblical case in Numbers. I discuss the treatment of the generation once it is dead in chapter 6.

15. God's memory of Amalek's treatment of Israel in the wilderness many years after the fact illustrates the act of remembering something in order to hold the object of that memory to account. See I Samuel 15:2.

16. Avraham Even-Shoshan, *The New Concordance* (Jerusalem: Kiryat-Sepher, 1979), 1782 (Hebrew). H. Eising's comment can be found in *Theological Dictionary of the Old Testament*, 71.

17. Martin Buber and Franz Rosenzweig, *Scripture and Translation* (Bloomington: Indiana University Press, 1994), 84.

18. Robert Alter suggests that the fear of a census among the Israelites is based on a sense that such an accounting creates a "vulnerability to malignant forces." *The David Story* (New York: W. W. Norton, 1999) 354. In Numbers 14 Moses attempts to soften the divine decree by asking God to delay the punishment or at least, as suggested by Milgrom, to distribute the divine punishment over a number of generations, visiting the transgressions of the fathers upon the children. See Milgrom, *Numbers*, 111, n. 18, and Excursus 32, 392–396 for a discussion of this phrase.

19. Note that the term also surfaces in Numbers 27 and 31.

20. While the adultery is stated initially as a fact, it becomes clear that it is only fact in the mind of the suspicious husband: note Numbers 5:14. However, see Michael Fishbane's detailed proposal that verses 12–13 and verse 14 refer to two different legal situations. Fishbane, "Accusations of Adultery," in *Women in the Hebrew Bible*, ed. Alice Bach (London: Routledge, 1999), 493.

21. Noting that in Numbers 5 the meal offering of remembrance does not incur an obvious benefit on the one offering it (the man for the woman?). Milgrom, *Numbers*, 39, n. 15 suggests that the phrase "recalling wrong-doing" was added by means of explanation. These terms have long been considered obscure in meaning. See George Gray, *Numbers* (New York: Charles Scribner's Sons, 1903), 45. Tikva Frymer-Kensky points out that these terms are "restricted to this passage." Frymer-Kensky, "The Strange Case of the Suspected Sotah," in Bach, *Women in the Hebrew Bible*, 472.

22. For a similar reading of the public humiliation of the woman, see Helena Zlotnick, *Dinah's Daughters* (Philadelphia: University of Pennsylvania Press, 2002), 29. Note also that זכר surfaces one last time in this ordeal in verse 26. This refers to the portion of the meal offering turned into smoke on the altar. For a discussion of the term, see Levine, *Numbers*, 199.

23. Pierre Nora, "Between Memory and History: Les Lieux de Memoire," *Representations* 26 (1989): 7–24, 12.

24. David Damrosch, *The Narrative Covenant* (San Francisco: Harper and Row, 1987), 265. For general descriptions of priestly themes and language that can also be found in Numbers 1–10, see Walter Brueggemann and Hans Walter Wolff, *The Vitality of Old Testament Traditions* (Atlanta: John Knox, 1952); Ralph W. Klein, "The Message of P," in *Die Botschaft und die Boten* (Neukirchen-Vluyn: Neukirchener Verlag, 1981); Menachem Haran, "The Character of the Priestly

Source: Utopian and Exclusive Features," in *Proceedings of the Eighth World Congress of Jewish Studies* (Jerusalem: World Union of Jewish Studies, 1983); and Sean E. McEvenue, *The Narrative Style of the Priestly Writer* (Rome: Biblical Institute, 1971).

25. Joseph Blenkinsopp, "The Structure of P," *Catholic Biblical Quarterly* 38 (1976): 275–292, 275–276.

26. McEvenue, *The Narrative Style*, 180.

27. Ibid., 14.

28. Brueggemann and Wolff, *The Vitality of Old Testament Traditions*, esp. ch. 6.

29. As defined by Milgrom, *Numbers*, xxii, a chiasm "is named after the Greek letter X and denotes a pair of items that reverses itself." For a detailed discussion of the structure and use of chiasm in the book of Numbers, see his introduction on pp. xxii–xxviii.

30. Numbers 2 lists the following marching orders: camped on the east and marching first are the divisions of Judah, Issachar, and Zebulun. Camped on the south and marching second: Reuben, Simeon, and Gad. Camped on the west and marching third: Ephraim, Manasseh, and Benjamin. Camped on the north and marching last: Dan, Asher, and Naphtali. In Numbers 10:13–28 the order of the march is the following: Judah, Issachar, Zebulun, Reuben, Simeon, Gad, Ephraim, Manasseh, Benjamin, Dan, Asher, Naphtali. In other words, the divisions march precisely in the same order as instructed in Numbers 2. The main difference involves the inclusion of the Levitical groups who transport the tabernacle in Numbers 10. They are given their instructions only in Numbers 3 and 4, after the marching orders of Numbers 2. Because chapter divisions are a later imposition on biblical scrolls, the use of chapter numbers in the chiasm is merely for convenience. Even without chapter numbers, the proposed structure works based on content.

31. Le Goff, *History and Memory*, 58, n. 12.

32. Robert Alter, *The Art of Biblical Narrative* (New York: Basic Books, 1981), 143.

33. Haran, "The Character of the Priestly Source: Utopian and Exclusive Features," 136.

34. On the identification of this phrase with the Holiness School, see Knohl, *Sanctuary of Silence*, 46–55. Note that I have altered the translation of the phrase from that of the JPS commentary to emphasize "law" instead of "institution." Finally, while I see Numbers 9 and 10 as reflections of the priestly goal of harmony and the means to obtain that vision, Knierim and Coats argue that they are in considerable tension. In their reading, Numbers 10 "relativizes the immediacy of Israel's response to Yahweh's theophanic cloud and voice by either offsetting it through the priestly calls to meetings or by delaying it through intermediary priestly signals. Num. 10:1–10 is hierocratic, Num. 9:15–23 theocratic." Knierim and Coats, *Numbers*, 134. That may be so. Yet I would suggest that the priests desired the picture of harmony of Numbers 9 to complement Numbers 10 but

would prefer the assertion of control over the children of Israel as represented in the blowing of the trumpets by the sons of Aaron. They expressed that preference in the order of the two chapters, having the blowing of the trumpets follow and perhaps supersede Numbers 9.

35. Blowing the trumpets is an act that requires commemoration through performance. It is precisely the performative aspect of memory that Paul Connerton claims as crucial to the preservation of memory: "we are likely to find it [social memory] in commemorative ceremonies; but commemorative ceremonies prove to be commemorative only in so far as they are performative." Connerton, *How Societies Remember*, 5.

36. Avishai Margalit points out that certain regimes exhibit an "urgent need . . . to control collective memory, because by so doing they exercise monopoly on all sources of legitimacy." Margalit, *The Ethics of Memory* (Cambridge: Harvard University Press, 2002), 11. The priestly strands within the biblical narrative, including the episode of the blowing of the trumpets, provide evidence of such an attempt within the biblical context.

37. Eric Hobsbawm and Terence Ranger, *The Invention of Tradition* (Cambridge: Cambridge University Press, 1983), 1.

38. For further details of their argument and analysis of more recent examples, see ibid.

39. Taken from Connerton, *How Societies Remember*, 11.

40. As pointed out in the introduction, the reliance on memory for theological purposes is examined at length in the work of Brevard S. Childs, *Memory and Tradition in Israel*. Yosef Hayim Yerushalmi also treats biblical memory in largely theological terms in *Zakhor*.

41. Bernard Lewis, *History Remembered, Recovered, Invented* (Princeton: Princeton University Press, 1975) 53.

42. Stephen Owen suggests a fascinating tension between memory and narrative when he suggests that memory and memoir may disrupt linearity due to the "very randomization of the past," which in turns leads to "the shattering of narrative models." See *Remembrances*, 139. Dennis Olson, *Death of the Old*, 119 and esp. 122, also identifies the abrupt way in which Numbers 11 interrupts the prior narrative. In general, Olson's work on the two censuses of Numbers lays the foundation for my own ideas. Yet Olson fails to link the generational shift he identifies with the necessary interrogation of memory that accompanies and results from the death of the old and the birth of the new in the wilderness period. For a different approach to the textual connections of Numbers 11 with what precedes it, see Milgrom, *Numbers*, 82, n. 1.

43. See in particular Benjamin D. Sommer, "Reflecting on Moses: The Redaction of Numbers 11," in *Journal of Biblical Literature* (Winter 1999): 601–624, nn. 8–10. Levine, *Numbers*, 66, has identified Num 10:29–12:15 as nonpriestly.

44. See my "Memory and Reflection: Jacob's Story," in *Journal of the Association for Graduate Students in Near Eastern Studies* 5, no. 2 (Spring 1995).

45. Richard Elliott Friedman, *The Exile and Biblical Narrative* (Chico: Scholars Press, 1981), 125.
46. I chose to use the JPS translation "gullet" for the Hebrew *nefesh*, as in Akkadian *napishtu*, pointed out by Milgrom, *Numbers*, 84.
47. As argued by George Gray, *A Critical and Exegetical Commentary on Numbers*, 103–104.
48. Jan Asmann, *Moses the Egyptian* (Cambridge: Harvard University Press, 1997), 12.
49. Owen, *Remembrances*, 14.
50. Ilana Pardes, "The Biography of Ancient Israel: Imagining the Birth of a Nation," *Comparative Literature* 49, no. 1 (Winter 1997): 37. The recurrent force of bodily cravings does indeed suggest a type of memory outside the realm of easy manipulation. Interestingly enough, the psychologist Daniel Stern has linked the formation of bodily memory directly to the experience of nursing. See Daniel Stern, *The Interpersonal World of the Infant* (New York: Basic Books, 1985), 91–96.
51. Ilana Pardes, "Imagining the Promised Land: The Spies in the Land of the Giants," *History and Memory* 6 (1994): 5–23, 17.
52. Richard Terdiman, *Present Past: Modernity and the Memory Crisis* (Ithaca: Cornell University Press, 1993), 346.
53. Milgrom, *Numbers*, 450. For Milgrom's discussion of the couplets, see 82–83 and excursus 50, 449–450.
54. Everett Fox points out that the argument hinges on the different meanings of דבר ב, which can be translated either as "speak against" or "speak through." See *The Five Books of Moses* (New York: Schocken Books, 1995), 716. In a comment on Numbers 21:5 Baruch Levine points out that the phrase is idiomatic. He translates it as "to speak against" and reminds us that it "recalls Numbers 12:1 Miriam and Aaron spoke against Moses." Levine, *Numbers 21–36*, 86. Focusing on reported popular speech in the formation of the nation's self-identity is suggested by the work of Nancy Ruttenburg, "George Whitefield, Spectacular Conversion, and the Rise of Democratic Personality," in *The American Literary History Reader*, ed. Gordon Hutner (New York: Oxford University Press, 1995).
55. See Milgrom, *Numbers*, 23, for his notion of the concept "measure for measure," which shapes biblical punishment. This biblical conception of punishment forms the basis of chapter 6 of the present work. Simon J. De Vries makes a similar point concerning the path of retreat for the condemned generation in his "The Origin of the Murmuring Tradition," *Journal of Biblical Literature* 87 (March 1968): 55.
56. I have used the same syntax as Everett Fox in translating this verse, in order to come closer to the Hebrew. See Fox, *The Five Books of Moses*, 728.
57. I am indebted to Robert Alter in a personal communication for suggesting the aptness of the imagery of Moses as wet nurse in response to the people's

hunger. In the present discussion of Numbers 11 I have omitted the story of the appointment of the seventy elders. That episode suggests a more positive response on God's part to Moses' complaint than the provision of the quails and illustrates the composite nature of Numbers 11. Both points are sufficiently made by Benjamin Sommer, "Reflecting on Moses: The Redaction of Numbers 11."

58. Terdiman, *Present Past*, 20.

59. Nathan Wachtel, "Introduction," in *Between Memory and History*, ed. Marie-Noëlle Bourguet, Lucette Valensi, and Nathan Wachtel (Chur, Switzerland: Harwood Academic Publishers, 1990), 218.

60. Hendel, *Remembering Abraham*, 33.

61. Anita Shapiro raises such questions in "Historiography and Memory: Latrun, 1948," *Jewish Social Studies* 3, no. 1 (Fall 1996): 20–61, 46, 60, n. 59.

62. For the full argument, see Knohl, *Sanctuary of Silence*. Knohl recently came out with *The Divine Symphony* (Philadelphia: Jewish Publication Society, 2003), which argues for the intentional redaction of the Torah as a multivocal text that preserves diverse points of view. That assumption certainly underlies the current reading of the book of Numbers.

63. Owen, *Remembrances*, 66.

64. A very interesting and provocative study of views of Egypt in the Torah can be found in F. V. Greifenhagen, *Egypt on the Pentateuch's Ideological Map* (London: Sheffield Academic Press, 2002). My understanding of the use of Egypt in the book of Numbers, arrived at independently of Greifenhagen, nonetheless is mirrored in and confirmed by his discussion of Numbers 11 (see, e.g., 165, 178–181) and its possible audience (184) as well as in his overall study of the complex attitudes toward Egypt found throughout the Pentateuch. Broader in scope, Greifenhagen's readings emphasize the use of Egypt in shaping collective identity, while my work focuses in much more detail on different conceptions of memory, including of Egypt, and their ramifications in the shaping of a usable past for a postexilic audience. Therefore, I am interested in the uses of memory by the priestly hierarchy that redacted the work, necessitating a greater analysis of the role of politics in shaping Numbers' final form.

CHAPTER 5 CRISIS AND COMMEMORATION

1. Catherine Bell, *Ritual Theory, Ritual Practice* (New York: Oxford University Press, 1992), 211.

2. It should be noted that other objects are described in Numbers, including the gifts for the tabernacle, the lampstand, and the trumpets. These particular objects are in the first ten chapters of Numbers, chapters that reinforce and celebrate the system of order and control that exemplifies the harmonious priestly vision of the wilderness camp. I discuss the trumpets in chapter 4. The remaining two objects lie outside the purview of the present discussion, which focuses on the series of rebellions.

3. In a personal communication Israel Knohl suggested that the Holiness School, the most likely source of the redaction of Numbers, not only edited earlier priestly materials but also contributed their own creative writing to the project.

4. Victor Turner, *Dramas, Fields and Metaphors* (Ithaca, N.Y.: Cornell University Press, 1974), 33. For a relatively recent critical consideration of the work of Victor Turner, see Mathieu Deflem, "Ritual, Anti-Structure and Religion: A Discussion of Victor Turner's Processual Symbolic Analysis," *Journal for the Scientific Study of Religion* 30, no. 1 (March 1991): 1–25, 3. Deflem describes Turner's theory in generally positive terms, while providing a useful and concise history of Turner's thought. In describing Turner's early work Deflem faults Turner for seeing rituals as "mere compensations, or redressive mechanisms for the tensions produced in the secular order" (3). Yet as Turner's theory develops, so do his ideas of ritual. Ritual is no longer exclusively considered in secular and/or political contexts. Deflem cites what he considers Turner's main theoretical advance: "rituals are processes, not states, in the social world, which itself is a 'world in becoming, not a world in being'" (19). Deflem provides a good case for using Turner, as he offers "a fruitful set of tools to discover the meanings of ritual performance" (21).

5. Turner, *Dramas, Fields and Metaphors*, 33.

6. Victor Turner, "Social Dramas and the Stories about Them," *Critical Inquiry* 7, no. 1 (Autumn 1980): 141–168, 152.

7. This according to Bell, *Ritual Theory, Ritual Practice*, 35. Renato Rosaldo complains that Turner's social dramas rely too heavily on structural principles: "his conclusions usually reduce complex human dramas to mere illustrations of supposedly explanatory structural principles.... Turner's conclusions emphasize principles of social structure more than the human processes he so thickly dramatizes." Renato Rosaldo, *Culture and Truth* (Boston: Beacon Press, 1993), 96.

8. Perhaps "community" should be considered a "world" as Frank Gorman reflects on that term: "the world of meaning and significance within which the ritual is conceptualized, constructed and enacted." Frank H. Gorman, *The Ideology of Ritual* (Sheffield: Sheffield Academic Press, 1990), 15.

9. Turner, *Dramas, Fields and Metaphors*, 39.

10. Ibid., 41.

11. Ibid., 38–42. Turner adds the term "recognition of schism" in his article "Social Dramas," 149. Even with that revision, Turner's last stage has come in for criticism. Because the targeted subgroup is often reincorporated into the group, restoring stability and strengthening the status quo, those interested in examining the building of diverse communities and the possibilities for change have become disenchanted with Turner's proposals as too restrictive and regulatory. An example of such criticism is that of Donald Weber. "Turner doesn't realize that he is privileging his sense of social leveling and attendant cultural bonding over what we now recognize as an encounter with identity politics and the

border." Weber, "From Limen to Border: A Meditation on the Legacy of Victor Turner for American Cultural Studies," *American Quarterly* 47, no. 3 (September 1995): 525–536, 530. In response I would suggest that a highly crafted and political narrative such as that of Numbers in fact has as its aim the restoration of the status quo. Thus Turner's fourth stage illuminates a highly purposeful and contentious use of social drama precisely to reinscribe hierarchies of authority.

12. Turner, *Dramas, Fields and Metaphors*, 32.

13. I would extend Bell's claim on behalf of ritual to include social drama. She argues: "Ritual actually constructs an argument, a set of tensions." Bell, *Ritual Theory, Ritual Practice*, 195.

14. Turner, *Dramas, Fields, and Metaphors*, 33.

15. Rosaldo, *Culture and Truth*, 141.

16. Bell, *Ritual Theory, Ritual Practice*, 98.

17. Victor Turner, *The Forest of Symbols* (Ithaca, N.Y.: Cornell University Press, 1967), 45. Turner also cited the associative and analogous qualities of a symbol in the same work (19).

18. Max Black, *Models and Metaphors* (Ithaca, N.Y.: Cornell University Press, 1962), 222.

19. E. H. Gombrich, *Symbolic Images* (London: Phaidon Press, 1972), 159.

20. Bell, *Ritual Theory, Ritual Practice*, 15.

21. Ibid., 54.

22. As quoted by Bell, ibid., 45.

23. I use Jacob Milgrom's translation "your carcasses are finished, consumed." See his note for 14:33 in *Numbers*, 115. I also use Everett Fox's phrasing "(for each) day a year" in *The Five Books of Moses* (New York: Schocken Books, 1995), 729.

24. Philip J. Budd, *Numbers*, Word Biblical Commentary, vol. 5 (Texas: Word Books, 1984), 188.

25. Ralph W. Klein makes the point more emphatically. The entire vision of life once the Israelites enter the land is meant to reassure a much later generation living in Babylonian Exile. See Ralph W. Klein, "The Message of P," in *Die Botschaft und die Boten* (Neukirchen-Vluyn: Neukirchener Verlag, 1981).

26. See Israel Knohl's reference to the work of Wellhausen and Keunen as he links chapter 15 of Numbers with Leviticus in *Sanctuary of Silence*. Knohl argues that chapter 15 is a later HS reworking of Leviticus 4, which originated in the priestly Torah. For his full discussion, see p. 53.

27. For a discussion of the Sabbath violator, see Milgrom, *Numbers*, 410.

28. Ibid., 127, for the argument labeling the fringes "tassels" as well as his comments on their placement along the edge of garments. At times, Milgrom's comments and my reading overlap, as is common when conducting a close reading of a biblical text. I try to cite him where appropriate. Yet as I argued in the introduction to the present study, in his incomparable commentary on Numbers, Milgrom does not raise or highlight the effects of different conceptions of memory, both on the narrative and in its use by the priestly editors. In

the present reading, I also try to account for the formation and concentration of three commemorative objects clustered together in chapters 15–17, in other words, at the very center of the book of Numbers.

29. Nehama Leibowitz, *Studies in Bamidbar*, trans. Aryeh Newman (Jerusalem: World Zionist Organization, 1980), 175.

30. Milgrom points out the link with the spy story in *Numbers*, 127.

31. In the qal form, the verb means "to explore," though it is also translated "to scout." It occurs fourteen times in Numbers, once in chapter 10:33 (the only time it is used to refer to exploring the wilderness instead of the land), seven times in chapter 13, five times in chapter 14, and only once in chapter 15. The strategic use of the verb in Numbers 15 suggests the allusion to the events of chapter 13–14 to which the tassels are a response. Elsewhere in Torah, the verb occurs only once more in Deuteronomy. See Gerhard Lisowsky, *Konkordanz Zum Hebraischen Alten Testament* (Stuttgart: Württembergische Bibelanstalt, 1958), 1513–1514.

32. See Knohl's description of the editing of Numbers 13–14, *Sanctuary of Silence*, 91–92.

33. On this point, see also Milgrom, *Numbers*, 127.

34. Baruch Levine, "Priestly Writers," in *The Interpreter's Dictionary of the Bible* (Nashville, Tenn.: Abingdon Press, 1976), 683–687.

35. Mary Douglas, *Purity and Danger* (London: Routledge and Kegan Paul, 1966), 114.

36. Ibid., 115.

37. Milgrom, *Numbers*, 83. I divide the book of Numbers into three sections based on each section's temporal focus. Chapters 1–10 focus on the present, 11–25 on the past, and 26–36 on the future. Hence chapter 11 becomes a "border" between the present and the past and between sections of text in Numbers.

38. Douglas, *Purity and Danger*, 125.

39. Gorman, *The Ideology of Ritual*, 21.

40. Milgrom, *Numbers*, links the wearing of tassels with the aspiration after royalty suggested by the phrase "a kingdom of priests" in Exodus 19. See his excursus 38 beginning on p. 413 and his comments on p. 127.

41. Milgrom, *Numbers*, 411. See also Ferris J. Stephens, who discusses the ancient Near Eastern context for the wearing of tassels in some detail in his "The Ancient Significance of Sisith," *Journal of Biblical Literature* 50 (1931): 59–71.

42. Knohl, *Sanctuary of Silence*, 186.

43. Bell, *Ritual Theory, Ritual Practice*, 124.

44. Knohl, *Sanctuary of Silence*, 90.

45. Ibid., 80–81.

46. Jonathan Magonet, "The Korah Rebellion," *Journal for the Study of the Old Testament* 24, (October 1982): 3–25, 5. See his genealogical chart on p. 24 as well as that of Milgrom in *Numbers*, 130. In *Sanctuary of Silence*, 82, Knohl points out that Korah and Aaron are made contemporaries in Exodus 6.

47. Magonet, "The Korah Rebellion," 5. In his reading of Korah's rebellion Magonet makes several observations that are quite similar to my own close reading of the material. These include providing a context for the rebellion that includes the connection between the deaths of Nadav and Avihu and those of the 250 who surround Korah. Both of us place a great deal of emphasis on the Levitical context, especially Korah's close family relationship, and the significance of the changing responsibilities of the Kohatites. Magonet identifies midrashic recognition of the tensions inherent in Korah's family situation (5) as well as an elaboration of the Jewish exegesis of Korah's rebellion. I do not. However, I develop the implications of Numbers 8 for the situation of the Levites in more depth. I also emphasize their indeterminate status and its dangers. In Numbers 16 I further elaborate on the links among Nadav, Avihu, and Korah's rebellion, partly in response to the agenda of the HS, a school not identified or addressed by Magonet in his work. In fact my reading is designed to expose the agenda of the priestly editors, while Magonet is more interested in the story than its redactors. I am also far more interested in the aftermath of the revolt and the use of the plating. Thus the current reading should be seen as complementary to that of Magonet, confirming some aspects of his reading while elaborating on points not touched on in his article.

48. Milgrom emphasizes the protective aspect of the ruling concerning the Kohatites in *Numbers*, 25. I stress how the psychological effects of the ruling will have an adverse influence over subsequent events. Magonet suggests that the episode of Korah becomes "a working out of the implications of this task of the Levites." "The Korah Rebellion," 11.

49. Magonet, "The Korah Rebellion," 13.

50. As also noted by Milgrom, *Numbers*, 62.

51. Milgrom devotes an excursus to this practice in *Numbers*, 425–426.

52. Victor Turner, *The Ritual Process Structure and Anti-Structure* (Chicago: Aldine Publishing, 1969), 171.

53. Milgrom, *Numbers*, 62.

54. Douglas, *Purity and Danger*, 96.

55. Milgrom, *Numbers*, 343. See also his excursus 40, beginning on p. 423 for his view of איש זר.

56. See Magonet, "The Korah Rebellion," 14, for the further exacerbation of tensions in the camp as a result of the Levitical duties. For the possible historical background to the introduction of the Levitical class as a separate institution, see Menachem Haran, *Temples and Temple-Service in Ancient Israel* (Oxford: Clarendon Press, 1977), 70–81.

57. Magonet, "The Korah Rebellion," 22.

58. Nehama Leibowitz, *Studies in Bamidbar* (Israel: Haomanim Press, 1996), 222.

59. Magonet, "The Korah Rebellion," 6–8, summarizes midrashic recognition of, and attempts to resolve, some of the inconsistencies in Korah's story. One can find a summary of various contemporary theories for the editing of Korah's

rebellion, including that of Knohl in *Sanctuary of Silence,* esp. 74, 79, 80–81. Milgrom, *Numbers,* 414ff., also discusses the editing of the rebellion in excursus 39.

60. Knohl, *Sanctuary of Silence,* 77–78, summarizes the evidence for editing, as well as the creative additions of HS to, the Korah rebellion. He argues that the revolt of the chieftains, the plague, and the miracle of the staff were part of an earlier layer of the story, while the narrative of Korah the Levite was added at a later stage of HS.

61. Milgrom, *Numbers,* 340. On the proximity of the Reubenites and Kohatites, see also Magonet, "The Korah Rebellion," 6 and 25.

62. Pierre Bourdieu, *Outline of a Theory of Practice,* trans. Richard Nice (Cambridge: Cambridge University Press, 1993), 120.

63. Milgrom, *Numbers,* 130, pointed out the reference to *nesi'ei* though not the allusion to verbal forms of the root in chapters 3 and 4.

64. Turner, *Dramas, Fields and Metaphors,* 41

65. Clifford Geertz, *Negara: The Theatre State in Nineteenth-Century Bali* (Princeton: Princeton University Press, 1980), 14.

66. I want to thank my former student from Hebrew Union College, Karen Rosauer, for pointing out an allusion to the establishment of Aaron's exclusive claim to the priesthood for all time in Exodus 29:9.

67. Douglas, *Purity and Danger,* 100.

68. Geertz, *Negara,* 113.

69. Ibid., 116.

70. Ronald L. Grimes, *Reading, Writing and Ritualizing* (Washington, D.C.: Pastoral Press, 1993), 64.

71. See Douglas, *Purity and Danger,* 114, for a discussion of Van Gennep's idea.

72. Grimes, *Reading, Writing and Ritualizing,* 67.

73. See also Magonet, "The Korah Rebellion," 21, on the image of Dathan and Abiram "going down."

74. Turner, *Dramas, Fields and Metaphors,* 37.

75. Menahem Haran argues that the fire pans were held by hand. Haran, "The Uses of Incense in the Ancient Israelite Ritual," *Vetus Testamentum* 10 (1960): 121.

76. Two of the more creative proposals concerning Nadav and Avihu include Julian Morgenstern, *The Fire upon the Altar* (Chicago: Quadrangle Books, 1963), which traces the possible historical background that would explain why fire from outside the tabernacle (or Temple precincts) could be interpreted as idolatry, and John C. H. Laughlin, who detects a Zoroastrian influence on the Nadav and Avihu story while linking it to Korah. He argues that in both stories they fail to take the fire from the altar. See his "The 'Strange Fire' of Nadav and Avihu," *Journal of Biblical Literature* 95, no. 4 (December 1976): 559–565.

77. Haran, "The Uses of Incense in the Ancient Israelite Ritual," 121. See also Milgrom, *Numbers,* 139.

78. Black, *Models and Metaphors,* 222.

79. I take up the use of plague as punishment as well as the different terms to describe it in the next chapter.
80. Magonet, "The Korah Rebellion," 11.
81. Milgrom, *Numbers*, 141. Note another parallel to the situation of Nadav and Avihu, but in reverse. By bringing strange fire into the tabernacle, they were killed. Now, by bringing fire out of the tabernacle into the midst of the people, their father Aaron saves the children of Israel.
82. Ibid., 141 for a similar suggestion.
83. For a different treatment of the story of the flowering staff and its significance based on the history of the text rather than the final form, see Knohl, *Sanctuary of Silence*, 79. See also William H. Propp, "The Rod of Aaron and the Sin of Moses," *Journal of Biblical Literature* 107, no. 1 (1988): 19–26.
84. Milgrom, *Numbers*, 143, n. 17, suggests that the individual's name, rather than the name of the tribe, is placed on the staff, because the test was designed to choose God's priest from among the tribal chieftains. However, with the background of recent tensions between Korah and Aaron, combining Aaron and the tribe of Levi on the staff certainly merits consideration as an attempt to resolve the tensions set up in the creation of the Levitical class.
85. Ibid., 143.
86. Instead of a phallic symbol, the flowering branch could be a symbol of Asherah, the fertility goddess who is represented as a tree. For a recent discussion of Asherah, see Mark Smith, *Memoirs of God* (Minneapolis: Fortress Press, 2004).
87. Victor Turner, "Social Dramas and the Stories about Them," 157.
88. Bell, *Ritual Theory, Ritual Practice*, 123.

CHAPTER 6 FALLING IN THE WILDERNESS

1. Gerdien Jonker, *The Topography of Remembrance: The Dead, Tradition and Collective Memory in Mesopotamia* (New York: E. J. Brill, 1995), 235.
2. Harrison, *The Dominion of the Dead*, 147.
3. *The Babylonian Talmud*, Baba Bathra, 74a. The citations of Bialik's poem come from Bialik, *Selected Poems*.
4. In this chapter I generally follow the translation found in Milgrom, *Numbers*; Tigay, *Deuteronomy*; and other JPS translations, But in this verse, I have chosen to translate יִפֹּל as "fall" rather than the JPS choice of "drop." Both are accurate, but the present chapter's title echoes the "fall" in God's condemnation. At times I follow the syntax in the Hebrew and I use "YHWH."
5. As put by Harrison, *The Dominion of the Dead*, x: "the dead exert their power, press their demands, grant or deny their blessing, become loquacious, and in general cohabit our worlds. Such places where the dead carry on a secular afterlife... include graves... images... rituals, monuments and the archives of literature, whose voices always have a posthumous character of sorts." In the

case of Numbers the dead exert their power by providing a horrifying deterrent to the living.

6. The way in which one identifies the results depends in part on the topic that organizes that reading. For instance, Mary Douglas is interested in the interactions between the returning exiles and those who remained behind, so she identifies an overarching rhetorical structure for Numbers that reflects that focus in her work *In the Wilderness*, 102–122. Aaron Schart is interested in the Israelite rebellions in the wilderness in their entirety. In consequence he offers a reading of the final form that includes not only Numbers but Exodus in order to trace the parallel series of complaints in both works. See *Mose und Israel im Konflikt*, OBO 98 (Göttingen: Vandenhoeck and Ruprecht, 1990). My interest in the politics of memory and tradition influences what I highlight in the final form of Numbers.

7. Armando Petrucci, *Writing the Dead* (Stanford, Calif.: Stanford University Press, 1998), xvi. Even in earliest times the impulse to provide a corpse a "written death" has been in evidence. In fact Denise Schmandt-Besserat argues that the inscription of personal names in funerary rites had a highly significant impact on the evolution of writing. See "The Personal Name in Mesopotamia: Its Impact on the Evolution of Writing," in *Proceedings of the First International Congress on the Archaeology of the Ancient Near East* (Rome: 2000), 1493–1499, 1493. She points out that around 2700–2600 B.C.E at the court of the Sumerian kings of Ur, "Royal scribes began writing on objects of gold, silver and lapis lazuli that were to be deposited in tombs.... For the first time in history the Ur scribes put writing to work for a function other than accounting. That new purpose was funerary." Denise Schmandt-Besserat, "Signs of Life," *Odyssey* (January/February 2002): 6–7, 63, 63.

8. See Rachel S. Hallote, *Death, Burial and Afterlife in the Biblical World* (Chicago: Ivan R. Dee, 2001), 31, 45; Elizabeth Bloch-Smith, *Judahite Burial Practices and Beliefs about the Dead*, JSOT 123 (Great Britain: Sheffield Academic Press, 1992), 18; and Alan F. Segal, *Life after Death* (New York: Doubleday, 2004), 142. Wayne T. Pitard makes the same point. "The relative elaborateness of a tomb, the types of funerary offerings found in it and sometimes its location may suggest a particular social standing of its owner(s)." Wayne T. Pitard, "Tombs and Offerings: Archeological Data and Comparative Methodology in the Study of Death in Israel," in *Sacred Time, Sacred Place*, ed. Barry M. Gittlen (Winona Lake, Ind.: Eisenbrauns, 2002), 145–167, 148. Brian B. Schmidt discusses the politics involved in the burials that took place in the Ebla court (27) as well as the treatment of dead kings of Mari (44) in *Israel's Beneficent Dead* (Tubingen: J. C. B. Mohr, Paul Siebeck, 1994).

9. For a detailed discussion of the role of the censuses in anchoring the materials in Numbers, see Olson, *The Death of the Old and the Birth of the New*.

10. For a broad discussion of the juxtaposition of chapter 11 with that of chapter 10, see chapter 4 of the present work.

11. This last point was made by a careful Israeli reader of an earlier version of this chapter that appeared in the journal *Prooftexts*. In the cited examples from Numbers 11–16, the root is אכל, but in Numbers 17 it is כלה.

12. See Douglas, *In the Wilderness*, 212, for an interesting suggestion regarding Miriam's half-consumed flesh.

13. In addition to the verb's use when God kills the Egyptians and the Israelite meat-eaters, a form of the root נכה is used in Numbers when Israelites kill foreigners: e.g., in the battles against the kings of Sihon and Bashan (21:24, 21:35); used by Balak in reference to his desire to smite the Israelites (22:6); used by Balaam against his poor donkey several times in Numbers 22; and used when referring to those killed by Phinehas: Cozbi (a foreign woman) and Zimri (though Israelite, attached to the Midianite woman, 25:14, 12:15, 25:18); and against the Midianites (25:17). Finally, a form of the verb is used when Moses strikes the rock in 20:11. In contrast, מגפה is usually used when God kills Israelites: the death of the spies in 14:37 and that of Israelites in 17:13–15. It is also used in chapter 25. But the use of מגפה in chapter 25 highlights the differences in usage between the two terms. מגפה refers to God's plague against the Israelites, but מכה refers to the deaths of Cozbi the Midianite and Zimri (25:8, 9, 18, 19). The use of מגפה in chapters 17 and 25 is noteworthy. In both instances, the priest steps in to stop the plague. For a further discussion of the use of מגפה and a different form, נגף, see the comments of Magonet in "The Korah Rebellion," 11.

14. Milgrom, *Numbers*, 107–117, 379, highlights the way in which measure-for-measure punishment pervades the narrative. Midrash Rabbah explicitly comments on the same notion in Numbers 14:2: "Said he to the man: 'I shall pass upon you the sentence which you have uttered with your own mouth. You shall get what you have said.' The Holy One, blessed be He, in the same manner said to Israel: As I live, saith the Lord, surely as ye have spoken in Mine ears, so will I do to you: your carcasses shall fall in this wilderness" (Num. xiv, 28f.). Unless otherwise noted, when citing midrash I will use the translation of Judah J. Slotki, *Midrash Rabbah* (London: Soncino, 1961), 688.

15. See Appendix C for a list of the reports of the dead in Numbers, including the length of each report. In considering the various redactional moves made in chapters 11–20 and the way in which divine punishment organizes the material, Thomas W. Mann notes that the general theme of rebellion in the camp can be broken down into two distinct units. Chapters 11:1–14:45 should be considered prophetic controversies and have to do with the fate of the entire generation, while chapters 16:1–20:13 have to do with priestly controversies and the fate of Moses and Aaron. See Mann, "Holiness and Death in the Redaction of Numbers 16:1–20:13," 190.

16. Petrucci, *Writing the Dead*, xviii.

17. Ibid., xvii.

18. Midrash Rabbah understands the specific manner in which Dathan and Abiram die as dictated by measure-for-measure punishment: "And they said: WE WILL

NOT COME UP. These wicked men were tripped up by their own mouth and there is a covenant made with the lips, for they died and WENT DOWN into the bottomless abyss [Sheol]." Slotki, trans., *Midrash Rabbah*, 719. Sheol as a separate land of the dead appears in Numbers only in this chapter. See Gerhard Lisowsky, *Konkordanz Zum Hebraischen Alten Testament* (Stuttgart: Wurttembergische Bibelanstalt, 1958), 1390. By the end of Numbers the entire wilderness has become the territory of the dead, effectively becoming the equivalent of Sheol. Note also that the passage includes a reference to the people of Korah in verse 32, even though the 250 die in verse 35. See Milgrom, *Numbers*, 138, n. 32.

19. Petrucci, *Writing the Dead*, xviii, identifies the ways in which death reports reinforce the status quo.

20. Rita J. Burns, *Has the Lord Indeed Spoken Only through Moses?* (Atlanta: Scholars Press, 1987), 117, considers the arrangement found in chapter 20 to be purposeful, because it narrates not only the deaths of Miriam and Aaron, but also the impending death of Moses.

21. The relevant sections of Deuteronomy that concern the death report of Moses, 31:14–15, 23; 32:48–52; and 34:1–12, have long been considered as belonging to the same block of material as that found in Numbers, particularly in the priestly narratives. For such an identification, see Gerhard von Rad, *Deuteronomy* (Philadelphia: Westminster, 1966), 188, 201, 209; E. W. Nicholson, *Deuteronomy and Tradition* (Philadelphia: Fortress, 1967), 36; Jeffrey H. Tigay, *Deuteronomy* (Philadelphia: Jewish Publication Society, 1996), 518; and Alexander Rofe, *Introduction to the Composition of the Pentateuch* (Sheffield: Sheffield Academic Press, 1999), 134. Thus, not only is it valid, but if one wants to understand the connections among the three death reports, it is necessary to consider the report of Moses found in Deuteronomy alongside those of Miriam and Aaron in Numbers 20.

22. Translation mine. Miriam remains enigmatic. Unlike the majority of other women in the Hebrew bible, her reputation does not rest on being someone's mother or wife. She has an independent existence, even accorded the title "prophetess" (Exod. 15:20.) That she is mentioned as late as the book of Chronicles testifies to "the tenacity of her place in Israel's memory," as pointed out in Burns, *Has the Lord Indeed Spoken Only through Moses?* 92, 129. That she is called "sister" suggests a status parallel to that of her brother Aaron as a member of an important founding family of Israel (96). Yet a more elaborate tradition has not been preserved. Perhaps she held such an established reputation as a leader of Israel that she threatened the interests represented by the Torah's editors. Therefore her voice was extinguished.

23. Ibid., 120.

24. Ibid., 117. The prophet Micah places Miriam on par with her brothers: "I brought you up from the land of Egypt and redeemed you from the house of slavery and I sent before you Moses, Aaron and Miriam" (Micah 6:4). Rita Burns's

conclusion recapitulates the fragmentary evidence for Miriam's status and is worth quoting:

> Six of the seven...texts which mention her represent her as a leader. In her initial appearance in the narratives (Exodus 15:20–21) Miriam officiates at a celebration of the foundational event of Hebrew religion.... In designating Miriam as "sister" of Aaron (Exod. 15:20) and of Aaron and Moses (Num. 26:59; I Chron. 5:29) the biblical writers use kinship terminology to express Miriam's parallel status in religious leadership vis-à-vis that of the two other leading figures in the wilderness.... Micah 6:4... [says] that Miriam (along with Moses and Aaron) was divinely commissioned as a leader in the wilderness. Ibid., 121)

25. Thomas W. Mann discusses God's verdict against Moses and Aaron at length in "Holiness and Death in the Redaction of Numbers 16:1–20:13," 189–90. Burns, *Has the Lord Indeed Spoken Only through Moses*, 118–119, lists several elements that the reports of Aaron and Moses have in common. They die on mountains, both are mourned for thirty days, and both leave successors in office. In what follows, I delineate how their death reports echo and resolve the political rivalry between the two that was hinted at in Exodus 32 and erupted in Numbers 12.

26. On Joshua as Moses' successor, see also Numbers 27:18. For a discussion of the tent of meeting as distinct from the *mishkan*, see Tigay, *Deuteronomy*, 293.

27. No successor to Miriam is announced. One could make the argument that Deborah is a fitting choice. She is a significant leader in the early tribal years before the monarchy. She is called prophetess, appears in the light of a military strategist (Judges 4), and is associated, as is Miriam, with a very early victory poem (Judges 5).

28. This is true in spite of a countermove to place the brothers on an equal footing at the moment of their deaths in the midrash. "'My decree retains in force; GET THEE UP INTO THIS MOUNTAIN OF ABARIM,' etc. AS AARON THY BROTHER WAS GATHERED: You are not better than your brother." Slotki, trans., *Midrash Rabbah*, 840.

29. Petrucci, *Writing the Dead*, 30.

30. Within the biblical texts, a corpse requires interment in a grave. See, e.g., Genesis 23:4, Exodus 14:11, and Isaiah 22:16. Yet a brief perusal in Lisowsky, *Konkordanz Zum Hebraischen Alten Testament*, 1233–1234, reveals that קבר appears remarkably little in Numbers considering the number of dead. It appears only once in qal (Num. 11:34), niphal (Num. 20:1), and piel (Num. 33:4), and twice as a noun (Num. 19:16, 18).

31. Brian B. Schmidt, "Memory as Immortality: Countering the Dreaded 'Death after Death' in Ancient Israelite Society," in *Judaism in Late Antiquity*, ed. Alan J. Avery-Peck and Jacob Neusner (Leiden: Brill, 2000), 88.

32. Several recent works discuss the treatment of the dead prior to exile in ancient Israel, including that of Schmidt, "Memory as Immortality," and his earlier

Israel's Beneficent Dead; William G. Dever, *What Did the Biblical Writers Know and When Did They Know It?* (Grand Rapids, Mich.: Eerdmans, 2001), 216–221; and Bloch-Smith, *Judahite Burial Practices and Beliefs about the Dead.* For a discussion of the treatment of the dead after exile, see Wayne T. Pitard, "Afterlife and Immortality," in *Oxford Companion to the Bible,* ed. Bruce Manning Metzger and Michael David Coogan (New York: Oxford University Press, 1993), 15–16.

33. Harrison, *Dominion of the Dead,* 143.

34. The matter most debated in the literature on ancient Israelite treatment of the dead concerns the existence, or extent, of an actual cult of the dead in ancient Israel, a topic that lies beyond the scope of the present argument. For a description of a variety of ancient Near Eastern practices in the cult of the dead, see Milgrom, *Numbers,* 17–18; Denise Schmandt-Besserat, "The Personal Name in Mesopotamia: Its Impact on the Evolution of Writing," in *Proceedings of the First International Congress on the Archeology of the Ancient Near East* (Rome: 2000), 1493–1499, 1494; and Alan Segal, *Life after Death* (New York: Doubleday, 2004).

For details of the argument for a cult of the dead *within* Israel, see Bloch-Smith, including the summary of her argument in *Judahite Burial Practices and Beliefs about the Dead.* Along with Mark Smith she identifies the period roughly around 750 B.C.E as a crucial time in which attitudes toward specific practices concerning the dead might have changed. See Mark S. Smith and Elizabeth M. Bloch-Smith, "Death and Afterlife in Ugarit and Israel," *Journal of the American Oriental Society* 108, no. 2 (April-June 1988): 277–284, 282. For some hint of the possibilities of such a practice, see Isaiah 65:4. If there were such a practice, the contemptuous way in which the God of Numbers treats the dead would no doubt shock an audience accustomed to worshiping and fearing their ancestors. Perhaps the narrative was meant to persuade the Israelite audience of God's superior authority and power in comparison to their dead ancestors.

More recently, Bloch-Smith reflected on the cyclical nature of the debate over the cult of the dead in Israel in "Death in the Life of Israel," 139–143. That essay was followed by Wayne T. Pitard, "Tombs and Offerings: Archaeological Data and Comparative Methodology in the study of Death in Israel," 145–167, which sharply critiques the excavation carried out by Claude Schaeffer in the late 1930s out of which later interpretations of a few Israelite archeological sites arose. His essay throws into further doubt whether an Israelite cult of the dead existed. However, as he concludes that there is a lack of evidence for whether the Israelites provided additional offerings of food or drink to their dead after burial, he reminds us that such lack of evidence "does not allow us then to conclude that the Israelites did not perform such offerings. That would be a very dangerous argument from silence. But it means that we need considerably more evidence before arguing the practice existed." Pitard, "Tombs and Offerings," 155. In his essay "How Far Can Texts Take Us?" Theodore J. Lewis cites a consensus position that there *is* a cult of the dead, which he describes as "characterized by an active existence of the shades, the quasi-deification of the dead, the practice of necromancy, and the post interment feeding of the dead" (169–217, 186). The three essays can be found in Barry M. Gittlen, *Sacred Time, Sacred Place* (Winona Lake, Ind.: Eisenbrauns, 2002).

For a straightforward statement against the presence of ancestor worship in ancient Israel, see Brain Schmidt, *Israel's Beneficent Dead*. He concludes that there was a "historical absence of ancestor worship or veneration in pre-exilic Israel and Judah" (165). He sensibly reminds us that the absence of an ancestor cult does not preclude an ongoing relationship with one's dead, including visitation, caring for the tomb, and some form of commemoration (275). For a detailed critique of his work, see Theodore J. Lewis, "How Far Can Texts Take Us?," 189–199.

In this chapter I take up the proper care of the dead, including their burial, but not the question of ancestor worship. If one accepts the conclusion of Smith and Smith, by the redaction of Numbers (most likely after 750 B.C.E) the question appears moot.

35. Schmidt, *Israel's Beneficent Dead*, 275, 284.
36. Ibid., 122.
37. See Segal, *Life after Death*, 95–97, for evidence of Mesopotamian burial in family tombs.
38. Cyrus H. Gordon, "The Marriage and Death of Sinuhe," in *Love and Death in the Ancient Near East*, ed. Pope et al., 43–44, 44.
39. In addition to Jeremiah, see the rituals surrounding David's burial of Abner in II Samuel 3:31–38 as suggested by Lewis, "How Far Can Texts Take Us?," 178. Outside Numbers, no better example of the intersection between politics and death exists in the bible. See also Appendix D for a partial list of other biblical evidence for the proper and improper treatment of the dead.
40. Bloch-Smith, *Judahite Burial Practices*, 63–64. The list and distribution of types of graves can be found on p. 62. Lewis, "How Far Can Texts Take Us?," 179, claims that "standing stones are well attested in every archaeological age ... primary usage being one of commemoration." The dead of the desert were also denied such markers.
41. Yitzhak Avishur, *Phoenician Inscriptions and the Bible* (Tel Aviv: Archaeological Center Publication, 2000), 112.
42. Ibid., 115.
43. Ibid., 135.
44. Brian Peckham, "Phoenicia and the Religion of Israel: The Epigraphic Evidence," in *Ancient Israelite Religion: Essays in Honor of Frank Moore Cross*, ed. Patrick D. Miller, Paul D. Hanson, and S. Dean McBride (Philadelphia: Fortress Press, 1987), 79–99, 82.
45. Some families apparently buried their dead under their family homes. See Hallote, *Death, Burial and Afterlife in the Biblical World*, 30. Hallote also discusses

the common practice of group burial (42), as does Bloch-Smith, *Judahite Burial Practices*, 37, 110. For the evidence that family tombs were maintained, see ibid., 150, and Dever, *What Did the Biblical Writers Know*, 217. On public recitation, see Schmidt, "Memory as Immortality," 99.

46. Jonker, *Topography of Remembrance*, 4.
47. Harrison, *Dominion of the Dead*, 24.
48. Bloch-Smith, *Judahite Burial Practices*, 111.
49. Herbert Chanan Brichto, "Kin, Cult, Land and Afterlife – A Biblical Complex," *Hebrew Union College Annual* 44 (1973), 1–54, 8–9.
50. Segal, *Life after Death*, 140.
51. Bloch-Smith, *Judahite Burial Practices*, 112, cites Deuteronomy 28:25–26; I Kings 13:22, 14:10–11; Jeremiah 16:4.
52. Excerpted from the *Classic Midrash*, trans. Reuven Hammer (Mahwah, N.J.: Paulist Press, 1995), 268.
53. Schmidt, "Memory as Immortality," 100.
54. Jonker, *Topography of Remembrance*, 21.
55. The linkage of space and memory is developed further by Pierre Nora, "Between Memory and History: Les Lieux de Memoire," *Representations* 26 (Spring 1989): 7–24.
56. Jonker, *Topography of Remembrance*, 37.
57. Ibid., 37.
58. I discuss Numbers 19 in much greater detail in the forthcoming *Women's Torah Commentary*, to be published by the UAHC Press. See also Thomas Mann's discussion of chapter 19 in "Holiness and Death in the Redaction of Numbers 16:1–20:13," 185.
59. Robert L. Cohn, *The Shape of Sacred Space: Four Biblical Studies* (Chico, Calif.: Scholars Press, 1981), 16.
60. Shemaryahu Talmon, "The Desert Motif in the Bible and in Qumran Literature," in *Biblical Motifs, Origins and Transformations*, ed. Alexander Altmann (Cambridge: Harvard University Press, 1966), 42. Talmon identifies three categories within the biblical materials meant by the Hebrew term for desert. His third category defines מדבר, wilderness, as imagined in Numbers and in this chapter. It denotes the true desert, the arid zones beyond the borders of the cultivated land. He concludes: "This meaning is well rendered in English by 'wilderness'" (40–41).
61. As quoted by Brevard S. Childs, "Death and Dying in Old Testament Theology," in Pope et al., *Love and Death in the Ancient Near East*, 89–91, 90.
62. Theodore J. Lewis, "The Abode of the Dead," in *The Anchor Bible Dictionary*, ed. David Noel Freedman (New York: Doubleday, 1992), 102. A series of reflections on Sheol can be found in James Kugel, *The God of Old* (New York: Free Press, 2003), 169–180. Segal, *Life after Death*, 136, also described Sheol as "far from the presence of God."

63. Talmon, "The Desert Motif," 37. Alternatively, the wilderness becomes a refuge for characters such as Hagar and David, who flee there to escape danger or ill treatment. For details, see Talmon, "The Desert Motif," 42.

64. I am referring to the wilderness as it is perceived by the end of Numbers. Deuteronomy poetically imagines the wilderness as a wasteland in 32:10. However, for a distinctly different memory of the wilderness period, see Deuteronomy 29:4. Within the prophetic tradition, note that the wilderness period is considered a time of great intimacy between God and Israel. See, e.g., Hosea 2:16–17, Jeremiah 2:2 and 31:1–2. Yet within Hosea can be found a starkly different view of the wilderness period, closer to that of Numbers. See, e.g., Hosea 9:10 and 11:1–4. A discussion of midrashic readings of the wilderness can be found in Daniel Boyarin, *Intertextuality and the Reading of Midrash* (Bloomington: Indiana University Press, 1994), 48–49.

65. Petrucci, *Writing the Dead*, 2.

66. Bialik, *Selected Poems*.

CHAPTER 7 INHERITING THE LAND

1. Jerome Bruner, *Acts of Meaning* (Cambridge: Harvard University Press, 1990), 47.

2. Mary Marshall Clark, "Speak, Memory," *Columbia Magazine* (Spring 2006), 24.

3. Frank Kermode, *The Sense of an Ending* (New York: Oxford University Press, 1967), 8.

4. As paraphrased by Bruner, *Acts of Meaning*, 90.

5. Ibid., 56.

6. Ibid., 47.

7. Knierim and Coats, *Numbers*, 8.

8. Ibid., 147.

9. Bruner, *Acts of Meaning*, 85.

10. As put by Bruner, they find a way to renegotiate meaning by means of narrative. Ibid., 67.

11. Kermode, *The Sense of an Ending*, 23–24.

12. Ibid., 17.

13. Knierim and Coats, *Numbers*, 274, point out that the term "drawing near" signals "a trial, a civil suit designed to determine the legitimacy of the daughters' claim for inheritance rights." Note also Milgrom's identification of the pattern of Numbers 27 as fitting that of three previous cases decided by oracle. For details, see Milgrom, *Numbers*, 230. For present purposes, it is the connection of Numbers 27 with the ending of Numbers rather than those earlier cases that is relevant.

14. Knierim and Coats, *Numbers*, 274, point out that the objection of the daughters presupposes a law or practice of inheritance that limits the succession to male

heirs. They point to Deuteronomy 21:16 as the probable source of such a law. For a discussion of "holding" versus "inheritance," see Milgrom, *Numbers*, 232, n. 7.

15. As put by Knierim and Coats, *Numbers*, 274: "The concluding formula proclaims the new ruling as the prevailing principle, an addition to the law."

16. Dennis Olson as quoted by Milgrom, *Numbers*, 296.

17. Loosely based on the JPS translation. Instead of "diminished," I use "lost" for purposes of the allusion to Numbers 27. See the alternative translation of Everett Fox, *The Five Books of Moses* (New York: Schocken, 1995), 836.

18. Knierim and Coats, *Numbers*, 330.

19. Milgrom, *Numbers*, 296, offers several other possible explanations for the placement of Numbers 36 where it is, including the proposal that it is an afterthought, added after the book had been completed.

APPENDIX B

1. Rabinowitz et al., *A Witness Forever*, 116.

2. Thomas W. Mann makes this point in "Holiness and Death in the Redaction of Numbers 16: 1–20:13," 184.

Bibliography

Allan, George. *The Importance of the Past.* Albany: State University of New York Press, 1986.

Alter, Robert. *The Five Books of Moses.* New York: W. W. Norton, 2004.

    The David Story. New York: W. W. Norton, 1999.

    The Art of Biblical Poetry. New York: Basic Books, 1985.

    The Art of Biblical Narrative. New York: Basic Books, 1981.

Alter, Robert, and Frank Kermode. *The Literary Guide to the Bible.* Cambridge: Belknap Press, 1987.

Asmann, Jan. *Moses the Egyptian.* Cambridge: Harvard University Press, 1997.

Avishur, Yitzhak. *Phoenician Inscriptions and the Bible.* Tel Aviv: Archaeological Center Publication, 2000.

Bach, Alice. *Women in the Hebrew Bible.* London: Routledge, 1999.

Barton, John. *Reading the Old Testament.* Philadelphia: Westminster Press, 1984.

Bell, Catherine. *Ritual Theory, Ritual Practice.* New York: Oxford University Press, 1992.

Bialik, Hayyim Nahman. *Selected Poems.* Trans. Ruth Nevo. Israel: Dvir Co., 1981.

Black, Max. *Models and Metaphors.* Ithaca, N.Y.: Cornell University Press, 1962.

Blenkinsopp, Joseph. *Sage Priest Prophet: Religious and Intellectual Leadership in Ancient Israel.* Louisville, Ky.: Westminster John Knox Press, 1995.

    "The Structure of P." *Catholic Biblical Quarterly* 38 (1976): 275–292.

Bloch-Smith, Elizabeth. *Judahite Burial Practices and Beliefs about the Dead.* Sheffield, England: JSOT Press, 1992.

Bloch-Smith, Elizabeth M., and Mark Smith. "Death and Afterlife in Ugarit and Israel." *Journal of the American Oriental Society* 108, no. 2 (April–June 1988): 277–284.

Blum, Erhard. *Studien zur Komposition des Pentateuch.* Berlin: Walter de Gruyter, 1990.

Botterweck, G. Johannes, and Helmer Ringgren. *Theological Dictionary of the Old Testament*, vol. 4. Grand Rapids, Mich.: William B. Eerdmans, 1980.

Bourdieu, Pierre. *Outline of a Theory of Practice.* Trans. Richard Nice. Cambridge: Cambridge University Press, 1993.

Boyarin, Daniel. *Intertextuality and the Reading of Midrash.* Bloomington: Indiana University Press, 1994.

Brettler, Marc Zvi. "Memory in Ancient Israel." In *Memory and History in Christianity and Judaism,* ed. Michael Signer. Notre Dame: University of Notre Dame Press, 2001.

The Creation of History in Ancient Israel. London and New York: Routledge, 1995.

Brichto, Herbert Chanan. "Kin, Cult, Land and Afterlife – A Biblical Complex." *Hebrew Union College Annual* 44 (1973): 1–54.

Bronner, Leila Leah. *From Eve to Esther.* Louisville, Ky.: Westminster John Knox Press, 1994.

Brueggemann, Walter, and Hans Walter Wolff. *The Vitality of Old Testament Traditions.* Atlanta, Ga.: John Knox, 1952.

Bruner, Jerome. *Acts of Meaning.* Cambridge: Harvard University Press, 1990.

Buber, Martin, and Franz Rosenzweig. *Scripture and Translation.* Bloomington: Indiana University Press, 1994.

Burns, Rita J. *Has the Lord Indeed Spoken Only through Moses?* Atlanta, Ga.: Scholars Press, 1987.

Carr, David. "Controversy and Convergence in Recent Studies of the Formation of the Pentateuch." *Religious Studies Review* 23, no. 1 (January 1997): 22–30.

Carter, Charles E. *The Emergence of Yehud in the Persian Period.* Sheffield, England: Sheffield Academic Press, 1999.

Cassuto, Umberto. *Biblical and Oriental Studies.* Jerusalem: Magnes Press, 1973.

Childs, Brevard S. *Memory and Tradition in Israel.* Naperville, Ill.: A. R. Allenson, 1962.

Clark, Mary Marshall. "Speak, Memory." *Columbia Magazine* Spring (2006): 24.

Cohn, Robert L. *The Shape of Sacred Space: Four Biblical Studies.* Chico, Calif.: Scholars Press, 1981.

Connerton, Paul. *How Societies Remember.* Cambridge: Cambridge University Press, 1989.

Cooper, Alan, and Bernard Goldstein. "The Development of the Priestly Calendars (I)." *Hebrew Union College Annual* 74 (2003): 1–20.

"At the Entrance to the Tent: More Cultic Resonances in Biblical Narrative." *Journal of Biblical Literature* 116, no. 2 (1997): 201–215.

Cornell, Stephen. "That's the Story of Our Life." In *We Are a People.* Ed. Paul Spickard and W. Jeffrey Burroughs. Philadelphia: Temple University Press, 2000.

Damrosch, David. *The Narrative Covenant.* San Francisco: Harper and Row, 1987.

Davis, Natalie Zemon, and Randolph Starn. "Introduction." *Representations* 26 (Spring 1989): 1–6.

Deflem, Mathieu. "Ritual, Anti-Structure and Religion: A Discussion of Victor Turner's Processual Symbolic Analysis." *Journal for the Scientific Study of Religion* 30, no. 1 (March 1991): 1–25.

Dever, William D. *What Did the Biblical Writers Know and When Did They Know It?* Grand Rapids, Mich.: Eerdmans, 2001.

Douglas, Mary. *In the Wilderness.* Sheffield, England: JSOT Press, 1993.

Purity and Danger. London: Routledge and Kegan Paul, 1966.

Eskenazi, Tamara. "Current Perspectives on Ezra-Nehemiah and the Persian Period." *Currents in Research: Biblical Studies* 1 (1993): 59–86.

Even-Shoshan, Avraham. *The New Concordance.* Jerusalem: Kiryat-Sepher, 1979.

Fox, Everett. *The Five Books of Moses.* New York: Schocken Books, 1995.

Friedman, Richard Elliot. *The Bible with Sources Revealed.* San Francisco: Harper, 2003.

The Creation of Sacred Literature. Berkeley: University of California Press, 1981.

The Exile and Biblical Narrative. Chico, Calif.: Scholars Press, 1981.

Funkenstein, Amos. *Perceptions of Jewish History.* Berkeley: University of California Press, 1993.

Gedi, Noa, and Yigal Elam. "Collective Memory – What Is It?" *History and Memory* 8, no. 1 (Spring/Summer 1996): 30–50.

Geertz, Clifford. *Negara: The Theatre State in Nineteenth-Century Bali.* Princeton: Princeton University Press, 1980.

Geller, Stephen. "The Religion of the Bible." In *The Jewish Study Bible.* Ed. Adele Berlin and Marc Brettler. Oxford: Oxford University Press, 1999: 2021–2040.

Geoghegan, Jeffrey C. *The Time, Place and Purpose of the Deuteronomic History.* Providence, R.I.: Brown Judaic Studies, 2006.

Gittlen, Barry M. *Sacred Time, Sacred Place: Archaeology and the Religion of Israel.* Winona Lake, Ind.: Eisenbrauns, 2002.

Gombrich, E. H. *Symbolic Images.* London: Phaidon Press, 1972.

Gordon, Cyrus H. "The Marriage and Death of Sinuhe." In *Love and Death in the Ancient Near East: Essays in Honor of Marvin H. Pope.* Ed. Marvin H. Pope, John H. Marks, and Robert McClive Good. Guilford: Conn.: Four Quarters Publishing, 1987: 43–44.

Gorman, Frank H. *The Ideology of Ritual.* Sheffield, England: Sheffield Academic Press, 1990.

Gottlieb, Isaac B. "*Sof Davar:* Biblical Endings." *Prooftexts* 11 (1991): 213–224.

Gray, George. *A Critical and Exegetical Commentary on Numbers.* Edinburgh: T. T. Clark, 1903.

Greenberg, Moshe. *Biblical Prose Prayer.* Berkeley: University of California Press, 1983.

Greenstein, Edward L. *Essays on Biblical Method and Translation.* Atlanta, Ga.: Scholars Press, 1989.

Greifenhagen, F. V. *Egypt on the Pentateuch's Ideological Map.* London: Sheffield Academic Press, 2002.

Grimes, Ronald L. *Reading, Writing and Ritualizing.* Washington, D.C.: Pastoral Press, 1993.

Halbwachs, Maurice. *On Collective Memory*. Chicago: Chicago University Press, 1992.

Hallote, Rachel S. *Death, Burial and Afterlife in the Biblical World: How the Israelites and Their Neighbors Treated the Dead*. Chicago: Ivan R. Dee, 2001.

Haran, Menahem. "The Character of the Priestly Source: Utopian and Exclusive Features." In *Proceedings of the Eighth World Congress of Jewish Studies*. Jerusalem: World Union of Jewish Studies, 1983.

"Behind the Scenes of History: Determining the Date of the Priestly Source." *Journal of Biblical Literature* 100, no. 3 (1981): 321–333.

Temples and Temple-Service in Ancient Israel. Oxford: Clarendon Press, 1977.

Harrison, Robert Pogue. *The Dominion of the Dead*. Chicago: University of Chicago Press, 2003.

Hendel, Ronald. *Remembering Abraham: Culture, Memory, and History in the Hebrew Bible*. Oxford: Oxford University Press, 2005.

Hervieu-Leger, Daniele. *Religion as a Chain of Memory*. Trans. Simon Lee. New Brunswick, N.J.: Rutgers University Press, 2000.

Hobsbawm, Eric, and Terence Ranger. *The Invention of Tradition*. Cambridge: Cambridge University Press, 1983.

Hurvitz, Avi. "The Language of the Priestly Source and Its Historical Setting – The Case for an Early Date." In *The Proceedings of the Eighth World Congress of Jewish Studies*. Jerusalem: World Union of Jewish Studies, 1983.

Jenks, A. W. *The Elohist and North Israelite Traditions*. Missoula, Mont.: Scholars Press, 1977.

Jonker, Gerdien. *The Topography of Remembrance*. Leiden and New York: E. J. Brill, 1995.

Kallai, Z. "The Wandering Traditions from Kadesh-Barnesa to Canaan: A Study in Biblical Historiography." *Journal of Jewish Studies* (Spring-Autumn 1982): 175–184.

Kermode, Frank. *The Sense of an Ending*. New York: Oxford University Press, 1967.

Klein, Ralph W. "The Message of P." In *Die Botschaft und die Boten*. Germany: Neukirchener Verlag, 1981.

Knierim, Rolf P., and George W. Coats. *Numbers*. Grand Rapids, Mich.: William B. Eerdmans, 2005.

Knohl, Israel. *The Divine Symphony*. Philadelphia: Jewish Publication Society, 2003.

The Sanctuary of Silence. Minneapolis, Minn.: Fortress Press, 1995.

Kugel, James. *The God of Old*. New York: Free Press, 2003.

Kushelevsky, Rella. *Moses and the Angel of Death*. New York: Peter Lang, 1995.

Laughlin, John C. H. "The 'Strange Fire' of Nadav and Avihu." *Journal of Biblical Literature* 95, no. 4 (December 1976): 559–565.

Le Goff, Jacques. *History and Memory*. New York: Columbia University Press, 1992.

Leach, Edmund. *Culture and Communication: The Logic by Which Symbols Are Connected*. Cambridge: Cambridge University Press, 1976.

Leibowitz, Nehama. *Studies in Bamidbar.* Trans. Aryeh Newman. Jerusalem: World Zionist Organization, 1980.

Leveen, Adriane. "Reading the Seams." *Journal for the Study of the Old Testament* 29 (2005): 259–287.

Levine, Baruch A. *Numbers 1–20: A New Translation with Introduction and Commentary.* New York: Doubleday, 1993.

Numbers 21–36. New York: Doubleday, 2000.

Leviticus: The Traditional Hebrew Text with the New JPS Translation. Philadelphia: Jewish Publication Society, 1989.

"Late Language in the Priestly Source: Some Literary and Historical Observations." In *The Proceedings of the Eighth World Congress of Jewish Studies.* Jerusalem: World Union of Jewish Studies, 1983.

"Priestly Writers." In *The Interpreter's Dictionary of the Bible.* Nashville, Tenn.: Abingdon Press, 1976: 683–687.

Lewis, Bernard. *History Remembered, Recovered, Invented.* Princeton: Princeton University Press, 1975.

Licht, Jacob. *Commentary on the Book of Numbers.* In Hebrew. Jerusalem: Magnes Press, 1991.

Lisowsky, Gerhard. *Konkordanz Zum Hebraischen Alten Testament.* Stuttgart: Wurttembergische Bibelanstalt, 1958.

Lowenthal, David. *The Past Is a Foreign Country.* Cambridge: Cambridge University Press, 1985.

Magonet, Jonathan. "The Korah Rebellion." *Journal for the Study of the Old Testament* 24 (October 1982): 3–25.

Mann, Thomas W. "Holiness and Death in the Redaction of Numbers 16:1–20:13." In *Love and Death in the Ancient Near East: Essays in Honor of Marvin H. Ed. Marvin H. Pope, John H. Marks, and Robert McClive Good.* Guilford, Conn.: Four Quarters Publishing, 1987: 181–190.

Margalit, Avishai. *The Ethics of Memory.* Cambridge: Harvard University Press, 2002.

McEvenue, Sean E. *The Narrative Style of the Priestly Writer.* Rome: Biblical Institute, 1971.

Medenhall, George. "The Census Lists of Numbers 1 and 26." *Journal of Biblical Literature* 77 (1958): 52–66.

Milgrom, Jacob. *Numbers: The Traditional Hebrew Text with the New JPS Translation.* Philadelphia: Jewish Publication Society, 1990.

"The Structure of Numbers: Chapters 11–12 and 13–14 and Their Redaction. Preliminary Gropings." In *Judaic Perspectives on Ancient Israel,* ed. Jacob Neusner, Baruch A. Levine, Ernest S. Frerichs, and Caroline McCracken-Flesher. Philadelphia: Fortress Press, 1987.

Morgenstern, Julian. *The Fire upon the Altar.* Chicago: Quadrangle Books, 1963.

Muffs, Yochanan. *Love and Joy.* New York: Jewish Theological Seminary of America, 1992.

Nicholson, Ernst. *The Pentateuch in the Twentieth Century.* Oxford: Clarendon Press, 1998.

Nora, Pierre. "Between Memory and History: Les Lieux de Memoire." *Representations* 26 (Spring 1989): 7–24.

Noth, Martin. *Numbers.* Philadelphia: Westminster Press, 1968.

Olson, Dennis. *The Death of the Old and the Birth of the New.* Chico, Calif.: Scholars Press, 1985.

Olyan, Saul M. *Rites and Rank.* Princeton: Princeton University Press, 2000.

Owen, Stephen. *Remembrances.* Cambridge: Harvard University Press, 1986.

Pardes, Ilana. *The Biography of Ancient Israel.* Berkeley: University of California Press, 2000.

"The Biography of Ancient Israel: Imagining the Birth of a Nation." *Comparative Literature* 49, no. 1 (Winter 1997): 24–41.

"Imagining the Promised Land: The Spies in the Land of the Giants." *History and Memory* 6 (1994): 5–23.

Countertraditions in the Bible. Cambridge: Harvard University Press, 1992.

Parunak, H. Van Dyke. "Transitional Techniques in the Bible," *Journal of Biblical Literature* 102, no. 4 (1983): 525–548.

Paul, Shalom. "Prophecy and Prophets." In *Etz Hayim.* Philadelphia: Jewish Publication Society, 2001.

Peckham, Brian. "Phoenicia and the Religion of Israel: The Epigraphic Evidence." In *Ancient Israelite Religion: Essays in Honor of Frank Moore Cross.* Ed. Patrick D. Miller, Paul D. Hanson, and S. Dean McBride. Philadelphia: Fortress Press, 1987: 79–99.

Petrucci, Armando. *Writing the Dead.* Stanford, Calif.: Stanford University Press, 1998.

Pitard, Wayne T. "Tombs and Offerings: Archeological Data and Comparative Methodology in the Study of Death in Israel." In *Sacred Time, Sacred Place.* Ed. Barry M. Gittlen. Winona Lake, Ind.: Eisenbrauns, 2002: 145–167.

"Afterlife and Immortality." In *Oxford Companion to the Bible.* Ed. Bruce Manning Metzger and Michael David Coogan. New York: Oxford University Press, 1993: 15–16.

Pope, Marvin H., John H. Marks, and Robert McClive Good. *Love and Death in the Ancient Near East: Essays in Honor of Marvin H. Pope.* Guilford Conn.: Four Quarters Publishing, 1987.

Propp, William H. "The Rod of Aaron and the Sin of Moses." *Journal of Biblical Literature* 107, no. 1 (1988): 19–26.

Rabinowitz, Isaac, Ross Brann, and David I. Owen. *A Witness Forever.* Bethesda: CDL Press, 1993.

Rauch, Angelika. *The Hieroglyph of Tradition.* Teaneck, N.J.: Fairleigh Dickinson University Press, 2000.

Rendtorff, Rolf. "Directions in Pentateuchal Studies." *Currents in Research: Biblical Studies* 5 (1997): 43–65.

The Problem of the Process of Transmission in the Pentateuch. Sheffield, England: Sheffield Academic Press, 1990.

Rofe, Alexander. *Introduction to the Composition of the Pentateuch.* Sheffield, England: Sheffield Academic Press, 1999.

Rosaldo, Renato. *Culture and Truth.* Boston: Beacon Press, 1993.

Rosenberg, Joel. "The Garden Story Forward and Backward." *Prooftexts* 1, no. 1 (January 1981): 1–27.

Ruttenburg, Nancy. "George Whitefield, Spectacular Conversion, and the Rise of Democratic Personality." In *The American Literary History Reader.* Ed. Gordon Hutner. New York: Oxford University Press, 1995.

Sandmel, Samuel. "The Haggada within Scripture." *Journal of Biblical Literature* 80 (1961): 105–22.

Schart, Aaron. *Mose und Israel im Konflikt.* Gottingen: Vandenhoeck and Ruprecht, 1990.

Schmandt-Besserat, Denise. "The Personal Name in Mesopotamia: Its Impact on the Evolution of Writing." In *Proceedings of the First International Congress on the Archaeology of the Ancient Near East.* Rome, 2000: 1493–1499.

Schmidt, Brian B. "Memory as Immortality: Countering the Dreaded 'Death after Death' in Ancient Israelite Society." In *Judaism in Late Antiquity.* Ed. Alan J. Avery-Peck and Jacob Neusner. Leiden: Brill, 2000.

Israel's Beneficent Dead. Tubingen: J. C. B. Mohr (Paul Siebeck), 1994.

Schniedewind, William. *How the Bible Became a Book.* Cambridge: Cambridge University Press, 2004.

Schwartz. Seth. *Imperialism and Jewish Society 200 BCE to 600 CE.* Princeton: Princeton University Press, 2001.

Segal, Alan F. *Life after Death.* New York: Doubleday, 2004.

Shapiro, Anita. "Historiography and Memory: Latrun, 1948." *Jewish Social Studies* 3, no. 1 (Fall 1996): 20–61.

Shils, Edward. *Tradition.* Chicago: University of Chicago Press, 1981.

Smith, Jonathan Z. *To Take Place.* Chicago: Chicago University Press, 1987.

Smith, Mark. *The Memoirs of God.* Minneapolis, Minn.: Augsburg Fortress Press, 2004.

Sommer, Benjamin D. "Conflicting Constructions of Divine Presence in the Priestly Tabernacle." *Biblical Interpretation* 9, no. 1 (2001): 41–63.

"Reflecting on Moses: The Redaction of Numbers 11." *Journal of Biblical Literature* 118, no. 4 (Winter 1999): 601–624.

Spickard, Paul R., and W. Jeffrey Burroughs, eds. *We Are a People: Narrative and Multiplicity in Constructing Ethnic Identity.* Philadelphia: Temple University Press, 2000.

Stephens, Ferris J. "The Ancient Significance of Sisith." *Journal of Biblical Literature* 50 (1931): 59–71.

Stern, Daniel. *The Interpersonal World of the Infant.* New York: Basic Books, 1985.

Talmon, Shemaryahu. "The Desert Motif in the Bible and in Qumran Litera-ture." In *Biblical Motifs, Origins and Transformations.* Ed. Alexander Altmann. Cambridge: Harvard University Press, 1966.

Terdiman, Richard. *Present Past: Modernity and the Memory Crisis.* Ithaca, N.Y.: Cornell University Press, 1993.

Tigay, Jeffrey H. *Deuteronomy: The Traditional Hebrew Text with the New JPS Trans-lation.* The JPS Torah Commentary. Philadelphia: Jewish Publication Society, 1996.

Empirical Models for Biblical Criticism. Philadelphia: University of Pennsylvania Press, 1985.

Turner, Victor. "Social Dramas and the Stories about Them." *Critical Inquiry* 7, no. 1 (Autumn 1980): 141–168.

Dramas, Fields and Metaphors. Ithaca, N.Y.: Cornell University Press, 1974.

The Ritual Process Structure and Anti-Structure. Chicago: Aldine Publishing, 1969.

The Forest of Symbols. Ithaca, N.Y.: Cornell University Press, 1967.

Ulrich, Eugene. *The Dead Sea Scrolls and the Origins of the Bible.* Grand Rapids, Mich.: Eerdmans, 1999.

Van Seters, John. *The Life of Moses.* Louisville, Ky.: Westminster/John Knox Press, 1994.

Wachtel, Nathan. "Introduction." In *Between Memory and History.* Ed. Marie-Noëlle Bourguet, Lucette Valensi, and Nathan Wachtel. Chur, Switzerland: Harwood Academic Publishers, 1990.

Weber, Donald. "From Limen to Border: A Meditation on the Legacy of Victor Turner for American Cultural Studies." *American Quarterly* 47, no. 3 (Septem-ber 1995): 525–536.

Weinfeld, Moshe. *Deuteronomy and the Deuteronomic School.* Oxford: Clarendon Press, 1972.

White, Hayden. *The Content of the Form: Narrative Discourse and Historical Repre-sentation.* Baltimore: Johns Hopkins University Press, 1987.

Wieseltier, Leon. "Washington Diarist: A Year Later." *The New Republic,* September 2, 2002.

Wilcoxen, Jay A. "Some Anthropocentric Aspects of Israel's Sacred History." *Journal of Religions* 48 (1968): 333–350.

Williams, Raymond. *Notes on Marxism and Literature.* Oxford: Oxford University Press, 1977.

Wiseman, D. J. "Books in the Ancient World." In *The Cambridge History of the Bible,* vol. 1. Ed. Peter Ackroyd, and Christopher Evans. Cambridge: Cambridge University Press, 1970.

Yerushalmi, Yosef Hayim. *Zakhor: Jewish History and Jewish Memory.* Seattle: Uni-versity of Washington Press, 1982.

Zlotnick, Helena. *Dinah's Daughters.* Philadelphia: University of Pennsylvania Press, 2002.

Index

Scriptural Index

Selected Hebrew Index

CPSIA information can be obtained at www.ICGtesting.com
Printed in the USA
BVOW021430170213

313422BV00001B/13/P